KINGDOMS IN THE AIR

ALSO BY BOB SHACOCHIS

The Woman Who Lost Her Soul
The Immaculate Invasion
Swimming in the Volcano
Easy in the Islands
The Next New World
Domesticity

KINGDOMS
IN THE AIR

Dispatches from the Far Away

BOB SHACOCHIS

Grove Press
New York

Published simultaneously in Canada
Printed in the United States of America

First published by Grove Atlantic, June 2016

FIRST EDITION

ISBN 978-0-8021-2476-0
eISBN 978-0-8021-9022-2

Grove Press
an imprint of Grove Atlantic
154 West 14th Street
New York, NY 10011

Distributed by Publishers Group West

groveatlantic.com

16 17 18 19   10 9 8 7 6 5 4 3 2 1

For Jonah, and those who gave their hearts to Petey

CONTENTS

KINGDOMS
IN THE AIR

Kingdoms in the Air

PART ONE
Journey to the Land of Lo
(2001–2002)

I could now prove what had long been disbelieved, that beyond the snows of the Himalayas, hidden from the world, there truly existed a lost kingdom.
—Michel Peissel, 1964

Then and Now and Then

Kathmandu, in the spring of 2001, lay dazed in its green bowl of mountains, suffering from an unusually fierce heat wave and a host of maladies of its own making, the city's pre-monsoon lethargy spiked with foreboding. Any day you expected the government to collapse under the weight of its own corruption, or the Maoists to march into the valley, or something more wicked and inconceivable to occur. Tourism was down, body counts up; a first wave of expatriates had begun to arrange its exodus. The capital's sense of dread pulsed with a surreal intensity, seemingly disconnected from the clear facts of the matter: gun battles erupting throughout the countryside, the beloved king's reluctance to deploy his army against the guerrillas, a venal ruling class of Brahmans who deserved tar and feathers, an infant democracy withering in its cradle. Like Kathmandu's legendary pollution, the dread simply hung in the air; you breathed in its thick, sour pungency and exhaled one thought—*Something so bad is about to happen, don't even think about it*—and the city forged ahead on fatalism and denial, at least for a few more weeks. Then all hell exploded and has exploded without mercy ever since.

By spring 2002, after a season of bombings and midnight arrests and assassinations, Kathmandu was still reeling from the battlefront news of what had become internationally known as "the killing terraces," Nepal's six-year-old civil war between time-warp Maoists and the constitutional monarchy. It was an expanding catastrophe that had claimed almost four thousand lives, more than half of them since the end of last November's truce, when King Gyanendra, assuming the throne after the massacre of his brother King Birendra and the rest of the royal family by Crown Prince Dipendra on June 1, 2001, unleashed the Royal Nepal Army on the rebels. By summer, Gyanendra and his prime minister had dissolved parliament, the nation's chief industry—tourism—was crippled, and the Bush administration had braided Nepal's tragedy into its all-consuming preoccupation, America's war on terrorism, throwing money (twenty million in military aid) and personnel (Special Forces advisers) into the cauldron. By 2003, the body count had again doubled upward toward eight thousand miserable souls.

Suddenly all the arguments I have ever had or heard about the deleterious effects of trekkers on traditional cultures seemed quaint and luxurious, if not utterly frivolous. In early May 2001, I was having just such an argument with myself as I headed up to the formerly off-limits kingdom of Mustang, a semiautonomous region of Nepal, with the photographer and author Tom Laird, our wives, and three friends, to see what ten years of open doors does to an insular culture. With the jackals of war ripping Nepal apart, it's tempting to look back now on that journey as a more innocent time and to think that the lessons of the journey no longer matter. But that too would be an illusion, and within the illusion, danger, and within the danger, who we are in the world.

We left Kathmandu for Pokhara on May 14, crossing paths with the Chinese prime minister at the airport, who had come to dispel any notion that China supported the Maoist insurrection in Nepal, a policy contingent upon Kathmandu's reassurance that it would crack down on the country's tenacious Free Tibet movement not just in the city but in the northern borderlands. That evening in the middle hills, strolling Pokhara's lakeside strip of shops, I chatted with the vendors and entrepreneurs and was alarmed by how thorough and deep ran the popular disgust for the current situation. Restore the old monarchy, give the Maoists a chance—anything but the unruly, greed-stricken child-beast of democracy sounded good to the Nepalese.

Much had changed for the worse, little for the better in the decade since King Birendra had unlocked the doors of democratic reform in Nepal, and with them the gates of the once forbidden kingdom of Mustang. The kingdom had been loosely aligned with Nepal since the eighteenth century and formally annexed in 1946. The first outsiders had arrived only in the 1950s, Tibetan refugees with goats and yaks, and Khampa resistance fighters from eastern Tibet plotting their doomed, CIA-sponsored war against the Chinese occupation. For the next two decades, Mustang was entirely closed to foreigners, Shangri-la shuttered up tight, and only a handful of scholars eluded the ban. In 1972, the southern third of the kingdom was opened once more, and Nepal's 1990 revolution pried open the rest. Upper Mustang officially opened in December 1991, and although tourist numbers were and still are restricted, close to 500 foreigners had come through by the end of 1992, a number that peaked at 1,066 in 1998. (Compare this rate with the number of trekkers visiting the nearby Annapurna Sanctuary that same year—61,292.) Not surprisingly, given Nepal's tourism slowdown, only 222 trekkers had registered to enter Upper Mustang by the time we arrived in 2001. If one thing terrified the Kathmandu government more than the Maoists, it was the decline of tourism, the backbone of Nepal's gross national product and the only modern economic force in the feudal-like agrarian society that came close to being egalitarian. Even the Maoists knew better than to bite the hand that fed Nepal, and they enforced among themselves a strict, hearts-and-minds no-whack policy toward foreigners. French tourists wandered out of the Maoist-controlled Dolpo, in direly impoverished western Nepal, starry-eyed with tales of the "wonderful guerrillas." In the government's desperation to keep hotel rooms occupied and trekking agencies booked, and to pacify its far-flung districts, which had seen their cut of the permit fee revenues, meant to be a never-initiated 60 percent, dwindle from 35 percent to 28 to 18 to 3 to nothing, the minister of tourism had recently announced the abolishment of all restricted areas but two—Dolpo and Upper Mustang—within twelve months.

Had ten years of exposure to the modern world—white people from the West, Chinese goods from the East—contorted Mustang with growing pains? we wondered, sitting for dinner on the patio of our hotel, surrounded by Pokhara's rice paddies, the water buffaloes being led to their pens for the night. We'd heard the rumors in Kathmandu: Mustang's traditional center of gravity was shifting to the Chinese, the Free Tibet movement, to art thieves and smugglers; shifting to mass tourism; to the charitable American Himalayan Foundation; to local nongovernmental organizations and the Nepalese themselves, in a deliberate campaign of assimilation.

Perhaps all of this was true, perhaps none of it, but one thing we knew for certain: Mustang's mysteries were no longer inaccessible, though perhaps no less elusive to our understanding. For Laird the questions and speculation were personal. Extremely personal, I should say, as most issues were for the impassioned Laird, who had spent the past thirty years—all of his adult life—in Nepal, documenting its marvels, absorbing its multilayered conflicts and pettiness. His association with the people of Mustang and their ménage of patrons would reveal itself to be more complicated than even he knew or dared imagine.

High above us, above the gathering clouds, higher than most airplanes fly, into the violet-blue of outer space towered the summits of Makalu and Machhapuchchhre, Annapurna and Dhaulagiri, their snowfields bloodred in the sunset. Behind these peaks, which had sheltered Mustang from the outside world for millennia, we would have our answers, and could only hope they would be free of the anger, betrayal, and confusion that had infected fabled Nepal.

PART TWO
The Roof of the World
(1997)

And the wildest dreams of Kew are but the facts of Kathmandu.

—*Rudyard Kipling*

The Profane

It's late for Kathmandu, already almost midnight, and I cling to the shoulders of photojournalist Tom Laird as we lurch down deserted, shuttered alleys on his motor scooter, cruising Sherpa pubs, two *queris* on the *chhang* trail of the Snow Leopard. *Queri* is Nepali slang for Westerners; it means "white eyes," a coy play on the word *quero*, meaning "cloud." *Queri ayo*, villagers might say mischievously, spotting a group of trekkers: The clouds have come.

Chhang is Tibetan-style homemade barley beer, and Laird, a veteran of the Rock and Roll Raj, lingers in the doorway of each dim establishment we visit, vacuuming up the sweet, fermenty harvest-fragrance of the brew, barking at me to Smell it! Smell it!, not hearing my recommendation to Drink it! Drink it! But the sad fact is that each *chhang* bar we come to, the Snow Leopard has already been there before us and closed it down with his prodigious thirst. Wobbly proprietors open their doors to wash us in the after-aroma of Sherpa revelry and tell us, "He was just here drinking, he just left," and then recede into their own fog.

I guess you could call Laird a Sherpaphile—who isn't in this town, the world capital of adventure, the Rome of the hip universe, where the Grand Tour in the sixties and seventies traveled east to become the Great Trek and the Great Pilgrimage, where 335 outfitters and agencies compete with the city's thousands of shrines, icons, and strange objects of veneration, squares and courtyards to rival the Piazza Navona, and enough public art to choke a Vatican curator with envy, or an art thief with greed.

Laird lived for several years up in the Khumbu region below Everest, home ground of the Sherpas, recording the community's traditional songs and folklore, chumming around with high-altitude heroes like the legendary Snow Leopard. The Snow Leopard is the nom de guerre of Ang Rita, the man who's summited Sagarmatha, the Nepali name for Mount Everest, more times than anybody else, alive or dead—ten times all together—and last week, on the north face with a team of Russians, Ang Rita turned back a couple of hundred meters short of his eleventh triumph, leaving behind a pair of *queri* corpses from another expedition.

An extraordinary achievement, but the excitable photographer doesn't really approve, single-mindedly disgusted by the Sherpa rate of attrition up on the summits. "Those peaks are sacred!" Laird rants over the whine of the scooter. "The white guys came in and bent the Sherpa worldview from mountain as god to mountain as goal. The Tengboche lama says he never gave anyone permission to climb Everest. He says it's a sin and always will be. The Sherpas know they're not supposed to be up there, but how can they say no to the money?"

We pull up to the entrance of a courtyard flanked on one side by a shabby concrete apartment building. Laird's eyes narrow behind his wire-rimmed glasses and he whips off his helmet, swinging it in a wide arc to emphasize his point. Even with the engine turned off, Laird is loud. I sort of like it when he yells; I like the passionate investment in the issues, the unedited emotion, the suddenly inflated meaning of everything.

"I'll hire Sherpas to haul my ass up Everest," he says, "when people start killing their caddies to play golf."

I don't know where we are exactly—some centuries-old neighborhood on the edge of Kathmandu, the low skyline broken by the fabulous tiered roofs of pagodas. We've been getting closer and closer throughout the night, and now we've come to the end of the trail, a clean, brightly lit, two-table restaurant with silk *khatas* draped along its walls and around the necks of its sunburned, wind-raked clientele. They just poured him into bed, Ang Rita's bunkmate tells us, pointing to a dark window across the courtyard. The Snow Leopard's plastered, wasting no time on his first day down from the upside. "The *queris* are leaving tomorrow, and he's got nothing to do," explains another Sherpa guide; they each have raccoon eyes from wearing snow goggles. Here at the end of May, with Ang Rita safely back in his bed in Kathmandu, the heavyweight climbing season is over for another year, and it's time to binge on glory.

Despite the mountain caddies turned into blocks of ice in the service of other people's obsessions, and even though Laird insists that just because the Sherpas have played along with our goals doesn't mean they have accepted them as their own, one thing's for certain: The *queris* have been very, very good for the Sherpas. In the thirty years that travelers have been storming Nepal, barrels of hard cash have rolled into the Khumbu region, and the Sherpas have used it to strengthen their community and fortify their culture, sinking money back into their shrines and monasteries. They've made an entrepreneurial assault on the adventure business too, starting their own trekking agencies, running teahouses and lodges, leasing Russian Mi-17 helicopters from Tatarstan for $1,000 an hour (with crew) and charging twice that to whisk climbers and hikers up to altitude. And of course there's the psychological payoff. Working for the *queris*, the Sherpas have earned a reputation as the world's most agreeable but tenacious studs, so much so that the word *Sherpa* itself, Laird reminds me, has entered the English language as an adjective to describe anyone with particular skill and prowess who prepares the way for others. Not the worst of all possible fates for an isolated Central Asian mountain tribe living in one of the planet's most impoverished countries.

Another round of *chhang* for my men and horses.

I'm not sure what we wanted from the Snow Leopard anyway, except perhaps a blessing, some gesture of grace from a man who has sinned his way ever upward toward the very heavens.

*   *   *

Our feet scuff a free-market strewing of happy-hour handbills as we walk through Thamel—ground zero in Kathmandu's tourist boom—headed for the Maya Pub, the only place that seems to be open, clomping up a steep, narrow flight of stairs to the funky bar. "Don't you just love the smell of shit and incense?" Laird says happily. Hepatitis has kept him away from Thamel drinking establishments for ages, and he squints through the murk, mildly shocked by the presence of three young Nepali women, their red-tipped fingers gliding over half-full bottles of San Miguel beer. You wouldn't have seen Nepali girls in a bar ten years ago, but since Laird has been teetotaling, Kathmandu's changed, become more cosmopolitan. Women have stepped a bit closer to the forefront of society, although it's questionable whether the first Miss Nepal contest, held in 1995, is evidence for or against this trend.

As recently as 1947, Nepal was the largest inhabited country on earth yet to be explored by Europeans, and the life expectancy was a prehistoric twenty-four years. When you enter the second half of the twentieth century as a medieval and in many ways prefeudal kingdom sandwiched between a newly independent India and a newly Communist China, and make a conscious decision to modernize, you probably ought to expect some whiplash. In rush the not-always-farsighted do-gooders, outfits like the World Health Organization, to take one example. They set up clinics, eradicate disease, train people to take better care of themselves, make a dent in the infant mortality rate, accomplish noble, generous objectives, but my goodness, someone forgot the birth control pills, the population triples, and here comes a housing shortage, accelerated environmental degradation, unemployment, and a bloated bureaucracy slurping on the platinum teats of the Lords of Poverty: competing donor nations, international developmental aid organizations such as the World Bank, self-righteous NGOs and vanity charities, carelessly recycling Big Money through the Third World. And Big Money, friends, leaves Big Footprints.

Thanks in part to the global homogenization of this subtle but virulent form of colonialism, Nepal's seemingly endemic problems are not especially unique. You give us your problems, we give you ours. The nature of migration only intensifies the dynamic. Adventure tourism: an outflow of the affluent into the tribal world. Immigration: a ravenous inflow of diversity into the established mainstreams. Two sides of the same postmodern coin. Yes, the gap between the haves and the have-nots in Kathmandu is widening, but that's true for London and New York, Moscow and Zurich, as well. Okay, Kathmandu is filthy and traffic-clogged, but compared to Mexico City or Bangkok or New Delhi it is downright user-friendly. Yes, the environment is under pressure, but on a day-trip stroll up the Annapurna trail, which hosts fifty thousand trekkers a year, I spotted only a single gum wrapper littering the footpath. Yes, the culture is eroding, but so is France's, so is everybody's as they ingest American pop culture, the most narcotic substance in the galaxy.

Still, it's tricky, this not-always-sincere experiment called development. Once you let the Coca-Cola out of the bottle, the landscape is going to change regardless of any effort to preserve it, but how much for the better and how much for the worse? Suppose you run a charity and decide to bring electricity to all the monasteries in the ancient kingdom of Mustang, which have somehow managed to survive without a hot plate for hundreds of years. Is this good or bad? What are the social parameters for such dramatic change? Hard to say. You want to help, but what if you hurt? Suppose you're an overconfident altruist who wires the Tengboche monastery at the base of Everest for electricity, yet maybe you overlook the necessity for a fire extinguisher on-site, and you forget to instruct the monks in the proper use of space heaters and circuit breakers, and the old monastery burns to the ground (this actually happened). Gosh, that's bad, we can all agree, but the intention isn't, is it? In 1992, almost 95 percent of Nepal's energy needs were still being met by firewood. The percentage hasn't decreased that much in the intervening years, despite the fact that this is the country with the greatest hydroelectric potential per square mile in the world. Burn a monastery, save a forest?

In the eighties, Tengboche became something of a microcosm of what adventure travel had done to Nepal. During the high season, a thousand trekkers a day were slogging through; monks would throw off their robes and join the expeditions, and the lama was hard-pressed to deal with the situation. Today, Tengboche, rebuilt since the 1989 blaze, is no less a freeway. Apple pie, peanut butter, brandy, satellite uplinks, fax machines, Everest has it all, and somewhere along the trail the concept that there are pure places that require a pure presence from us became too heavy a load.

"Democracy," proclaims Laird, "has unleashed the floodgates of desire without any of the structures to fulfill them!"

"What?" I stare at my immoderately eloquent companion over a glass of local vodka. "What did you say?" Laird, I think, must stand in front of the mirror and practice these lines.

Nepal's infant democracy, in fact, has been the photographer's ticket to ride. From the eighteenth century until 1950, power in the kingdom was jockeyed between two dynastic families, the Shahs and the Ranas—not exactly a civic-minded bunch. An India-sponsored mini-revolution ended with the creation of a coalition government in 1951. Nine years and ten governments later, the king turned off the lights—too much hubbub in Nepal's fledgling democracy—and the lights stayed off until 1990, when Nepal's outlawed political parties decided they were destined for a greater existence than life underground. Throughout the country there were marches, protests, the mass defiance only ballooning when police began to shoot demonstrators. On April 6, the Movement to Restore Democracy rallied two hundred thousand people, who surged down Durbar Marg toward the royal palace, where the police opened fire. Weaving in and out of the demonstrators on his scooter was Tom Laird, documenting the bloodiest day in the history of modern Nepal. The official death toll was ten, including a young British tourist. Laird, however, had photographed the police beatings and had heard, as many had, of the police hauling off truckloads of bullet-riddled bodies. His images of the atrocities were broad-sheeted and by the following morning pasted on walls throughout the city. Several days later the good King Birendra "converted" to democracy, elections followed in '91, and the new prime minister, G. P. Koirala, mentioned that Nepal owed the brave photographer a favor. Name it, said the PM. Taken by surprise, Laird couldn't remember his dream-come-true list and declined the offer.

After a sleepless night, Laird got back in touch with Koirala. In 1952, the Swiss geologist Toni Hagen had been the first and virtually the last Westerner permitted to visit Mustang, the magical high-desert valley north of the snow peaks on the old salt-trade route between Tibet and India. But with the end of the Cold War, the gates to off-limits border areas were being cautiously unlocked by erstwhile foes. That spring of 1991, Dick Blum, the well-heeled chairman of the American Himalayan Foundation, a fellow who apparently cannot be identified without the encumbering appellation "the husband of Dianne Feinstein," became the first *queri* to see Mustang in decades.

Laird wanted to go to Mustang too, record the antiquities with his camera. Done, said the PM, have a nice trip, and Laird became the first foreigner ever to live in Mustang for a year, and the first to get a permit to cross the border to visit Mount Kailas, Tibet's most sacred peak. For years, the tribal people of Mustang had been begging the Nepalese government to open up the valley for a slice of the touristic pie, and now it happened, the ancient kingdom intimately married to the world for better or worse, richer or poorer, in no small part because of Laird's collaboration with Peter Matthiessen, who later joined the photographer in Mustang and wrote the text for the published collection of Laird's mesmerizing images, *East of Lo Monthang*. But nobody, not even the rabidly sensitive Laird, can go to such far-flung places without dragging in the microbes of transformation. His own demand to prohibit the use of outside porters, he tells me, caused the price of

17

wheat to double, and he frets, however belatedly, that Mustang would soon become an anthropological zoo.

Nepalese politics have continued to be steadily unsteady, as befits a newborn democracy. In 1991 the Nepali Congress Party won a majority in the elections, but despite the dismantling of Marxist-Leninist regimes in the Soviet Union and Eastern Europe, the Communist Party of Nepal placed a red-hot second. Six years later, even as Laird and I sit in the Maya Pub, ballots for another election are being tallied, and the Communist Party is walloping the opposition.

But there's more, an ominous blossoming of extremism. Among the reds is a splinter group of pyscho-rad Communists who identify themselves as Maoists and broadcast nothing but contempt for their in-house comrades. Thus, in early 1996, to gear up for the forthcoming election, the lunatic faction announced it was starting a people's war. For the last week, every time I picked up a Kathmandu newspaper, I was treated to alarming headlines about Maoists terrorizing voters and disemboweling local functionaries with Gurkha *khukris*.

The geopolitics of tourism can tilt either way: the foreigner as valuable friend and ally (Tibet) or the foreigner as enemy, scapegoat, and pawn (Kashmir). "Is it true," I ask Laird, "what I've been reading about the Maoists?"

"Yeah." He nods. For the moment at least, the guerrillas have been operating mostly in the jungles and in the midwest hill country, nontourist regions, though he recently heard about a Maoist demonstration at Jiri, the road head for the Everest trek. I had been told that the American embassy was under pressure from the Nepalese government not to publicize Maoist shenanigans, allegedly because it might complicate plans to launch a nationwide tourist campaign in 1998.

"Is it true," I asked the secretary of tourism and civil aviation, the affable D. P. Dhakal, who sat behind his desk in Kathmandu's palatial parliamentary compound, jiggling his head in that curious way Nepalis have, "that you're trying to start a tourist campaign over the top of a Maoist insurrection?"

"Tourism is a thing which is totally aloof from politics," Dhakal said with the fine assurance of a man who works and lives in the capital of a country with a centralized government. "Yes, the Maoist thing grows, but it cannot be there forever. They did it for the elections. They did it for attention." Surprisingly, Dhakal cited the "positive" example of Sri Lanka, how the violence there was never targeted at the tourists, who flew in indifferent to the bloodshed and headed straight for the beaches. "Here, even if we have an insurrection," he said, "the foreigners will not be affected."

When the minister sighed that "the attention of the media gets attached disproportionately" to negatives, I mustered a thimble of sympathy and let the whole bizarre mess of disconnection drop, wondering instead what sort of push he was involved in to inaugurate Visit Nepal '98. (Motto: "A sustainable habitat through sustainable tourism.") He shrugged and sat back cavalierly in his chair. "Our society is not built up to do our homework," he said. "Even for me, I can only plan for this week, not next week. Revolutions here are only planned fifteen, twenty days in advance. Tourists are going to come anyway."

As I left his office, Dhakal had urged me to put the Maoist situation into the "proper perspective," whatever that perspective was.

The Maya Pub closes down around us, people stumbling for the door, and we're back on the streets of Thamel, swarmed by insomniac teenage rickshaw drivers. "Come on," says Laird. "Let's drive around."

We glide down twisting alleys, lines of freshly outdated election posters crisscrossed above us like the city's forgotten laundry. Laird points out the former Cabin Restaurant, infamous during the Nepal gold rush for its hashish menu. We cruise Freak Street, park, duck through a doorless entrance, and Laird proudly shows me where he used to live in the Third Eye Lodge, only now this section of the hostel has fallen down, his room a pile of rubble. Taped to a remaining wall is a photocopied advertisement: *Attention Adventure Seekers. Karnali*

19

Video Expedition—My name is Matthew from Australia. Our expedition requires over-the-top enthusiasts who don't mind getting themselves bent out of shape. I guarantee this adventure will be well catered.

Yeah, right. Fly-by-nighters like this drive the more responsible agencies nuts. "Things are going down-market," Steve Webster told me. He's the director and sales manager for Mountain Travel Nepal, one of the oldest and most reputable firms in the city. "The free market has allowed anybody to open up an agency, so quality has eroded. People are running trips out of their homes—no overhead, one or two groups a year, very little profit—and that seems to be enough for them." Webster wants less mass-tourism backpackers, more top-end clientele. "We'd prefer to see fewer people paying more money," he said, "because it has less impact on the environment and less impact on the culture."

"You can't imagine how far away this was in 1972," says Laird, peering into the dark at his memories, his face aglow with nostalgia. "Santana was booming out on the street the first night I spent in this room. You can look around and just see those fucking psychedelic hippies coming out of the corners. We were so desperate to get somewhere. When you came over and saw those mountains, that was *it*, this was the end of the world."

Ah, Freak Street, the epicenter of the countercultural fantasy, the Haight-Ashbury of Asia, where the Rock and Roll Raj reclined on pillows of dreamy hash, having traveled the overland route from Europe across the Near East and Middle East to the Buddhist heart of the biggest playground ever. Freak Street, where yesterday's hippies came to lose themselves in one set of myths and coincidentally started creating another. Shiva's Slaves Motorcycle Club, the long-haired brothers astride Indian-made Enfields. Peace Corps puppies over-assimilated into goofy enlightenment. Dharma-droids and born-again Buddhists. Hump-a-Yeti Trek Agency. Too-Loose-to-Trek Outfitters and Guides. What fun to be a ne'er-do-well in Kathmandu. If you were a freak afoot in the world in, say, 1968, this is where you stopped, this was the end of an imaginary beginning, and there was nowhere else to go unless

20

you were in some profound way damaged by your own restlessness: China and its Cultural Revolution, Southeast Asia and its wars—too far fucking out for this world or any other.

Kathmandu became Asia's emblematic antithesis to Vietnam and the lurid Conradian lust for darkness, the apparent antidote for all the bad knowledge Western civilization seemed to be coughing up like blood clots. Light was Kathmandu's essence. Butter lamps instead of napalm. *Puja* instead of paranoia. Here in Kathmandu the exotic was timeless and transcendent, immune to complacency, inherently hospitable (and therefore inherently exploitable), hinting of eternal life, in serene opposition to the exotic as a hostile plunge toward the death of the soul. Apocalypse not now or ever. That was Kathmandu's self-defined identity, its embracing presence, and it made perfect sense to blond-haired kids raised on *The Dharma Bums*, the Beatles, the draft, the dope. You could get a room for less than a dollar a day, a bowl of *dal bhat* cost pennies, and the reefer was like a spiritual can-opener, prying open the tin of your consciousness to the full pulse of the sublime, mystical weirdness of the place. "Another willing convert," wrote Gita Mehta in *Karma Cola: Marketing the Mystic East*, "to the philosophy of the meaningfully meaningless."

Finally Laird scoots me back to the Kathmandu Guest House, legendary for being the Ritz of the downscale *queris* all those many years ago. The proprietor has just built a deluxe hotel in Nagarkot, on the ridgeline above the city, which gives you some idea about how eagerly the citizens of Kathmandu have invested themselves in the adventure travel phenomenon. Dawn comes with a village sound track—roosters crowing, laundresses gossiping in the courtyard below my window, the interminable wake-up call of the cuckoo bird—and when I emerge, bleary-eyed, for breakfast, the hallway is blocked by student types lined up in front of the computer room, waiting to e-mail home, and an ensemble of Eurotrash slackers have hunkered down on the vinyl-covered couches in the lounge, their expressionless faces turned toward the television, watching an Elvis Presley movie.

The Sacred

From the *Kathmandu Post*, May 22:

"MORE FANFARE THAN DEVOTION MARKS
BUDDHA'S ANNIVERSARY."

"It is not only the political chaos which hindered the people of the land of the Buddha from celebrating heart and soul the 2,541st birth anniversary of the Lord Buddha, the light of Asia. . . . Most of the pilgrims at Swayambhu were there to freak out than to celebrate the holy day. Vendors selling cold drinks, music albums, pictures and handicrafts got prominence than devotees, and the stalls were the focus than the stupa. People's indifference to Buddhism here will certainly lead our existence to the pit, a monk complained."

In the quirky English of the subcontinent, the lament still sounds all too familiar. Even the divine takes it in the cosmic balls when insular kingdoms get drop-kicked out of their pasts into the age of globalism.

On the outskirts of Kathmandu is a modest hill called DevBhumi, Home of the Gods, and it lifts the shrine of Swayambhu toward the nearby heavens, which reproduce the immensity of the stupa, magnifying and multiplying the dome of whiteness into the most soul-boggling horizon on the planet—the snow peaks of the Himalayas. The land of the Eight Thousands, blasting up from sea level five miles into the atmosphere. And all those divine wannabes—countless other mountains exceeding 20,000 feet—tightly accordioned into a crest known as the Roof of the World. Roof of your mind is more like it.

This is Nepal, where you climb a hill to expose yourself to the sacred, not shelter yourself from the profane—not Tuscany, where you might reasonably expect to find a fortress atop this breast of land jutting skyward off the valley floor. Kathmandu—never actually invaded, never actually colonized—has been forever too preoccupied with its conversation with the gods to have bothered much with defending itself against the material designs of men. Three million deities, or 30 million, or even, say some texts, 330,000 million of them in the Hindu pantheon, not to mention Buddha and the bodhisattvas or countless trickster woodland spirits in need of constant propitiation. "It's like Greek mythology," I heard Dubby Bhagat, another one of the city's resident infatuees and a manager at the Everest Hotel, say, "only it's happening now. That's the fantasy we should be selling." Karma, not cappuccino.

DevBhumi is where I'm headed this muggy afternoon to do something Kathmandu's expatriate community seems loath to do, which is walk, walk anywhere in the urban morass, sucking in a dun-colored haze, the diesel fumes and the wood smoke and the dust and the atomized holy cow shit all bottled up in the valley's thermal inversion to plunge Kathmandu's air-quality index to a level synonymous with black lung disease. But even polluted Kathmandu has rivers of eucalyptus purity running through its metropolitan groves, downdrafts of alpine freshness, the brisk exhalations of mountains, that leave me buoyant on my grateful march through the ever more endangered enchantment of the city.

I step past the rug merchants idle on their stoops, past Pilgrims Book House, its windows full of trekking maps, and the Himalayan clinic whose lucky American doctor has just choppered down from an inaccessible part of the Tibetan border with Dick Blum following a walkabout around Mount Kailas. What fun to be a do-gooder in Kathmandu. Helicopters, advocates argue, don't leave footprints—but they're infamous for collateral damage: not just ruined potato fields-cum-landing pads or hopping up to altitude without proper acclimatization, but the troublesome compression of experience, like the one-day junket a French television station sponsored for its advertisers. They flew the clients in from Paris, helicoptered them up to the base of an almost twenty-thousand-foot peak for breakfast, whisked them down for a riverside lunch among elephants and one-horned rhinos, and then brought them back to dinner at a Kathmandu monastery, where the lamas chanted prayers for the executives' long lives.

I cross Durbar Marg, one of the city's most Westernized boulevards, past pricey artifact outlets, the jewelry stores and gem retailers and vacation wholesalers, past Wimpy hamburgers with its coterie of hometown punks—McDonald's execs are in town, smoothing the way for the Himalayas' first franchise—and on up toward the royal palace, where Nepal's constitutional monarch, King Birendra, sits brooding behind the sky-high spears of an iron fence, its most contemporary function to keep the rogue elephants of democracy at a comfortable distance. A few blocks westward I step around a woman emptying a pan of goat's blood into a gutter drain and walk into Thamel.

If Thamel has changed much since its halcyon days, I couldn't know and wouldn't care. You should have been here twenty, thirty years ago, the graying remnants of the hip community chide with dismissive smiles and the sagging body language of bittersweet loss, staring off into a Felliniesque kaleidoscope of images that compose the melancholy of their collective past. The increasingly geriatric veterans of the countercultural road trip have wearied of all that drug nonsense; they're decamping back to the States, putting their kids into college, retooling their ambitions to be swashbucklers of the free market or heading into the foothills to become cave-dwelling mystics, reserving beds at Om's Nursing Home on Lazimpat should they need a place to really cool out, come the millennium. Right—I should have been here a hundred years ago, I wish I could be here a hundred years hence, but I seem to be one of the few *queris* around unwilling to bitch unchastely about Kathmandu. Be here now, I know, works better when you're not part of the gang responsible for popularizing a destination.

"We discovered these places, Afghanistan, Nepal, Goa," an old hippie named Jasmine told the writer Gita Mehta. "When we arrived everybody loved us. Now the whole damn world is on the trail we opened up, and the same people who loved us, fucking hate us. There's too many of them. They're not in the same class as those of us who got here first."

As far as life on the planet goes, we are certainly the last of the last generations to get there first. The postwar baby boomers, Kennedy's children, heirs to the Boeing 707, presided over the deconstruction of any and all remaining frontiers and the death of myriad traditions. We are the last to see true, unboxed wilderness, the last to see life as it had been lived for centuries. Thirty years ago I was a high school junior with my first driver's license, the roof of my thirdhand Volkswagen stacked with surfboards, rolling down the wild empty beach from Sandbridge, Virginia, to the Outer Banks of North Carolina, all but deserted except for the families of migrant fishermen who had worked the tides for three hundred years. We surfed ourselves into sweet exhaustion, strutted around bare-assed, built bonfires as big as dump trucks, grilled bluefish given to us by the migrants, and slept in World War II bomber-spotting towers in the midst of sand dunes peppered with unexploded ordnance dropped in practice runs. I have never since known such freedom, never since known such a wide-open America.

Now the rickety wooden towers are gone, replaced by condos and private clubs and tony restaurants; you can't drive on the beach from Virginia to Carolina; the migrant fishermen exist only in history books; and I moved out of Hatteras forever ten years ago. Be here now? You can't, not in a place where you have a history, however short. That's the traveler's ace in the hole—no memories, no regrets; the irrelevance of hope. Jasmine's more right than not; the dynamic is an internecine class issue among restless, shameless consumers. The irony is souring and self-indicting: Hatteras, the last good place on the East Coast, is ruined, for me at least, and I mourn it, but I'll take Kathmandu almost any way it is delivered.

So I walk, making the city my own. I turn down Tridevi Marg, deep into Thamel, one of the many neighborhoods in Kathmandu that have transformed themselves into base camps for Adventure with a capital A. Shingle after shingle of local and international companies—one for every thousand of Nepal's visitors each year—hawking their services for trekking, rafting, climbing, mountain biking, hot-air ballooning, hang gliding; armies of guides and porters to shepherd you through wildlife parks and high-altitude death zones. Mr. Dhakal's apathy toward the Visit Nepal '98 campaign was a bit disingenuous. His Majesty's government and the private sector have whipped up dozens of "tourism products" to bolster the effort: wildflower walks, snow leopard treks, angling trips, a monkey watch, honey hunting, fossil hunting, elephant polo, and thirty-four other "culture" offerings, including ethnological tours, festival tours, yoga tours, even a brewing tour that will bus you around to local moon-shiners to sample *chhang*. The exotic as free-for-all growth industry, the global capitalization of adventure.

But where might you start to prevent Nepal's macrocosmic drift toward cultural decline and deracination? Is tourism the problem? Is adventure travel a form of designer imperialism? Hard to say, when tourism is just about the only industry Nepal can depend on to democ-ratize its rural economy and spread a little of the wealth, rupee by rupee.

"Nepal has to have tourists," says Nirmal Chabba, manager of the famed Hotel Yak & Yeti. (If you're the type who likes to dress elegantly and piss away money, the hotel hosts a swank casino. Richard Gere and Bernardo Bertolucci prefer to rent the luxurious fairy-tale Tibetan palace suites on the seventh floor and meditate on their private terraces overlooking the city.) As I've heard so many Nepalis say, thank God for Everest. No tourism would turn us into beggars.

In Thamel, every few steps someone is hawking a *khukri*, a brass idol, a baseball hat embroidered with Buddha's feminine eyes, but Nepalis are either too proud or too shy to confront you with the hard sell, and history has so far spared Nepal from a culture of resentment toward foreigners. At the end of Tridevi Marg, I veer south and arrive at the old pilgrims' junction that leads west out of Thamel, where I am ceremoniously joined by eight-year-old Sham, merry-eyed ragamuffin, and we indulge in a not always rewarding game. "I'll show you the way," Sham offers when I answer his question about where I'm going, but I know the route myself and decline his service. Just in case I am bluffing, as a courtesy Sham briefs me on the route—"Down, right, over, up"—and tells me that Washington, D.C., is the capital of America. "Are you sure?" I tease. Oh yes, he read it in a book. Sham flits around me like a snot-nosed hummingbird, an adroit combination of urchin charm and beggarly boyish cunning. He's not annoying, he's brilliant, wonderful, yet still I want him to go away, earn his future without me.

"When you leave," he says, an identical silky black gleam to his eyes and hair, "will you give me your extra shirts and pants?" Sham's head only comes up to my belt buckle, but the discrepancy doesn't faze him. All over the mountains, porters are walking around in tattered oversize down vests and tattered undersized sneakers. He's used to wearing big clothes, he tells me, but the thought is so absurd that we both laugh.

"Okay, no clothes," says Sham. "Milk."

He wants milk. How coldhearted do you have to be to say get lost to a kid whose final appeal in this most clichéd of Third World shantytown vignettes is for milk? Still, I'm skeptical. I insist on accompanying Sham to a nearby shop to make the purchase myself, but it's not a twenty-cent pint carton he wants. He points behind the wooden counter to a top shelf holding a huge, family-size box of powdered milk. The little bastard probably works for the Milk Baba, I think, a local Hindu ascetic who for sixteen years has squeezed out a life for himself by refusing to put any nourishment other than milk into his body. "What are you planning to do, break it down into dime bags to sell to four-year-olds?"

Sham doesn't miss a beat. He has a flock of brothers and sisters who apparently do nothing but sit around wailing for him to bring milk to comfort their hungry stomachs. "It is my duty," he says manfully.

I balk at the price—three hundred rupees, a fortune in the shadows of Kathmandu's kiddie economy. Sham might well grow up to become one of Central Asia's biggest criminals, perhaps even prime minister. "Why am I letting you talk me into this?" I wonder out loud, tugging a lump of bills from my pocket.

"Because it's Buddha Jayanti and you are going to the monkey temple."

Good answer: It's Buddha's birthday and I'm going to Swayambhu. Far be it for me, on such a day, on such a journey, to be the one to impede the flow of milk into the mouths of babes, innocent or otherwise.

"Are you a Buddhist?" the expats I pal around with in Kathmandu eventually get around to asking. They are, I'm not, but the answer is never so simple. I confess I feel disconnected from the great theologies of man, abandoned to the scientist's god, Technologia. I have no place reserved inside myself for Catholicism, the religion I was raised with, and little warmth for Christianity in general, finding nothing in its central image of crucifixion to stir my devotion. The unforgiving severity of Islam appalls me, and being a Jew is not simply something for which you sign on the dotted theological line.

Despite Buddhism's ubiquity, Nepal has ordained itself the world's only Hindu kingdom, but as religions go, forget it. On my scorecard, Hinduism falls into the orbit of the biggest freak shows ever conceived, one outrageous carny act after another. I do, however, bow to one of Hinduism's defining rituals and feel that cremation should be a spectator sport, especially for death-defying Westerners, and whenever I'm in Kathmandu I make a point of visiting its most holy Hindu shrine, Pashupatinath, on the banks of the sacred, scuzzy Bagmati River. This trip, on an early-morning pilgrimage to the temple, I sat on the

Bagmati's eastern bank along a row of stone monuments, each housing a linga, a polished marble phallus, the ancient Hindu symbol of masculine power. I was quietly appreciating Pashupati's sobering essence as a living place of worship, its compressed cycle of life and death, when I was approached by a sassy, twentysomething sadhu, dressed flamboyantly in blue satin pajamas and a pink silk vest, who wanted to cadge a cigarette. "You want to see my dick?" he asked. He was one of those afflicted, grotesque ascetics who renounce their carnal passions by tying heavy stones around their penises to "break" the erectile tissues. As we talked, an old woman across the river lost her footing on the slippery steps leading from the cremation ghats to the main temple, cracked her white-haired head on the stone embankment, and, to the mortification of her assembled family, expired then and there. The sadhu burst into weaselish laughter. "What's so funny?" I asked. "She's very lucky," he snickered. "She died in a sacred place." To anyone who might imagine that I lack the cultural sensitivity to correctly understand the sadhu's response, I would suggest that hip and holy are a poisonous and often reprehensible mix.

I try to explain my feelings to the Kathmandu crowd—my relief in the presence of the Buddhist sense of humor, the lightness of the pleasure I find sometimes in a monk's guileless grin, my appreciation for Buddhism's spiritually generous posture of whateverness. Yet what I find most profoundly compelling about Buddhism is predoctrinal, post-dogmatic, and has little to do with monasteries or myths or received wisdom. I'm in love with the exquisite Buddhist tension between the animate and the inanimate, the aesthetics of the mountains. The sight of a row of prayer flags rippling upward toward the snow peaks astounds me, penetrating deep into the marrow, a visual haiku more potent in its simplicity than the epic poetry of a cathedral. The juxtaposition of the colorful, weather-shredded flags and the floating Himalayan snowfields is the only beauty I ever witnessed that did not ultimately make me melancholy. Various whiteboy Buddhists have regarded me with contempt for this minimalist perspective of the religion they drape and adorn themselves with, but that's what Buddhism is to me: the graceful simplicity of its attempt to articulate the never-to-be-comprehended Himalayas, the mountains that fit no earthly scale of proportion and explode into the spirit with rupturing disbelief.

"Oh!" Heads nod. "Then you're a Buddhist."

Well, not so fast. An affinity is not faith, nor need it be, and there's plenty about the religion I find disheartening. I believe in the marvelous immensity of mountains and oceans, billowy flags whispering our frailty to the void, the accrued sanctity of places like Swayambhu, and I try—an effort made both significantly easier and impossible by the Nepalese—to believe in the goodness of people. All the rest can be nicely gift-wrapped into the Hindu concept of maya—trivia and illusion and dream—starting with the tasty Buddhist baloney about nirvana.

At the foot of DevBhumi I cross a stone bridge and fall in step with a parade of celebrants headed up a low ridge under a leafy canopy of trees. The entrance to the shrine looks like a refugee camp on holiday. Groups of families rock on their heels, sipping tea from thermoses, munching on fried dough or snow-white crescents of coconut. Laughing children run about with no sense of direction or purpose other than to be laughing children. Through the gate, a prayer wheel the size of a wine cask creaks in perpetual motion and three enormous stone Buddhas the color of marigolds doze at the foot of the 365 breath-robbing steps that ascend the steep gradient of the hill. Mothers grip their toddlers by the shoulders as they slide down the long, scary iron handrail separating the up and down traffic. Three hundred steps to go and already I'm soaked through my shirt, but this is why I'm sold on Swayambhu, the hill and the ascent and the summit a perfect metaphor for the sweaty elation of the trail. Everything holy in Kathmandu has been built with visual cues to divert the eye upward, Dubby Bhagat suggested to me, "just mysterious enough to tempt you further."

And perhaps no greater proof of such temptation than the daunting approach to Swayambhu: on the steps, when you drop back your head and raise your downcast eyes, so attentive to your feet, and finally notice the pair of *shikara*, monolithic stone-and-brick towers like fat white rocket ships, stationed on each side of the highest landing. *Shikara* translates as "mountain peak," and their forms are architectural expressions of the soaring peaks of the Himalayas. It's hard to look at *shikara* without thinking ice ax, rope, oxygen. Desire. Fear. And where the steps terminate, it's not the ready-to-launch *shikara* you first see, but what they frame: a gigantic gold thunderbolt, called a *vajra*, the Buddhist symbol for the absolute nature of reality, or, in my own rescrambled interpretation, the absolute reality of nature.

I hump upward, my ears slowly filling with a glacial splintering of sound, the gravelly crackle of hundreds of human beings in motion. My eyes slide along the hemispheric curve of the stupa, along rising and converging lines of fluttering prayer flags, like permanently suspended confetti, toward the inevitable symmetry of the shrine's little metaphysical joke. When you set your sights high enough, you're looking straight on at the Buddha and the Buddha's looking at you: the all-seeing eyes of the supreme enlightened one painted on each side of the square base of Swayambhu's golden spire, gazing out across the Kathmandu valley toward each cardinal point on the compass, each pair of eyes like a parasol balanced on the red curling staff of a stylized question mark signifying dharma, the path to self-awareness. Today, the path is being shared by soft drink vendors doing a brisk business under a makeshift awning. Awareness, I'm forced to conclude from my own dust-parched mouth, is preceded by great thirst for the real thing, ice cold.

I sit down on a stone ledge, my sweaty back against the wall of a tiny shop and its interior breath of coolness, trying to get a fix on how it is, amidst this chaotic swirl of humanity, that one celebrates Buddha's birthday in the land where the historical Siddhartha himself was born. For anyone who has tied his or her piety to churches or mosques or synagogues, Swayambhu and its robust venerations probably won't click. Round and round the pilgrims flow in clockwise circumambulations of the stupa, slapping the hundreds of copper prayer wheels that ring its base, poking their heads inside the small dark shrine rooms recessed into the dome, flinging in offerings of rice, vermilion, incense. Like a large, gaudy caterpillar, a saffron-vested monk crawls into view in the circling tide, sprawls flat on his belly, arms extended in front of him, pushes himself slowly back on his feet, takes a few steps forward, and falls again, trailed by a white man snapping pictures. The monk has flat wooden blocks strapped to his hands to protect the skin of his palms from the friction of incessant, mechanical supplication.

From Kathmandu's quasi-punk point of view, Swayambhu is a terrific venue for girl-watching. In the courtyard in front of the rest house the Nepali lover boys congregate, sniggering at a trio of fornicating dogs, their horny eyes tracking cliques of sensual young women. With muffled snaps, a breeze steers the prayer flags toward the north and east, toward Everest, where climbers are bottlenecked at the South Col, where they are making it or not making it. Yesterday a member of a Nepalese youth expedition made it. Last week, five others—four foreigners, one Sherpa—died trying, one of them simply blown off the peak into space.

The wind lifts the dust and flies. Trash blows across my feet. There's birdsong and the bumblebee buzz of throaty chanting. Bells ring always but without a pattern, bells like Sunday church bells, like fire bells, like dinner bells, like we-have-another-winner. Out of nowhere, suddenly, monkeys scamper onto the stupa, playing Tarzan on a limp rope of old prayer flags, swinging their mangy selves up to the fretted tin roofline above the prayer wheels. The prostrating monk reappears on his circuit, rising from his knees more slowly, a white-haired old man, a slowly tumbling rock in a racing streambed. Another monk, in a porkpie hat, enters the herd holding a fat bundle of burning joss sticks like a smoke bomb, and it's this smell of junipery incense that tells me, as much as anything else, that I've returned to the Himalayas, a promise—perhaps the only one—I keep making to myself. The wheels never stop spinning, the flags never stop lifting, the beasts never stop fucking but stagger in a three-headed dance between the legs of the celebrants. In this holiest of shrines, it is the joy of existence, the ascendant laughter of its everydayness, that makes the loudest statement. Just as on the mountains one glimpses with the deepest and most self-questioning awe the stunning dimension of death, at Swayambhu, from this summit, one views the miraculous, astonishing expanse of life, the light within life.

As shadows lengthen, aproned Tibetan women begin filling the four tiers of brass butter lamps that ring the base of the stupa, a signal for me to unfold my legs and wander over to the observation platform that overlooks the valley and watch the sunset. But it's the northeastern view that most engrosses me, out across the city, beyond the knob of otherworldly Bhaktapur and the honey-colored sweep of terraced fields, toward the valley's rim, four thousand feet above, where, were it another season, one could reasonably hope to see the clouds opening and closing on the high peaks, the illusion of ideal worlds appearing and disappearing.

Here's the story of Swayambhu and it begins with a geologic fact: Once upon a time, the Kathmandu valley was a vast shimmering lake cradled by its present-day bowl of mountains, where the first Buddha pitched a lotus seed. Eighty thousand years later, the darn thing blossomed magnificently, rising out of the water as big as a chariot wheel, a thousand-petaled flower bursting with rays of light: Swayambhu, the light of the self-created. For the next however many aeons, the first tourists, gods and kings, crowded onto the surrounding mountaintops to marvel at the paradisiacal radiance of Swayambhu, adding to the future Nepal's growing expat community of deities, since plenty of the drop-bys determined the lake-filled valley with its dazzling lotus to be a pretty good place to settle down. Then one day another Buddha, Manjushri, showed up and smote the valley rim at its lowest point with his sword, creating the Chobar Gorge at the valley's south end, through which drained the lake. But the immutable light of Swayambhu remained, its lotus transformed into a hillock upon which, sometime around the fifth century, Buddhist monks began to build a stupa, burying the god-sent light beneath a stone slab to protect it from the dark age that humans have dwelled in ever since.

A fine tale, of course. Another cartoon-colored, hallucinogenic panel in the frescoes of Kathmandu. And yet what did the sage Dubby Bhagat tell me? "It's the mythology that keeps this country together—the stories, the narratives of the people." Even the ruins of a nation exhale its stories.

I stare off across the luminous nightfall of the world's most exotic valley to observe another Swayambhu levitate in the east above the storybook kingdoms of Bhutan and Sikkim, a glistening white stupa that swells and completes itself and becomes the full moon, and I suddenly recall that the wonderful Spanish phrase *a dar luz*—literally, "to give light"—means to be born. Buddha is 2,541 years old today, which is about how many butter lamps, now lit, encircle the shrine, the spectacular birthday cake of Swayambhu, innumerable tiny petals of flame winking in homage to the awakened self, like the starlight within jewels, or within Kathmandu's ancestral heart, a mystery so consolingly beautiful that you never want to have to explain it, or hear it explained.

The night turns milk-blue, ghostly, vaporous. The city animates light, and amplifies everything within a life. The self crackles in the ether like a sheet of electricity, and the celebrants flow back down the hill to suffer the contentments of mortality, having communed however briefly with the dreaming mind of god.

Darkness, said Martin Luther King, cannot drive out darkness. Only light can do that.

PART THREE
The Land of Lo
(2001)

The Land of Lo

One hundred and fifty million years ago, when there were not yet Himalayas to climb or die on, the air currents bouncing our little plane were a sea breeze, moderate or not, and these mountains lay darkly within the ocean floor, a chain of eggs from an underworld serpent, unimaginable in their greatness, and no one to imagine them anyway except the gods.

But in the expansive geologic minute, eighty million years later, the Indian subcontinent shuddered into wakefulness and began to butt its crown into the vast landmass of Central Asia. Where the plates met, the earth's crust folded upward, ever upward to the present day—Everest's summit rose three inches last year alone—thrusting snow peaks through seabeds and into the stars, forming a virtually unbroken axis fifteen hundred miles long. Only in a few places along this axis from Pakistan to Burma did the Asian continent's rivers breach the dam of the Himalayas, creating in one such place—like a cosmic ax-chop eighteen thousand feet deep between the Annapurna massif and Dhaulagiri—the second-deepest gorge in the world, cut by the Kali Gandaki River, which is where we found ourselves flying this early morning in May, the sheer flanks of the gorge thrusting far above our wings.

One learns immediately that any traveler's tale of Mustang begins with the cruel and ubiquitous wind. The tectonic instability of the Himalayas expresses itself in occasional earthquakes, but the clash of atmospheric forces is a daily affair, especially during the monsoon season, when the subcontinent's moisture-laden low pressure systems slam headlong into the Himalayas' southern face, and the arid high pressure systems of the Tibetan plateau push and push against the northern slopes. In this breach—the Kali Gandaki Gorge—the isobars of wind pinch like an ocean current through a narrow cut in a barrier reef. Planes flying up the gorge from Pokhara, in the southern foothills, to Jomsom, on the northern slope, leave shortly after sunrise or not at all. Any later, and the surge of subcontinental winds tossed by high-altitude thermals and pop-up squalls make the flight reckless, if not impossible.

"There are a hundred thousand ghosts flying in those Kali Gandaki winds," Nepal's aviation pioneer, the Swiss pilot Emil Wick, once remarked. It is, however, one of the world's most spectacular and thrilling flights, needling between two of the highest mountains on earth—a flight where you never see much sky but look up, at the snowfields, or out, at the waterfalls and rhododendron forests on the vertical hillsides. Down changes moment by moment, from treetop level to plunges measured in thousands of feet. The flight takes less than forty minutes in a De Havilland Twin Otter STOL. To walk the same distance takes a week, up and up out of the dripping, flowered forests into the Himalayan rain shadow, a land so barren and unforgiving that the Lobas themselves—the indigenous people of Mustang, called Lo in Tibetan—describe their own geography as the desiccated, bleached carcass of a horse, the wind trumpeting through its rib bones on an endless heap of rocks.

Despite Mustang's harsh enchantment, we would ride from Jomsom for thirteen days, to the Tibetan borderlands and back, and rarely think otherwise.

Past Dhaulagiri's sinister icefall tumbling out through a ceiling of charcoal clouds, the Twin Otter begins its nauseating descent toward Jomsom's landing strip, and in the sudden pitch downward, I stop thinking it's so hilarious that my seat belt is attached to an eyebolt by a bungee cord.

No sooner are we out of the plane with our gear than it reloads with trekkers and traders and pilgrims and begins to taxi for the return hop to Pokhara, the orange windsock above the terminal offering a limp salute. Though we are a hardy group, we are not professional mountaineers, and we stand stunned, astounded, there on the apron, gaping at 23,166-foot Nilgiri, rocketing into the heavens from the opposite side of the airstrip and glazed with brilliant sunlight, as close as most of us will ever get to a Himalayan summit. Then the cloud bank to the east shifts, revealing the back side of the Annapurnas and a cornice the size of a supertanker, hung on the crest of a frozen tidal wave. The miracle of the Himalayas is this: Every time you look, every second you look, you are seeing the mountains, trying to believe the mountains, for the first time. There is no sense of *Oh I get it*, no internal message of *Been there, done that*. For once in your life, the newness is eternal.

And for the sunny, frontier town of Jomsom, so, apparently, is change. The airport's paved apron, begun two Decembers ago, would be completed in five days, allowing turboprops to land. Then, the construction crew tells us, the government will begin to build a road up the gorge from Pokhara to Jomsom, which will eventually continue on to Lo Manthang, the traditional capital of Mustang and Asia's only surviving walled city, already connected by a Chinese-sponsored road to the Tibetan border. The project, though, has more than enormous financial and technical difficulties to overcome. The mule skinners, who freight cargo between China and Pokhara, and pack trekker's gear up and down the old salt trade routes through Mustang, have objected. So have the agencies and individuals who don't want mass tourism in the kingdom, although the Nepalese government was mulling the idea of lifting Mustang's restricted status and lowering its seven-hundred-dollar entrance fee. And so, most significantly, has New Delhi, which abhors the doomsday possibility of Chinese troops trucked across Mustang and down through the Himalayas to the Indian border.

But with or without a road, Jomsom thrives, its guesthouses and cafés filled with windburned Germans and Australians and Israelis. As a destination, Jomsom is a way station or the end of the road for trek-kers on the Annapurna circuit coming down from Thorung La pass. Or a staging area for expeditions like ours up to Lo Manthang, fifty linear miles and three centuries away, and a rendezvous point for thousands of Hindus making a pilgrimage to the sacred cave of nearby Muktinath, many of them affluent Indians who stay in the comfort of a five-star hotel built on a mesa above the town. As a political entity, Jomsom is the seat for Mustang's elected governor, the liaison between the government in Kathmandu and Jigme Dorje Palbar Bista, the twenty-fifth raja—or, as he is commonly but incorrectly called, king—of the autonomous region of Mustang. As a cultural and ecological entity, Jomsom, and all of Mus-tang, is regulated by the Annapurna Conservation Area Project (ACAP), a Nepalese nongovernmental organization funded by the royal family's King Mahendra Trust for Nature Conservation. ACAP's influence, as evidenced by its sign forbidding the use of plastic bags in Mustang, was a benign force to be reckoned with by both foreigners and locals, a sort of Big Didi watching over the land and its creatures.

Breaking the spell of Nilgiri, we transfer the elation of our arrival from the snow peaks to the gleaming smiles of Ang Tsering, who will be the trip's *sardar*, Chhundi, the cook, and their crew of Sherpas, already organizing our mountain of gear. The Sherpas, who live in the Solu-Khumbu, the Everest region of eastern Nepal, have never been to Mustang either, though they share a Tibetan lineage, language, and religion with the Lobas. A reunion takes place: Laird and his wife, Jann, seasoned trekking guides throughout the Nepalese high country, have worked with the cheerful Ang Tsering and Chhundi before and they have joined the expedition at the Lairds' request, their competence essential to our success on the trail. In the whirl of activity, hasty introductions are attempted. There are seven of us *queris*, including my own wife, Cat; Mark, our friend from Santa Fe; and the Bangkok Bachelors, Captain Jack, a Vietnam vet, and Michael, a former Peace Corps volunteer in the terai, friends of the Lairds who arrived in Kathmandu from Thailand two nights earlier like beaming monkeys, stewed in whiskey and well ingested with recreationals. With Ang Tsering and Chhundi are four porters—Ang Dawa, Ang Naru, Chaapten, and Biri. By my count, the expedition has expanded to fourteen members, including the central government's liaison officer—Raju, we'll call him—who attached himself to us in Pokhara, since it is illegal to journey into Upper Mustang or any restricted area without some variety of cop shambling along. We stroll up Jomsom's one rocky street to a nearby guesthouse for tea. The time is 6:40, with the fullest of days ahead of us.

In the courtyard of the guesthouse, we concentrate on the serious business of repacking our duffel bags for the mules that will carry our kit up through the gorge to the Tibetan plateau. Although the Sherpas will tote the kitchen on their backs in Mustang, ACAP, for environmental reasons, and local mule skinner politics, for reasons of survival, discourage the use of trekking porters, so common to Himalayan expeditions. With the gear reshuffled, we face a four-hour wait for the horses to be brought in from the countryside. Laird and Jann disappear on errands; the Bangkok Bachelors are laid out under the blanket of their hangovers; for Cat, Mark, and myself, the stress of traveling halfway around the world, the four-thousand-foot jump in altitude from Pokhara, and the adrenaline of arrival have made us squirrelly and disoriented and so we head out into the crisp, sun-blasted air of Jomsom for a calming stroll.

The road out of town is lively, an Old West mix of animals, villagers, and pilgrims—horses and mule trains, goats and shepherds, solitary *dhzos* like shaggy Texas longhorns, self-involved schoolchildren, porters hauling lumber north into the desert, shopkeepers on their stoops, orange-robed sadhus off to Muktinath, a toylike Chinese tractor hauling a wagonload of laborers. We pass a Nepalese army outpost and its mountain warfare training school, a sleepy bivouac unconcerned about the Maoists shooting up police stations to the south and west. The Kali Gandaki, out of sight below the airstrip, now parallels the road, its khaki-colored water foaming across rapids. Ahead, a perfectly reliable steel-girded suspension footbridge spans the fast-rushing river, leading to the more serene streets of Old Jomsom, its mud-walled houses and government offices, and over we go but slowly, holding my wife by the hand, since swinging bridges give her vertigo and usually, now in fact, she has to be dragged across them, eyes closed or at least averted from the imaginary fall.

At the edge of town, we cross back over the river and sit upon a pedestal of rocks at road's end, gazing up the valley, the spare pasture-land hugging the west bank filled with herds of goats that move in the distance like swarms of dark brown bees, the vast expanse of the Kali Gandaki's rubble-strewn bed and graveled floodplain, a thousand-lane highway rolled down between canyon walls, a slumbering monster undulating extravagantly across its Mississippi River–size bed, the bald, tormented hills beyond rising to the Tibetan plateau, and to the east and west imposing twin fences of twenty-thousand-foot peaks that box the northward thumbing of Mustang into China.

What we are about to do—ride horseback up the canyon—wouldn't be possible in another month, when the monsoons win their elemental battle with the Himalayas, and the river turns furious, its torrents swelling across the glacial plain, expanding to a hundred times its dry-season level and forcing travelers to the harrowing footpaths along the cliffs. Even now, on the eve of the rains, riders bound for Lo Manthang exit the canyon early for the trails over the high passes at Chelli, avoiding the overnight journey through the fabulous but virtually impassable upper gorge of the Kali Gandaki, but we are going through the gorge as well.

I had grown up riding horses, spent much of my life around them, have owned them, broken them, foaled them, swam with them, fallen with them, watched them die unnecessary deaths, but up that canyon, and on the loose-rock walls above it, I was about to find out that I had never really known before just what a horse can do, or what I would be willing to do on a horse, or the insanities that could be enacted by horse and rider.

Up-Canyon to Kagbeni

Time to mount up, but where are the horses?

Laird knows. The horses—the king's horses, mind you; Laird has cut some sort of deal that will end badly—have been brought down from Lo Manthang, where they have grazed and galloped all their horsey lives in agrarian bliss, never having to bear the insult of sharing the road with a diabolic machine. Their handlers—Mahendra, the king's horseman, and his young round-faced assistant, Tomay—are afraid that an encounter between the horses and one of Jomsom's Chinese tractors will not go well, and they wait for us on the northern edge of town.

The wind, which started to make its presence felt around midmorning, bowls powerful gusts at our backs, churning dust into the air. Across the river past the Jimi Hendrix Rooftop Restaurant, our horses cluster on the dirt lane near the second bridge, standing in the precious shade of neem trees planted on the bank above them. The king's horseman begins the inexact science of sizing us up and assigning mounts. Laird and I are the only experienced riders in the group; the Bangkok Bachelors, unadulterated greenhorns, are cocksure they can manage anything they are required to straddle. Our grimacing wives are overtly brave but secretly panicked. In her incipient life as an equestrian, Cat, with a mere two hours' credit on a lazy trail ride in Florida, is nevertheless game to bond with her pony, a doe-eyed white mare that she is hoisted upon, Mahendra on one side lifting, untangling her swing leg from the saddlebags, and Tomay on the opposite side counterbalancing the saddle and, if necessary, catching, since our heavy day packs skew our balance.

"What's her name?" my wife asks, settling her backside into the Tibetan carpets spread over the broad wooden frame of the saddle. Mahendra says a word that sounds like *cow*. "Cow? Oh no!" Leaning to pat the mare's neck, she rechristens her *Cowgirl*. Apparently invigorated by her new name, Cowgirl takes off, shoving her way through the pack toward the empty road ahead. Dashing forward, Mahendra grabs the reins from her fists and we are all instructed in Loba horse-talk. The command *Cho*! or *tchew*!, a phonetic cousin of *Whoa*!, means *Move it*! *Go*! The same double-click of the tongue that Westerners use to tell a horse *Giddyap* is the Loba command for *Stop*! The information is of course counterintuitive. Our brains absorb the lesson but our tongues are readily confused and the horses, neither bilingual nor mind readers, are doomed to be continually puzzled by our desires.

Mahendra hands the reins back to my wife. Cowgirl plods ahead. "Stop!" yells Cat. Cowgirl won't. We yell at Cat to click her tongue, pull harder on the reins, but now the stubborn horse has a stubborn, advice-resistant rider, and Tomay ties Cowgirl's lead rope to a rock so we can finish mounting the rest of the expedition.

Jann, unhappy with the enterprise, is helped up onto a second small white mare that, Mahendra tells her, is the rani's personal mount, and although she seems momentarily cheered to be riding the queen's horse, the honor quickly fades into a type of punishment Jann had not foreseen. The horse, graced with a comalike docility, won't move. The Bangkok Bachelors are led to a handsome pair of good-size "blue" geldings, the Loba description for gray-coated horses. For a guy who's never been on a horse, Michael, loose and gangly, pours well into his saddle and assumes a very credible slouch, the veteran of many cavalry charges down Bangkok's Pamdong Road toward the front lines of hedonism. We all watch expectantly as the dandy Captain Jack, an air force intelligence officer during the Vietnam War, is led to the second blue by Mahendra and his left boot placed carefully in the stirrup. The captain takes a moment to gesture grandiosely and, being a well-read fellow, pronounce a bon mot or two. Then, as he attempts to mount the blue, a type of well-meaning struggle takes place between Mahendra and the captain, which climaxes with the horrifying sight of Jack catapulting completely over the horse, Tomay breaking the fall before the captain breaks his neck. A second attempt seems as if it will prove equally disastrous, but at the last moment before flying off the captain awakens to the moment and grabs the horse's mane, and Tomay slides a stirrup over his right boot. Mahendra, intimately aware of the perils that await us on our journey, looks ashen, and you wouldn't blame him for coming to the conclusion that we are not, by the most basic criteria, serious people.

The liaison officer sits rigidly atop Mahendra's own white pony; without fanfare or guidance, Laird mounts a large, sturdy walnut-brown gelding. The remaining two horses are the biggest and the smallest of the herd, the most spirited and the most ridiculous: by Tibetan standards, a huge white prancing gelding named Jamling, and, by petting zoo standards, a round, diminutive chestnut mare with a graying face that, after our first river crossing, we will rename Submarine. I glance over at blond-haired Mark, shorter than I and lighter by forty pounds, and shrug. Mark sits astride Submarine like a sullen, overgrown child on a sawhorse, his legs almost scraping the ground.

The king's horseman has a look of grave concern on his otherwise optimistic face as we approach Jamling. He wants to be reassured that I know what I'm doing; I flip up the saddle carpets and begin, until Tomay takes over, to lower the stirrups to their last notch. The horse tosses its head; Mahendra seizes the reins. Tibetan horses were never bred to carry tall, bulky Westerners like myself.

I raise my foot to the stirrup and test my weight against the saddle, trying to determine if it is too loose and will rotate when I mount, and Tomay wisely exerts his own weight against the opposite stirrup. The moment I'm in the air, Jamling sidesteps nervously; my pack shifts, knocking me off balance, and the horse lurches, but I flip my leg over its rump and hold tight, grabbing the reins and pulling the bit back through its skull until the horse's nose is on my knee and it cha-chas backward into the other mounts, who begin biting one another. This acting up, I know, can go on for a while before a high-spirited horse resigns itself to a rider, but before I can subdue Jamling, Mahendra grabs the lead rope and halter and escorts the horse to the front of the pack, where it settles down.

"This horse likes to go," says Mahendra.

"He's all right," I say. I like to go too.

And just like that, we are moving out, down the bankside and out of town and onto the rocky floodplain of the Kali Gandaki. Cowgirl muscles through the scrum until she walks head to tail with Jamling; the blues jostle side by side behind her, trading places every ten seconds, unrestrained by their riders. Tom hangs back with his wife to offer encouragement and soothe her anxiety. Mark straggles aboard the sluggish Submarine, and Mahendra, who handed off Jamling's lead rope to Tomay, dashes along the line like a frantic mother duck, attempting to convince himself, I presume, that he has not lost his mind by mounting up such a dubious band of *queri*. And although I am at the head of the caravan, it exasperates me to no end that I am being led, however merrily, by Tomay. After five minutes of picking my way across the rocks, I rein Jamling to a stop, summon forward Laird and Mahendra, and object.

Although I had deferred to Laird's experience on most things Mustang, in our months of planning I had initially nixed the use of horses because of the expense, yet Tom had persuaded me not only that we would fail to get through the upper gorge without them but that there were social and cultural perceptions to be attended to, and that without horses, and good ones, we would be looked down upon by the class-conscious Lobas, for whom the horse is a traditional embodiment of prestige, and lose respect among the very people we would need to depend on for our well-being. *Well of course,* I thought cynically, a few hundred yards out on the Kali Gandaki floodplain, *the king and his court are certainly going to think less of us if we don't pay them a fortune for their horses.*

Laird and Mahendra have come up, surprised to find me snarling. "This is like a pony ride for a six-year-old at the circus," I explain, "and if that's the way it's going to be, I'd rather walk." Mahendra purses his lips at my unseemly anger and gives Laird a quizzical look, awaiting a translation while I rave on. "Is this horse uncontrollable?" I demand. "If it is, let's go back to Jomsom and swap it out of the pack for another."

Mahendra blinks with innocence, understanding the gist of the problem: How much might he trust my horsemanship? Straight-faced and guileless, he directs his answer at Tom. "I rode it myself from Lo Manthang."

"Then I'm riding it too," I say resolutely, taking the lead rope from Tomay to loop into the saddle straps. I jam my heels into Jamling's ribs and off we go again, set free. My wife, who's been wheeling Cowgirl in circles trying to make her stop, comes trotting ahead but Jamling will not let her pass, and I have no inclination to rein him in. Still, we can move across the difficult clutter of the stony riverbed only marginally faster than a man can walk, and, at least for today, the horses are in control and obey their own hierarchy of prejudice and competition.

Here at the end of the dry season, the river is down to only a fraction of its width, though by no means feeble, its dark flow contained in a serpentine channel that bends sluggishly across the plain from one side of the canyon to the other. We are immediately sobered by the desolation we ride into, its lifeless, lunar magnitude, the dense stacking of scorched, scoured mountains, so unwelcoming, we had quickly learned, that even the Maoists were giving Mustang a wide berth. Ahead of us, dust storms and dust devils form and unform like writhing spirits. Fortunately, judging from the bent, hooded faces and invalid steps of the infrequent trekkers and pilgrims staggering down the canyon toward the refuge of Jomsom, the wind, which I judge to be a steady thirty-five miles per hour, is at our backs, which intermittently receive a buckshot blast of rain although we're riding into a furnace of high-altitude sun.

Behind us, horses and riders are spread in a line for perhaps a quarter mile; perhaps another quarter mile behind the last riders comes our mule train, angling up out of the plain toward the cliffside trail. We have lost sight of Jomsom and its modern comforts, but the panorama of the Himalayas remains unobstructed, and what I see up in the heights when I turn in the saddle is worrisome—a massive storm dropping east off Dhaulagiri, plugging the breach and consuming the Annapurnas. The clockwork monsoons are two weeks premature, and it's unusual to find this much weather nudging into the rain shadow this early. The river rises measurably every afternoon from snowmelt, and surely any precipitation on the Tibetan plateau in the coming days will complicate our return journey.

Out come the sweaty rain jackets, Mahendra and Tomay hovering nearby to assist those of us who can't quite manage the acrobatics of removing our packs and donning clothes while on horseback, in a wind strong enough to blow an inattentive rider out of the saddle. The trail across the rocks is patchy but easy to follow, or not follow, as you please, and the sure-footed horses, invested in their steady clopping plod, pay close attention to the endless supply of next steps, sometimes faltering with indecision. After several rugged hours in the wind and rocks, our exhilaration is muffled but we're enjoying a Class B sort of sore-assed, mindless fun, occasionally glancing up at the footpath chiseled high into the cliffside and happy to not be on it.

So far the Kali Gandaki has remained mostly invisible, playing by itself in some other part of the neighborhood, but now it cuts a swath toward the eastern wall of the canyon; its hissing penetrates the throaty drone of the wind, and we can smell its stone-wet iciness. The trail branches, straight to the fording, right to the wall. Ever-vigilant Mahendra hobbles across the rocks to stop me. In any language, the meaning of Mahendra's words would be self-evident—the river here is too dangerous to cross; we have to go up. Well and good, but we are only a dozen feet above the rapids when Mahendra halts again, pointing ahead to where the canyon wall is raw and sagging, scooped out by recent landslides. "Go fast down this section," he says, his eyes alarmingly wide, and before I know it he bolts across the slides, dashing under the sickening, rotting overhangs in a crouch, like a soldier sprinting across Snipers Alley. My level of alertness skyrockets into focus. I pass the word down the line, their view of the horror obscured by the rise and dip of the path, then kick Jamling down and through this boobytrap at a brisk walk, preventing him from trotting out of the fear that a trotting horse sends sharper vibrations into the unstable ground than a walking horse, and that the last riders might find themselves the victims of our haste. There are many ways to kill yourself in the Himalayas, and here by God is one of them.

Horse by horse, we cross to safety without incident, our senses humming, but the real terror waits just ahead. Returning to the flood-plain, before too long we have been pressed back against the canyon wall by the bending river and dismount at the base of a stair of boulders, threaded by a narrow trail rising steeply to a landing some fifty or sixty feet above the bed. I do not yet believe or trust in the horses wholeheartedly, as I will in the days to come, and I truly doubt that these animals, which are not goats, powerful but not spry, deft but not limber, can ascend this vertical, rock-studded path without wings, or a crane to lift them. But in this case, to be wrong is to be astonished, and delighted, by the skill of the Tibetan horse.

Up the horses go, like dogs at the circus climbing ladders; we scramble behind them, clumsy apes, and remount on the flat shelf where the path worms out along the bulge of the cliffside. Mahendra smiles, pleased, but offers no forewarning. I lead us with some confidence out over a drop of hundreds of feet to the rocks and rivers below, and although the path is broad enough to accommodate mistakes of footing, it isn't long before the margin for error recedes to zero, the path attenuates, the up slope and the down slope sheer off, and I find myself the point man in a nightmare, riding a horse high on a cliffside along an eighteen-inch-wide trail of crushed rock, the river slurping the base of the wall far beneath me. To the left, I would be required to dismount into thin air. To the right, should the need arise, I could only dismount by pushing my horse over the brink, where it would splatter like a watermelon on the stones below. Jamling's hooves boot pebbles into the abyss.

My heartbeat thunders; my eyes swim when I chance to look down. I lack the composure to turn in the saddle for a glance behind me, to judge the welfare of my height-freaked wife and companions. You don't rope together horses as you might climbers on an icefall. We are, at times like this, woefully alone, outside the circle of a helping hand, and if we perish, we perish separately, for traveling through the vastness as we are breeds a powerful inwardness, a sense of solitude that seems a counterpoint to our collective destiny. Nothing we *queri* do out here requires much teamwork, and at least while we're in motion, the most intimate bond that forms is between horse and rider.

For twenty minutes the horses defy gravity, stepping with unflappable determination along the slippery thin line of catastrophe. When we finally descend to flat earth, I pull back on Jamling and take a minute to see how the crew has fared. Laird, a veteran of these canyons, is flushed with the nostalgia of previous risks. My wife, grim and gasping, admits she rode blind along the precipice, reins loose, eyes wide shut, and the stalwart Cowgirl in control. Jann, all nerves and still trembling, swears she'll never do anything like that again, and she means it. The wasted Bangkok Bachelors dozed through the entire drama, dreaming of nurses and gin-and-tonic IVs. For Mark, the geriatric, unwilling Submarine succeeded in making even this, the Pony Ride from Hell, tedious and slightly boring. Our liaison officer, an accountant by training and an immigration officer by necessity, is pale and grumbling. His fifth trip to Mustang, he can't figure out what the attraction is. By mutual agreement, he will leave us in the morning and, without informing his superiors, return gratefully to his family

50

in Pokhara. He is a bureaucrat, not an adventurer, a useless, inept, and frightened member of the expedition, and in a corrupt and violence-torn nation, his actual presence with us is pointless and the pretense of that presence a meaningless transgression.

More than four hours out from Jomsom, wind-blasted and parched, our asses and knees terribly sore, we arrive at the beautiful mud-and-stone village of Kagbeni, the last outpost before the restricted area of Upper Mustang, and dismount on a knoll above shockingly green terraces of barley. Mahendra and Tomay lead the horses to pasture, and, stiff-legged, we enter the town's medieval warren of streets beneath flapping rows of prayer flags, past turnip-shaped chortens and tea shops serving apple pie, apple cake, apple crumble, past a satellite dish and a huge protector deity with an erect wooden penis. Whooping and hollering, four teenage boys jog around a corner into my path; with both hands, one holds a painted clay god above his head, one wields an ax, and the other two slash the air with shiny butcher knives. Whatever hash of mythologies they're working with I can't say. We exchange nods and they run on to complete a ritual I can hardly imagine. Eventually at the top of town we find the Red House Inn, our lodging for the night, where we reunite with Ang Tsering and the Sherpas. By twilight the mule train arrives, the wind calms, and Chhundi, our artist in residence, has taken over the kitchen. Dandelions of light appear throughout the town's darkness; Kagbeni has had the pleasure of electricity for only one year, and a television flickers blue in the house below the tearoom where we sprawl. Three foreigners, like us on the way up-canyon to Lo Manthang, share the inn for the night. The youngest is a twenty-one-year-old, rosy-cheeked Swede, full of enthusiasm and energy and charm.

"Why are you reading that book?" Laird asks him gruffly, pointing to his copy of Michel Peissel's *Mustang: A Lost Tibetan Kingdom*, the account of the French ethnologist's 1964 journey to Lo Manthang. It seems Laird's subtext here is, Why aren't you reading *my* book, you hatchling? "It's almost forty years old! It's ancient history."

"Yes," says the kid, whose untested life is floating on the perfect answer, "but it makes you dream." Ah, Laird grins and mimes a swoon, falling back in love again with the concept of youth, this 2001 model of his yearning, footloose boyish self.

In the rough beds of our fatigue, we fall asleep dreaming of the dull brass chorus of horse bells, an echo, a lightness, fresh in our ears, the world so far away.

Wandervogel

His father was a Mississippi cracker, a tech sergeant in the air force, sent to Vietnam; his mother was a frustrated artist who quit cooking and started going away for the summers to Provincetown to paint. Their son Tom was pounded on all the time by the other kids, changing schools five times in Florida and Tennessee and St. Louis; by the time he was twelve he was reading Dostoyevsky and Kierkegaard and considered himself an unrepentant atheist. Graduating from high school at seventeen with no discernible honors, he understood that he hated his father, hated everything about America as well, and told his mother there was no sticking around, that whatever he was going to do in this life he wasn't going to do it here in the South, or in his parents' orbit. He didn't know where that place was where he would meet his destiny, but within a week of graduation he left to find it. Three times, he hitchhiked back and forth between Florida and San Francisco. Delaying college for what he thought would be a year and not a lifetime, he saved money for a trip to Europe working the night shift at a cardboard box factory in Murfreesboro, where his sister lived, and started reading Hemingway, Kerouac, Huxley. Within a year of high school, he was in Nepal and never came back.

Tom Laird was, in 1972, part of the great transcontinental traveling freak show that began in the States and Europe, pirouetted its way across the Bosporus into Asia, followed the Silk Road or the Spice

Trail into India, and finally nestled into Kathmandu, where it became infamously known as the Rock and Roll Raj. From London to Paris to Rome to Athens, Laird became slowly infatuated with his mother's supreme passion, art—the Babylonian display at the Louvre, the evolution of angels evident to the attentive eye in every museum in Europe, the inexplicable sensation that Michelangelo was speaking to him as he gazed adoringly at the *Pietà* at the Vatican. On the Spanish Steps he purchased a copy of French adventurer Alexandra David-Neel's *Magic and Mystery in Tibet*, an extremely inaccurate, romanticized account of Tibetan Buddhism, almost a nineteenth-century fantasy, but it gave him the dream of remote kingdoms where diamonds lay about on the ground. It was the classic *wandervogel* reinvented by the counterculture, the Grand Tour with free sex and psychedelics, kids looking for themselves and opening doors into their snow-white consciousness, but by the time Laird arrived on the islands of Greece he was fed up with Europe, it was too much like America, and on Santorini he met a Jewish kid who had just returned from Kathmandu who told him he could go overland to Nepal on public transport for sixty bucks. Laird had four hundred, with which he could either make his way back home or continue forward.

There were no maps, only travelers exchanging information. He went to Istanbul; at the legendary Pudding Shop he joined a group of kids on a four-day train ride to Tehran. In Iran, the knot of traveling companions changed again and he found himself on a bus to the Persian border and another bus through Afghan customs and another bus into Herat, which just had the worst blizzard in living memory, the nomads had lost all their animals, and here were all the naive young hippies getting off the bus into a catastrophe, women throwing their babies at them, tearing their breasts with their fingernails in desperation, people assaulting them as they scuttled in turtle formation to the nearest shop and closed the door and the shopkeeper explained they're dying, all the people of Herat are dying. There's an eye-opener, kids!

Already Laird was beginning to feel that Kerouac was a coward, a chickenshit, he didn't go far enough—fucking Marrakech, big deal. He started to see French and Italian kids OD'ing on heroin in filthy hostels. The girls had bruises on their breasts and ass from being pinched incessantly, and so did Tom, but it had become clear that Afghanistan was taking people away, far away from their former lives; Afghanistan was really the *beginning* of the adventure, where both the mind and the body began to alter in a way that proved difficult to reverse. Before Afghanistan they were just traveling, but now everybody dressed themselves in local clothes in a silly attempt to blend in; they were hanging out in the bazaars, eating weird food from the stalls that made them constantly sick.

He took a forty-eight-hour bus ride to Chicken Street, the hippie meeting place in Kabul, passing through the horrible searing bleakness of Kandahar, where three Frenchmen had recently been decapitated by a mob for looking a bit too longingly at a local woman. Kabul was teeming with a pan-ethnic tribe of freaks from across the world, broken into subcultures—drugs, antiques, religion, art. He took another bus to the Khyber Pass and down to Peshawar and then a night train across the Pakistani plains to Lahore, where he booked a thirty-six-dollar flight to Amristar because this was the Indo-Pakistani War of '72 and the border was closed. By now he had separated from his pod of fellow wanderers and was alone. He rode the bus to Delhi but India was immediately tiring, butt to chest people, the intolerable heat, the filth, the never-ending diarrhea. To escape the heat, all the hippies were bugging out to Kashmir or Kathmandu, take your pick, and after a few sleepless nights he was on the train to the Nepalese border and then standing by the roadside in the savanna-like terai with his thumb out.

An old American-made cargo truck stopped for him and he crawled in the back under a canvas tarp protecting a load of sacked sugar. It was the monsoon season and it rained all night while they motored up into the hills, and for the first time in months he crawled into his down sleeping bag to warm himself. He awoke at dawn because the truck had stopped and a Gurung woman with twenty gold earrings in both ears had flung the tarp back and the wind was cold. They were on the Damang Pass above the Kathmandu Valley, 9,000 feet high. Given the monsoons, it shouldn't have been a clear morning and he shouldn't have been able to see the Himalayas, but there they were in a spectacular panorama, from Annapurna to Everest, the clouds curdled below the peaks.

Immediately he knew he was at that place he had told his mother he was looking for, and that whatever he was going to do in life, he was going to do it here; just the details had to be worked out. Which sounded insane, of course, but he couldn't deny the exhilarating physical sensation of his life about to assume its shape, to grasp its purpose. Foreigners visiting Nepal fell under the spell of the mountains and the culture all the time, and now Laird was one of them. He was nineteen years old, halfway around the world from his childhood, and convinced he had come home.

After a month in Kathmandu, though, his money ran out and he hitchhiked back to Europe destitute, his last five dollars stolen in Kabul, starving and begging his way to Turin, Italy, where he telephoned a Kathmandu contact for help. By then he was possessed with an absolute faith, an iron flame of self-belief burning in his chest, that he could do anything, that nothing could deflect him, but he weighed less than a hundred pounds, parasites were eating his intestines, and he had a kidney infection. Alberto, his Italian friend, put him to work as a gardener at a Baptist missionary school; he was fed huge meals and sent to a doctor and the old missionary ladies gave him *The Chronicles of Narnia* to read and chamomile tea and he started putting on some weight and scheming about a return to Nepal.

Alberto invited him along to a party in Geneva; Laird shaved his shoulder-length hair, put on an Afghani skullcap, wrapped himself in a Tibetan *chuba*, and went as the exoticism of the moment. Encouraged to speak his callow mind, he launched into a soliloquy about the spirituality of Nepal and wrapped up with a sales pitch: All he wanted to do, he told the gathering of beautiful people, was to make a movie about the efficacy of Tantric Buddhism—the philosophic notion that you could employ any human activity to achieve enlightenment, an idea the hippies had seized upon with great vitality, using it to legitimize the two pursuits—sex and drugs—at the pinnacle of their enlightenment list.

Inconceivably, Alberto's patron, an eccentric Italian millionaire living in Geneva, gave Laird $50,000 after listening to his rap. Glory, glory. He had won the lottery, his karma runneth over, and the one remaining question of his good fortune was: Would he piss it all away? With the money, Tom persuaded three contacts back in Provincetown involved in photography to fly to Geneva with several trunkloads of film and equipment and then travel overland with him to Kathmandu. The filmmakers had all just finished college and were on their way up in the world: Frank, who would become a professor of photography at Amherst; Gary, a future computer wonk at NASA; and Billy, who would eventually come back to earth as a software specialist in Silicon Valley. Because it was a living Buddhist homeland, they went to Solu-Khumbu, Sherpa territory, for a year documenting tribal society—the same thing Laird would do in Mustang almost twenty years later.

Laird rented a house, began taking Nepali lessons, carried his own water, cooked his own food, trying to live like a Sherpa peasant, and was very proud and arrogant for his efforts at assimilation. He found Buddhism from the ground up; saw, felt, and touched the quotidian culture; did his homework; learned the mythology, the cosmology; stayed at the monasteries where he was offered a graduated understanding of the basic forces that govern our lives; and slowly comprehended that he would be a much more difficult person to be around if he had not studied these things. Maybe other people didn't need to learn these lessons but Laird did, over and over.

Here Laird met an old man living in a cave who would become one of his three Buddhist fathers, the men he encountered who most expressed the ideal of humanity, the models he most wanted to be like himself. (The second was the Dalai Lama; the third, the old *amji*, the practitioner of Tibetan medicine, in Mustang.) The first, Au Leshe, was the greatest living Sherpa *thangka* painter, now dead. Under the Au Leshe's mentorship, Laird began to look at the murals on the temple walls and pay hyper-focused attention. Art isn't art, the old painter told him, music isn't music; these are tools for developing your consciousness, created for the purpose of diverting us from greed, anger, ignorance, lust, and pride—the five sins. With these tools we develop compassion, wisdom, and love for our fellow human beings. Unlike the five sins, these virtues were not natural human states, they were cultivated.

Tom idolized the sage and the team took a thousand pictures in the cave and temples for a slide show that he hoped would capture the spirit of Au Leshe. The show premiered at Asia House in New York and the annual conference of the American Ethnomusicological Society, and the team released an LP with Lyrichord Discs, the first reproductions on a high-end Nagra recorder of Tibetan *puja* music. By 1974, Laird wasn't yet twenty-one but was proving to be somewhat of a wunderkind.

Back in Geneva sorting through the team's raw material, he sought refuge with the sixteenth Karmapa, the head of one of the four main sects of Buddhism, who was living in Geneva at the time and had a physical presence as commanding as a quarterback for the Denver Broncos. Laird, increasingly inclined toward mysticism, read every available Buddhist text in translation at the time and, casting aside his atheism, became one of the first, quote unquote, Western Buddhists, absorbed by the spiritual fantasy that had spellbound the West for so long—Shangri-la, Shambhala. The Karmapa threw a monkey wrench into the plan, however, forbidding him to record any more Tibetan music. Laird, who had been the team's soundman, thought the Karmapa's reasoning was primitive; it made him depressed but he obeyed the dictate. He had come out of Solu-Khumbu with a wealth of pictures and tape recordings, a book in progress, and a firm commitment to live in Nepal, but all the camera equipment had been stolen in Kathmandu, and he had squandered the fifty grand. I forgive you, said the patron in Geneva, but now I want you to do some work on Hindu medicine and the Vedhyas. I really want to continue with Sherpa mythology, said Laird. No money, said the patron. Tom sailed back to the States and promptly decided he'd made a terrible mistake, a blunder that would take him three years to resolve, but in 1977 he had saved enough money to return to Nepal, and this time he was back for good.

For two years Laird lived by himself in Solu-Khumbu, interviewing the Sherpas, writing on a tiny portable typewriter, cutting and pasting, finally publishing "Mountains as Gods, Mountains as Goals," in 1979 in the *CoEvolution Quarterly*, a long article translated into a half-dozen languages and cited by mountaineers—Rheinhold Messner et al.—in debates about the misuse of Sherpas by Western climbers. Laird's point of view was derided as "hippie philosophy" at the time, but he had interviewed Edmund Hillary for the piece, who agreed with Tom that climbers were letting Sherpas take the risks, the whole dynamic that led to guided commercial tours and the tragedy described by Jon Krakauer in *Into Thin Air.*

Instead of Switzerland, he started junketing to Japan, teaching monthlong English classes to make the rent. For years he had been shooting pictures compulsively, as a hobby, but now he started to think more seriously about photography and in 1981 in Japan he contracted as a stock photographer with his first agent, who gave him credentials and letters of introduction and suddenly he was getting visas when nobody else was, taking bullshit pictures for tourist brochures, and the Nepalese apparatchiks found him enormously useful.

For the next several years he went back and forth between Japan and Solu-Khumbu, snapping pretty pictures and working "on this fucking book" about Sherpa mythology. One day someone in Kathmandu said to him, "Hey, Tom, you speak English and Nepali—you want to lead a trek?" Thirty-five bucks a day sounded damn good to someone without steady or reliable income. By the late '80s he's leading treks, eventually for most of the agencies in Kathmandu, and he'd been picked up by stock agents in Paris, London, New York, and three in Tokyo. He was leading a trek in the Everest region when his father died in 1989, a soul-battering event that for Tom, then thirty-six, finally marked the overdue end of the weird, peripatetic party that was his childhood. Nepal's revolution began immediately thereafter, and in the fall of 1990, on his last commercial trek, he met the woman who would become his wife, Jann Fenner, his staunchest ally and fiercest defender. That year had been a tumultuous one for Nepal, which had only recently installed its first television network, exposing the population to the fall of the Berlin Wall and the overthrowing of dictatorships throughout Eastern Europe. For three months in the spring of 1990, the Himalayan nation came under intense scrutiny itself from the international media as its own masses took to the streets demanding democracy, culminating with riots in front of the king's palace in Kathmandu, a bloody massacre, and the end of the two-hundred-year-long Shah dynasty's grip on absolute power, although the royal family remained, in the hearts of the people, living gods.

Laird wasn't the only Western photographer on the streets that day, and he wasn't the only foreign journalist being shot at—we have argued about this before. Nothing about his role in the sequence of events had been scripted, but he emerged transformed. "Regardless of what others say about me," he had told me, "I did become the photographer of the revolution." Well, okay. There's no doubt that the revolution provided Tom (and plenty of others) with a bonanza of high-profile opportunities. Before a crowd of one hundred thousand demonstrators, he pushed aside guards and kicked in the glass doors of a hospital to photograph Ganesh Man Singh, the father of Nepalese democracy, who was being held inside under arrest. Laird's pictures of corpses in front of the palace were photocopied, enlarged into broadsheets, and pasted on street corners. He sold his first pictures to *Time* and *Der Stern* ($5,000 for one shot). *AsiaWeek* ran a six-page spread of his work, then put him on the masthead as a reporter. For a guy whose formal education disappeared with high school, and whose one and only fairy godmother had quit the case fifteen years earlier in Geneva, the revolution was a hell of a break, and the new Nepalese parliamentarians loved the exposure—as far as they were concerned, Laird had total access.

Laird himself would describe his political savvy as naive, but the ideal, his ideal—democracy—had come to Nepal and he was on the bandwagon, part of the team. Before being sworn in as the country's first prime minister, G. P. Koirala took him aside and said in effect, We owe you, what can we do for you? Laird had no response. The next day again Koirala repeated his offer. Laird had thought about it, falling asleep the night before with Jann, who had just moved in with him, and he had an answer—he wanted to be the first foreigner since Michel Peissel in the early 1960s to live in Mustang. The prime minister took his oath of office in the spring of 1991; by summer's end, the home minister had granted Laird permission to enter and remain in Mustang to document its history, its culture, and, most significantly for him, its art. He kissed Jann good-bye and was gone.

Like Peissel, Laird had arrived inspired with almost fanatical purpose: to record and disseminate, in Peter Matthiessen's words, "the extraordinary artistic expression in the unfrequented monasteries and palace-forts of the Kali Gandaki River trade route." Which is what, for eleven months, Laird did, with the assent of Mustang's king and nobles (though with the disapprobation of their former serfs). In 1995 when their collaboration, *East of Lo Monthang*, was published, the prime minister hosted an exhibition in Kathmandu's Patan Durbar Square to celebrate the occasion. Twenty thousand Nepalis came to view Tom's photographs and Robert Powell's paintings of Mustang. The politicians had successfully opened the Land of Lo, but people like Laird and Matthiessen, Robert Powell and the journalist Manjushree Thapa had opened the world to Mustang, irreversibly, and, for better or worse, it was no longer the lost or hidden kingdom.

Yet in his incarnation as a bridge, Laird ultimately felt walked on by everybody. His early dream, and supreme ambition, was to shoot the art—centuries-old frescoes, *thangkas*, and sculptures as accomplished and significant to civilization as anything in existence, and deserving of equal stature—show it to the world, and then become involved with the people restoring the precious work, perhaps be anointed as the cultural liaison. Whatever, whomever—the Getty Foundation, the American Himalayan Foundation, it didn't matter to Laird, not at first; he only wanted the art preserved, and its admirers to multiply. But nothing happened—he was out of the loop. At dinner one night in Kathmandu, he offered Richard Blum his Mustang files gratis—ten thousand photographs—and never heard back. He had walked out of Mustang $25,000 in debt on Jann's gold card. Like most books printed as an act of love, neither he nor Matthiessen ever made anything off of *East of Lo Monthang.* On he went with his life. *AsiaWeek* upgraded him to a contributing reporter, publishing hundreds of pages of his photos and text. He wrote *Into Tibet,* a book-length chronicle of the CIA's history in China and the Buddhist kingdom, and, with the Dalai Lama, he began compiling a history of Buddhism for a second book. Still Mustang haunted him, as if somehow he had misplaced himself there, as if he had left things unfinished. Dreams. Redemption. Expiation. I don't know.

The Upper Gorge

Ten years before our adventure, in a conversation with Mustang's King Jigme, Laird heard a bit of information that seemed extraordinary. The raja mentioned that, since a recent flood, at certain times of the year it was now possible to ride a horse through the upper gorge of the Kali Gandaki. Laird and two other Americans were the first foreigners to traverse its cavernous depths; the following year, Laird guided Peter Matthiessen through its labyrinth. Now we are attempting to be the third party of Westerners to enter the upper gorge, with its swift water and countless river crossings— nothing glorious about that, but an uncommon challenge nevertheless, especially since Tom is fulfilling his decade-long promise to take Jann to Lo Manthang and so we are dragging our spouses along, as well as our friend Mark, and the two bons vivants from Bangkok.

In the chill of sunrise, the mules are hobbled together on the flag-stones below the Red House Inn, snorting into feed bags packed sweet with corn. Several more mules have been added to the train to carry fresh barley hay and extra sacks of grain for the upper gorge. At all costs, reincarnation as a beast of burden is to be avoided. One of the animals has a bloody fist-size patch of hide ripped from its side where the wooden frame of the panniers was inadequately padded, and every mule displays white-haired scars along its spine, the flesh rubbed raw by the incessant shift of its load. I can't conjure the physics of crossbreeding the toy-like Nepalese burros, not much bigger than standard poodles, with the comely mares of Mustang, until Mahendra explains the process: The Lobas dig a pit, back the mare into it, and thus facilitate the romantic designs of the pipsqueak donkey, a stud by any other name.

No one dawdles at breakfast; we shovel in the porridge, gulp coffee and tea, refill our bottles with boiled water, and leave. Where we must go, past an ancient *mani* wall and its canister of prayer wheels, is to the government checkpoint on an elevated plaza at the edge of town to present the permits allowing us to enter the restricted area for thirteen days. Inside the low, dark building, the stone walls are hung with ACAP anthropological displays and photo boards (many of the pictures taken by Laird), maps and regulations. "Oh, Americans," says the sleepy young policeman behind the bare wooden counter as the group crowds in to sign the registry. He hasn't seen many Americans this year, maybe because of the Maoists. I wander around, scanning bits of Loba lore from ACAP's earnest posters:

Total population, 15,492, although only a third of those people live in Upper Mustang. Serfdom abolished, more or less, in 1956. In the late '50s, Tibetan refugees fleeing across the border brought with them large herds of sheep, goats, and yaks, overgrazing the high-altitude pastures. Equally problematic for daily life in Mustang, in 1960 the kingdom became the base of operations for the Khampa guerrillas from eastern Tibet and their doomed, CIA-sponsored war against the Chinese occupation of their homeland.

Mustang ranks among the most unspoiled wilderness areas in the world, home to the snow leopard and a variety of other rare and endangered species. Loba society practices a polyandrous marriage system. A woman has two or three husbands, usually brothers. And here's a Loba saying: "A woman with two husbands laughs, and a man with two wives cries." The last sign I read is handwritten on a scrap of paper and tacked to a post—BEWARE OF MASTIFFS IN LO MANTHANG, FOUR PEOPLE HAVE BEEN BITTEN.

We shake hands and bid farewell to our liaison Raju, happy as a prisoner being paroled, promising we won't stray from our route, shoot wild animals, chop firewood, liberate Tibet, or otherwise misbehave, and that we will check in at the police garrison in Lo Manthang the minute we arrive. We regather in the sunlight on the parapet overlooking the canyon, where three gleeful little boys at the water pipe play with a green condom, slinging it at one another, until a townswoman passing by sees what they're doing and smacks them and they rub their close-cropped heads and bawl and we're off.

The way out of town descends a steep slope to the riverbed, and at its bottom Mahendra and Tomay wait with the horses. A minor rebellion ensues. Laird mounts up and so do the recovering Bangkokers (once again, Tomay saves the captain from flinging himself headfirst over the saddle into a concussion). Ang Tsering has never been to Mustang, and never ridden a horse, but wants to try it out. Jann is adamant about walking, and Mark, disappointed in Submarine, seems to feel the same. The stirrups have aggravated Cat's old knee injury and she thinks the exercise will do her good. Myself, I'm wondering if there are fossils in the millions of rocks underfoot. Mahendra cocks his head and shrugs, bewildered—it doesn't make sense to walk across this blazing, ankle-twisting wasteland if you don't have to, but some foreigners, he has observed, are essentially stubborn and stupidly dedicated to unnecessary hardship.

The horsemen ride ahead. The rest of us, we walk, we trudge, we straggle across the immense, vacant floodplain, empty and quiet, stupefied by the heat and the scenery, mere particles of animation to anyone glancing down from the mesas high atop the canyon. I lag behind the general pace, picking up rocks and throwing them down like a crazy person, searching for saligrams—the smooth, blackish, ovoid stones containing ammonite fossils, considered sacred by Hindus and Buddhists alike. I pocket two small but likely candidates but Laird later tells me no, we're too low in the canyon, and these are what the Lobas call "cold eggs," the right shape and color but without the surface aberration that signals a fossil within.

After a mile or so the river forces us back to the horses for our first water crossing, an unremarkable event, accomplished without incident.

By now we have joined up with a second group of riders, the only other people we've seen since Kagbeni. We ride together for perhaps an hour, telling one another who we are, where we're going, where we're from. They are Lobas, headed to Lo Manthang for the festival, as we are—a young monk in his garnet robes, sent away ten years ago to study in India, plus his sister and uncle, who have ridden down to Jomsom to meet him and another uncle who sells cloth in Assam while his wife tends the house and fields in Lo Manthang. Their company, like all encounters on the lonely trail ahead, where you can go all day without seeing another face, eases the monotony of the journey, blooming and dissolving with agreeable conversation, and then they are gone, or rather we are, turning up from the riverbed to the village of Chuksang to deal with a logistics problem that now must be resolved.

To enter the upper gorge, we need extra horses for two days for the Sherpas and camp staff, who cannot otherwise accompany us without great difficulty, and we need packhorses to carry the staff's heavy baskets of gear and the extra feed required by the extra horses and mules. These we expect to rent in Chuksang from a local wrangler. When it seems the negotiations are going to take some time, the walkers—that would now be everybody but the Bang Boys—decide to go on to Chele, marching through the shade-cool apple orchards of the village and back down to the river. (By the time the full party moves out, we constitute, according to Chuksang's headman, the biggest caravan he has ever seen heading up-canyon—twenty-two horses and fourteen mules.)

In our slog to Chele, for us nothing more than a bridge of decaying planks suspended across the river, we come of age as (illegal) saligram hunters, meandering aimlessly across the gullies and washes and bars of the receded Kali Gandaki, zombies in the wind tuned to an inner voice whispering, *Fill your backpack with rocks so you'll drown in the river.* We wander alone, mesmerized by the naked planet, glancing up intermittently to note our companions off in the distance. To find whole saligrams, rather than shards, one must summon a bit of aggression, and expect to be bloodied for it. Serendipity directs you to just the right grenadelike rock in the zillions lying around; you pick it up, find a bigger rock, and pitch the one in your hand against it with all you've got. If your luck holds, the rock will burst open with neat, clean lines, like a jewelry box, and for the first time in 150 million years, one of earth's earliest creatures is exposed to sunlight, its nautilus-like whorls sparkling with golden crystals. If, on the other hand, your luck is somehow deficient, the rock you pitched, or a razor-sharp fragment of it, comes zinging back like a line drive and takes you out.

Both Mark and I arrive at the Chele footbridge wounded; all of us arrive sweating and shivering, thanks to the drastic swings in temperature throughout the morning, a fan of clouds opening and closing over the sun. For the second day the southern horizon is blackened by storms, which threaten to slip off the Himalayas and engulf us.

Chele, out of sight above us on a mesa to the west, marks the end of the dry weather route up the riverbed from Jomsom. Anyone continuing north must climb out of the canyon here on the main trail leading to Lo Manthang, or have exited earlier at Chuksang to track a punishing goat path around the eastern side of the upper gorge to Tange, where the canyon broadens out again. We stand for a moment awestruck by the gorge's portal, to our left a dislodged block of canyon wall that looks like the top third of a World Trade Center tower, to our right a sheer red-rock face rising out of the river with an inaccessible line of man-made caves about 150 feet up, and then the river itself, burrowing ahead about a hundred yards until the opposite walls seem to clap together, as if we are about to enter a subway tunnel in this Manhattan of solid stone. We stare uncertainly at the river's muscle and force as it races from the gorge and then get out of the rising wind to play listlessly with our packed lunch of eggs gone rotten and curried potatoes.

Our mules finally arrive, and all the extras, and the extra wrangler, the dashing Rajendra on his dashing white pony, prince of the upper gorge, and his sidekick, a half-clothed kid who looks about thirteen, and there's much hubbub, biting, and head butting, a lot of kicking and attempted run-aways. Ang Tsering, who didn't care for his inaugural experience on a horse earlier this morning, encourages the Sherpas to mount up for the first time ever and it's clear, as the mountaineers sway and slip and bounce like rag dolls, that they were not born for the saddle. Mahendra, on a white horse half the size of Jamling, trots up to the front of this scrum and then we're off, splashing into the dark glacial water, and the column of our enterprise is so long and winding and in different time zones that it's not until the next day that I learn how we barely averted disaster right at the start, when Biri was unsaddled as his horse dropped off the bar into the river but grabbed by his terrified comrades before he was swept away. Sherpas, and porters in general, as you might expect, given their customary occupation—not riding horses through rivers in Mustang—don't know how to swim.

The sky itself has been reduced to a blue serpent held overhead in the jaws of the gorge, and when we are not sheltered by the nearness of the bulging walls, the sun pours down on us with dazing intensity. If the Grand Canyon is geology's Rome, the upper reach of the Kali Gandaki is its Athens, less grand but more finessed, elegantly sculpted and ethereal. We ride through amphitheaters and stacked galleries, through vaulted passageways with pigeons and swallows nesting along narrow ledges; we ride past grotesque monuments to the fury of water and sinuous curtains of rock carved by the persistent wind, past Olympian thrones, past soaring temples as long as city blocks, and always, always, we are in and out of the rushing river, which sometimes fills its bed from wall to wall.

At the fordings, Mahendra pauses to consult with the horseman from Chuksang; their dark eyes read the flow, determining entries and exits. Sometimes he and Rajendra will ask the column to wait while they ride ahead to test the bottom, and at every crossing Mahendra wants us to strictly follow his line into the rapids, often completing the ford and coming back to position himself midstream, down current, as insurance. Most of the fords are relatively shallow, but before long we come to our first deep crossing, the current shouldering the horses with real force. I can feel Jamling struggling to keep his footing, the brief loss of gravity each time he lifts a leg until, my hand wrapped into his mane to keep from falling backward, he thrashes up the steep, crumbling gravel bank of the opposite shore. Behind me I watch my wife and Mark entering the river, Submarine earning his name, the dark water foaming above Mark's knees. They've allowed their horses' heads to turn downstream and are losing ground with each step, inching toward violent water, and I shout to them to rein the horses at an angle upriver, so that they fight the current, rather than submit to it, as they move across. The Bangkok Bachelors, loath to discipline their horses or themselves, plunge ahead, crashing into each other and whomever else might be in the way. Still on the far bank, the queen's horse refuses to budge, despite Jann's pleading, until Laird whaps its hindquarter. Halfway back on the bar come the bedraggled Sherpas, and the lead mule, its colorful plume bobbing above its ears, is just in sight around the bend, the mule skinners with their pants tied around their necks, having no choice but to wade belly-deep into the ice-cold torrent.

Again and again, we ford the river, so many crossings that I lose count after thirty-five, kicking the reluctant horses into the flow, holding tight as they scramble out, Mahendra singing to calm his nervousness, Rajendra whooping with cowboy joy, because we are an impressive sight, so many people, so many animals, picking their way through the spectacular gorge. Only once am I flushed with alarm, when my horse and Cat's step into the same hole, lose their footing, and threaten to go down. The most dangerous part of the passage is not in the river but out of it, when we encounter one river bend too extreme to ford and must dismount to walk our horses up a steep, rocky bankside to a shelf of hardened slurry, around and down a pile of boulders, and back to the river.

Atop the shelf, Jann barely escapes being crushed when her horse sits to roll in the sand. Everybody's boots are waterlogged, our asses are raw, our backs stiff, knees throb, and our legs are unsteady. My wife, off her horse, is crippled, her left leg swollen, and as I help her through the rubble I dislodge a forty-pound rock that nearly breaks her ankle. By the time we regain the river, we're beginning to show the stress of the journey, our brains going numb with the mantra of the horse bells ringing out into the overwhelming emptiness of the landscape.

Late in the afternoon, the fords get deeper, colder, and the wind sharpens. We pass several good campsites with room enough for the livestock but none seems to be, in Laird's memory, the Matthiessen campsite, which he is obsessed with finding but it's been ten years. The sun lowers and we push on despite the advice of Mahendra and Ang Tsering, because Rajendra keeps assuring Laird that the site he's looking for is just ahead. It isn't. The day has been rugged and dramatic and exhausting, twilight sinks into the gorge, and finally we're stuck for the night at a cramped, eroded campsite that appeals to none of us—a narrow ten-foot-high flood shelf with an abrupt drop to a rock-strewn shoreline.

Now the wind howls, lashing our faces with sheets of dust from off the platform of dried mud where the mules and horses have their legs in the air, rolling on their backs. Scouting around, I discover a small riverside cave, the perfect spot to pitch our tent, I think, but then the wind bowls into it and a cloud of grit and sand stings me as if I've disturbed a hornet's nest. The Sherpas attempt to pitch the kitchen tent on the gravel below the shelf but it blows over. We're all getting pissed about pushing too far and ending up with only this—no shelter from the brutal and increasingly cold wind. Laird and I have a short, tense discussion about how we might possibly arrive at decisions that are more agreeable. Mark waddles behind a rock with dysentery. My wife's wet boots have given her the shakes, and she can't bend her left knee. The Sherpas are maxed out, and I find Rajendra and the mule skinners huddled in the gloom behind a boulder, half-naked, soaked and freezing. Somebody starts a campaign to round up dry socks for these guys—they have no socks at all. "This is no time to be socially sensitive," someone snaps. "It's always time to be socially sensitive," someone else says back. Cat and I slip away to hit the vodka.

The tents are finally pitched, the guylines weighted down with huge rocks. The mule skinners' new high-tech socks are delivered with packets of M&Ms; naturally they throw the trash on the ground, not because they're morons but because what does it matter here at the absolute center of nowhere, where cheap tennis shoes are the only litter we've seen for two days. The mules are hobbled for the night, their faces stuffed into feed bags. Mahendra has taken the horses back downriver in search of forage, where he and Tomay will sleep with the herd to keep them from running off. Thanks to the intrepid Sherpas, camp is set, a latrine dug, wash water provided, tea made, a dinner of spaghetti and mashed potatoes served; the wind dies down, everything's good again, and we separate into the starry darkness and collapse into our sleeping bags.

In the morning, after a round of ibuprofen cocktails with our porridge, we expect another long, demanding haul through the second half of the gorge to our day's destination, the village of Tange. Jamling, as is his habit, vies for the lead and I have to rein him back to allow Mahendra to trot forward on his pony. Within an hour even the Lobas are amazed when the canyon flares open in front of us, providing the strange sense that we have exited an Earth-size small intestine into the large intestine, which shits us out who knows where. The upper canyon between the gorge and Tange is as rarely traveled as the gorge itself, but the difference in habitat is striking. The inner gorge, too severe to support wildlife, void even of insects, was as biologically dead as it was geologically lush, but here in the high canyon the air above us stirs with the satin rustle of feathers—the ubiquitous ravens certainly, and now eagles and hawks, enormous condors and vultures. Animal tracks lead from the riverbed up the austere slopes; four blue sheep study our caravan from a ledge high atop a palisade, and when we dismount to collect a few saligrams, which are everywhere, my wife identifies the print of a young brown bear (*Ursus arctos*) faintly pressed in the dry mud. Here too are hundreds and hundreds of man-made caves high on the canyon walls, undisturbed for centuries or perhaps millennia, Mustang's last great mystery.

The first argument of the day is about lunch—Shall we stop here? Here? No, says Mahendra, uncustomarily peevish. He's intent on another place he thinks he remembers where there's a windbreak and better grazing, but when we go ahead, no such place seems to exist. We stop anyway, craving the shade in the basin of a sandy amphitheater, a need almost immediately cast aside by the changing atmosphere. "What happened?" Mahendra says after lunch, surveying the torrent with a grave expression. "The river is high and black." Barbarian clouds sweep in, a monsoon front has successfully assaulted the Himalayas, and the weather takes a dramatic, wintery turn as we turn ourselves into a side canyon and ride ahead bowed over our horses to the beautiful, stunningly primitive oasis of Tange, population 140 souls who might as well be living on Mars.

A long ramp rising up the escarpment off the floodplain of two merging rivers leads to the village and we ascend into the greening of the desert, awed by the laborious magic of the terraced fields. The exotic fragrance of wet earth wafts from the ancient irrigation ditch, its banks thicketed by yellow rose of Sharon, poplar trees, and, the closer we get to Tange, big cottonwoods. The ground turns grassy, then marshy; the marsh expands to a small pond, and beyond that we bivouac in a stone-walled corral at the entrance of the town, a weird and marvelous place.

To describe Tange and other equally remote hamlets in Mustang as neglected would be politically accurate but metaphysically inadequate. Ditto with *forgotten*, which implies substantial foreknowledge. Even *lost* would not be enough. The humanity here is like a seed in a prelapsarian garden, borne by the primal wind an unfathomable distance from its source, to root in complete oblivion. Like ghosts, we appear from an unseen world, passing through a corridor of high walls. At the first house we come to, a stooped, gray-haired *ama* cringes at the sight of us. "We're afraid," she cries, her voice flutelike. "Go. Go." Laird asks how old she is. "I'm not going to tell you," she says, scurrying behind the door of her well-built stone house.

We stroll self-consciously through the seemingly deserted village, its fabulous construction of connecting houses, a medieval warren of narrow alleys twisting into courtyards, tunneling below second-story spans, dark passageways into darker interiors stabling livestock, notched logs propped as ladders into haylofts, a miniature urban skyline of flat rooftops shaggy with eaves of cut brambles capped by firewood. Made of mud and stone and hand-hewn timber, Tange as a human creation mirrored its natural environment with an eerie, breathtaking perfection, its colors the land's colors, its solitary mood the land's mood, a coarse harmony that seemed the very essence of a permanent peace forged from permanent oppression.

Drifting into a tiny square at the heart of town, we shock the five women and self-amused gang of their ragamuffin children sitting in its dirt. We sit too, uninvited; greetings are exchanged, the silence slowly broken. One woman returns to combing out the braids of the woman in front of her; two more sitting nearby resume spinning sheep's wool with drop spindles. The fifth is off by herself in a corner of the walls, cross-legged at the end of a long hand loom, weaving a striped bolt of woolen cloth. Like bees, the children swarm to my wife's honey-colored hair and, after some preliminary tickling, arranged themselves in rows for English lessons.

"Hello."

"Hello," they sing.

"How are you?"

"How are—" and then a cascade of giggles. They are the filthiest and merriest children in the universe.

The cutup of the group, a boy no older than six whose obsidian eyes contain a mischievous charm, struts over to one of the big grinding stones in the plaza, pulls down his pants, and sits atop the mortar, his bare bottom a perfect fit into the bore. Aghast, we assume he's going to take a crap here where the village grain is pestled into flour, but what he does—he thinks it's hilarious and it is—is make air farts, suctioning his ass up and down in the bowl. The women laugh, we laugh, the other kids cheer. This goes on long enough for his mother, one of the younger women, to put a stop to it, hopping over on one leg to drag him off the stone. When she sits back down, from the way she arranges the skirt of her navy-blue dress, I can see she's missing the other leg. Oh, she says, she injured it and it wouldn't heal and so after a while her family carried her down to Jomsom where she was sent to Kathmandu and the doctors amputated her leg. Gangrene, says Laird. Fucking agony. This tale of woe inspires the *ama* of the group to declare that she gave birth to twelve children but seven died.

An elderly man turns a corner into the square and straightens up, blinking through mended eyeglasses at this apparition of *queri* in the middle of town. His name is Temba Lama; he's sixty years old, the village headman, and now a hostage of our curiosity. No, he says, when we wonder if life in Tange has changed much since the opening of Mustang—the village is ten people smaller than a decade ago, but everything else is the same. A lot of foreigners have come, but they haven't changed anything. Ten years ago the villagers had to go to the big towns for medicine and they still have to go there today, but if you're really sick, he says, you stay here and die.

"Some people feed the body to the vultures," says Temba Lama, "some people throw it into the river, some people burn it but not many, because there's not much wood. There's a ritual to call the birds [for the sky burial] and if you don't do the *puja* the birds won't come.

"No, nothing's changed. Drinking water would be nice, but electricity we only see in our dreams, so why talk about it? Nobody's done anything for us up here. But we're happy. The foreigners come, we get to see strange things, things we've never seen before, and we like that. We're just raising our food and tending our goats just like before." Before, I guess, would be the year 1500.

But the length of polyurethane irrigation hose we follow to the backside of town, and the empty Chinese beer bottle on the path to the ruins of a fort above town, whisper of the arrival of the world. The ancient fort's history is as decayed as its walls; like bloody Ireland, Mustang can boast abandoned fortresses and castles everywhere, melting back into the landscape, taking with them a dim epoch of forgotten wars, nomadic invasions come and gone, and a past that barely survives in legends. But the view from the ruins is a panorama of magnificence. Tange, built atop a promontory above the floodplain, faces out across the canyon to an opposite wall carved top to bottom with the most exquisite fluting, rumpled stone drapery tall as skyscrapers. Beyond that, the horizon accordions upward, peak after peak, into the snow line, where angry clouds smother the Himalayas. On its western flank, the headland drops into a ravine made beautiful by a mint-blue river, the Tange Khola, gushing through it, and across the ravine a coal-black mountain of loose soil that Laird believes to be the sedimentary layer of thrust-up-sideways seabed running from up north to here, where saligrams erode from the deposit, and farther south to Muktinath, where it leaks natural gas to the surface.

The wind reverses itself, blowing out of Inner Asia and into our bones. Cold and tired, we make our way downhill, past a lone woman herding hundreds of baby goats along the base of the scree into the high pasture. Where the slope flattens below us, an assortment of lovely chortens, perched above the barley fields, striped with the pigments of the Tibetan plateau—ocher, gray, skeleton-white—speak of Tange's ageless piety. At a manger back near camp, we stop to admire a mare and her week-old foal—it's birthing season, babies everywhere—and our conversation with the village continues. Tashi, the owner of the horses, comes to lean on the stone wall of the pen with us and watch the foal dance and wobble on its matchstick legs. Unlike the village women in their wraparound wool *bukkhoos*, Tashi dresses like a Westerner in chinos, a collared shirt, cheap running shoes, and he wears a marine flight jacket from the USS *Saratoga*, a gift from a trekker. Laird, who had just completed a book chronicling CIA involvement in Tibet's loss of sovereignty to the Chinese, asks Tashi about the Khampas.

"Ah, yes, there was a Khampa camp above Tange," he says. "If you leave now you'll get there tomorrow night, but be careful. Nobody has gotten hurt yet by the weapons up there, although across the valley at other Khampa camps people have had their hands and faces blown off by the caches of explosives left behind. At night we could see the American planes dropping weapons to the Khampas on the mesa top north of here. They lit fires and the planes came over. We had never seen planes before and the animals went crazy; all night the cows were crying. I was a small child and went up the next day with my father and saw all the boxes full of guns. The Khampas lived good, with yaks, sheep, mules. Then they all left and went to live in Kathmandu and Pokhara." Here for Laird at last is confirmation of the long-suspected fact that Americans were supplying the Khampas inside Nepal's border, an officially forbidden activity. Tashi asks for a cigarette and I give him a pack and his expression turns warm and playful.

"The guys who work for you," he teases, "say you foreigners have it easy." Behind Tashi, the sunset pries open the skies, and the snow peaks in the Dolpo shine like a row of wolf's teeth.

"In my idea," Tashi continues, becoming serious, "the life before tourists came was better. In your accounting, we are poor. Because you come, things are more expensive for us. People aren't more expensive, things are more expensive. The rich people make money from tourism but we don't. We don't have houses or horses to rent. You guys came up here and ate all the eggs so the price of eggs went up. You guys came up with more horses eating more corn and the price of corn went up."

But the problem's complex. Although the price of wheat has more than tripled in ten years, the trucks now coming from China to Lo Manthang—about thirty last year—bring lumber and kitchen utensils, stoves and beer, but mostly they bring rice. Chinese rice has become so cheap—half the price of Kathmandu's—that Lobas are eating two meals of it a day. Mahendra had already told us that the people of Lo Manthang don't buy anything from below, from Nepal, anymore. Still, no Chinese are allowed in, and you have to be ethnically Tibetan, and well-known in Lo Manthang, before you can drive one of the trucks. Yes, it looks good now, the Lobas say, but what will become of this? Grain, in fact, has become so inexpensive that many of the fields on Lo Manthang's Plain of Prayer lay fallow and abandoned; it made more sense to buy from China. Thus a difficult but centuries-old way of life slowly passes into obscurity.

More villagers have wandered up. It's a fine horse, we all agree, pleased to have something to agree on, and then everybody turns to Tashi to see what he'll say.

"You guys have toilet paper—that's what money is now," says Tashi, never less than amiable despite his jeremiad. "People who have it treat it like toilet paper, but for us one hundred rupees is a big thing. You just gave me cigarettes that cost thirty rupees, so I'm obeying you big-time."

My sudden ownership of this good man causes mirth among the growing crowd, but I'm at a loss for how to respond, and all I really have to give him is my attention, which he guzzles. In a strange way, in a way that's not pathetic but is indeed sad, Tashi's having fun.

"Your money is very big," he says without bitterness, and not to cause shame, I think, or beg pity. He says it to be real. "That's why you can come here and roam around. We can't even think about going to your country with our weak money. That money that you give to the government to come here—where does it go? Where does it go? I don't know, and I don't think anybody does. Look at our clothes—they're torn and dirty. We're poor people working really hard here, and I look really old."

"How old are you?"

"I'm forty-four."

"You look forty-five," I say, because it must end this way, with a joke, with everybody entertained and laughing, with good-natured back slapping and handshakes of gratitude for the moment, however brief, when we connected, because we must go back to our camp, our lives, and ride away forever in the morning, and Tashi must go back to his house and his life, and nothing here can be exchanged honestly, or permanently, except memories and goodwill.

Tsarang

There's these kids, a pack of excited children, their faces freckled with dirt and unstoppable green snot flowing from their noses, who seem to be ours now. Back at our bivouac, the cranks among us grumble at this noisy intrusion onto our turf, quickly forgetting who exactly is doing the intruding here, but Cat and Mark rise to the occasion and the corral fills with the singsong of games, the same games children play all over the world, Ring Around the Rosy, Red Rover, everybody loves to fall down, everybody loves to be sent over. Mark has the odd notion that he will teach the kids calisthenics. Now we're doing jumping jacks, now we're touching our toes. The exercise quickly devolves. We're roughhousing, we're wrestling. Now the big kids, as big kids will, are beating up on little ones, the victims wailing, and the cranks are inflicted with a case of the nerves. The party comes to a screeching halt when a woman rushes past our gate, headed toward the pond with a chaffing basket piled with . . . what? Fetishes? Guts? The children shriek in unison and hurry after her, spitting furiously, hollering at the woman whom it seems they might attack, but she pays them no regard. At the edge of the pond, she stops and flings the grotesque contents of the basket into the water—painted cones of soft clay and barley flour, tiny butter sculptures, red chilies, animal skin, something made of string, sticks with calligraphic markings, something grisly, perhaps an animal organ, which a dog slinks out of the reeds to eat. Onshore the children clap and spit; the woman wipes her hands on her hips, satisfied, everybody goes home, and we realize we have just witnessed a spontaneous cleansing of the village, a version of Tange's, or one of its families', annual Tiji ceremony that will take place a few days hence in front of the royal palace in Lo Manthang. What the woman carried in her basket were sins, demons, transgressions, illnesses, bad spirits, all the troubles visited upon Tange the past year, and now the village is rid of them.

The second controversy of the day arrives with dinner, when I am delighted by the appearance of an entrepreneur at the flap of our dining tent, a young woman toting a pail of river-chilled beer and soda. Back in Pokhara, Laird had pulled me aside and asked me not to drink on the expedition, in deference to the Bangkok Bachelors, especially the alcoholic captain, who were using the trip to crawl on the wagon, dry out, straighten up, kick the habit or habits, and otherwise renovate themselves as clearheaded, upstanding citizens. To ensure the no-booze policy, Laird doses himself and the Bachelors with Diamox, which prevents altitude sickness, because when you mix Diamox with liquor, it makes you piss all the time, a potential deterrent to drinking. Mark and Cat and I have chosen to ignore this protocol because we were already well acclimated to Mustang's relatively low elevations—9,500 feet at Kagbeni, 10,600 at Tange, 12,600 at Lo Manthang—and we rather enjoyed our moderate routine: a cocktail at the end of the day, perhaps a beer or glass of wine with dinner, and good night.

You must be joking, I had told Laird. If the captain was trying to lose weight, would I have to diet too? It was nice that Tom felt compassion for his wasted friends, but what's he doing, running a medical tour? The Mustang Detox Trek? No, I had begun to warm to the self-indulgent charm of the captain, who had become more droll and clever in his endless monologues of Asian girls and Asian wars, the same material repeated as fatuous tales in a slurring loop until he sobered up, but Jack was still responsible for his own problems, certainly not me, certainly not anybody else.

All to say before Laird can shoo her away, Mark and I happily purchase the woman's inventory of four San Miguels, four Sprites, and a Coke. Laird narrows his eyes at me, expecting, I suppose, intemperance, maybe brawling or sobbing, but adulthood prevails upon us all. Mark and I uncap bottles of beer, which we sip throughout dinner. Michael farts a steady stream of indifference into the enclosed tent, causing my wife to change seats. If the Bangkokers are tempted, they don't let on, and in two days they'll have swan dived off the wagon anyway in the *rakshi* emporiums of Lo Manthang. The captain leans back in his chair and begins a discourse about porno on the Internet. Michael, digging an index finger deep into his nose, allows that the Japanese have as many different names for cum shots as the Eskimos have for snow. With modest fanfare, Mark shits in his pants and must leave to hover outside over the squat hole, holding a packet of Huggies Wipes like a prayer book in his clammy hands. Sensing the advent of a headache, Cat excuses herself to bed.

Here in the badlands of the Tibetan plateau, among ourselves we are an exceedingly ill-mannered, immoderate, irreverent, bawdy, smartalecky, half-decadent–half-prissy overmedicated collection of white people glued together for a whiff of adventure, but we keep our teeth brushed, our faces washed, and our egos loaded but holstered, doing our best to get along and somehow be kind to if not love each other while storm clouds gather over Annapurna and Kathmandu sinks into its own darkness. As the rest of us are about to clear the dinner tent, a tribe of women appear out of the depths of the night, wanting to dance for us, the one thing they could proudly sell, but we have finally accepted our fatigue and only want our tents. The women are crestfallen. An old hag shoves a filthy red plastic pitcher of *chhang* toward my mouth, trying to sell us a drink, but two good bottles of beer sit untouched on the table.

Mahendra gives them a little money—these are his people, Bhotias, the king's people. I give Mahendra a little more to give to them, fifty rupees, less than a dollar, and they clap with thanks and bid us a respectful good night. "It's only by seeing the cash economy in the last ten years that they think of themselves as poor," says Laird, but they're not poor of spirit, he adds, like so many other people in other places are. Tomorrow he will tell me that the more he talks with people like Tashi, the more he realizes civilization is a description of technology, not of humanity, and I am reminded once again not to stay mad at Tom for too long, because he indeed has a heart, difficult to preserve and nourish in the Third World or I suppose anywhere, and always manages to find his way back to it.

In our tent, my wife lays groaning, her head split open with pain made worse by a pulled shoulder muscle from her heavy day pack. Even inside her down bag and its felt liner, she's quaking with cold and I hug myself around her until her chill is gone and then crawl into my own sleeping bag, worried and guilty, because I won't let her take her medication. As long as I've known Cat she's been susceptible to regular migraines, which only in the last few years she's been able to overcome, thanks to a new drug called Imitrex, but it's not possible to determine if what she's experiencing is the result of altitude sickness, or the stress-and-hormone kick of a migraine, or how the Imitrex might complicate either condition here in the high country.

She lapses into fitful sleep but wakes up nauseous shortly after midnight and vomits in the vestibule of the tent. Throughout the night she writhes and moans and at dawn I slip over to Tom and Jann's tent for consultation. Migraines are not on the long list of problems the Lairds have dealt with in the mountains, nor does the thick high-altitude medical textbook Jann carries with her on treks say anything about this particular affliction. We decide to let Cat take the Imitrex and see what happens. Meanwhile, Laird and I sit down with Ang Tsering and Mahendra to discuss our options. Initially we agree to let the group go ahead, Mark and my wife and I to follow with a Sherpa—who will carry her across the river if she can't ride—and one of the horsemen at midmorning. Reconsidering this plan, Mahendra objects to breaking up the expedition—Tomay doesn't know the river crossings well enough—and Ang Tsering agrees it would be best for everyone to wait until my wife recovers. "A group moves forward only as fast as its weakest link," says the *sardar*, who has been on Everest three times, summited once, and turned back a second time five hundred feet from the top. His own wife has forbidden him from a fourth attempt, but I know he lies awake at night dreaming of the North Col.

The snow peaks to the east and west of us along the Tibetan border flare into being but within the hour are snuffed out by the low-pressure system that refuses to retreat to the lowlands. Back in our tent, my wife is in terrible shape, lying very still to keep from vomiting up the Imitrex, but when I check on her an hour later, her condition has improved and she swallows a second pill with a weak smile. Chhundi serves breakfast and the Sherpas break down camp around her. On the hillside above the village, Laird and I consider the bucolic illusion of Tange, the surrounding landscape like the Canyonlands National Park in Utah on steroids. Everything's quiet except for the ravens cawing and the high-key drawling of Tibetan music coming from a cassette player in a house below and the click of Tom's shutter. Lower still on the green terraces, a woman returns from weeding her barley field. In town, no dogs bark, no children skip to school because the school has no teacher. The only person we see is the old woman in the plaza weaving her endless bolt of woolen cloth, as if her only plan in life was to die at her loom.

Finally back on her feet, Cat is woozy but able, and we mount up and leave Tange with no more ceremony than when we arrived. The result of her illness is that we will bypass the ten-hour side trip tomorrow to the monastery cave of Luri, have a more leisurely day, and stop short at Tsarang, Mustang's second-biggest town and the gateway to the valley of Lo Manthang. Not a bad idea, we all concur, to slow the pace, which has taxed both horse and human, and allowed us to pay only glancing attention to the wonders of so alien a world. Still, Jamling's frisky this morning, perhaps he's caught the smell of the king's rich pastures on the flux of currents, and back down on the floor of Tange's canyon we gallop on the sandbars, chased by Laird and Mahendra and Rajendra and the mountaineer Ang Tsering, who has grown fond of the cowboy's life and whipping a horse's ass.

At the confluence where Tange's canyon spills into the Kali Gandaki's, we wave farewell to Rajendra and his extra horses, who turn south back into the gorge toward Chuksang and quickly vanish into the resounding emptiness. The main canyon is windless, its baking heat abrupt, and we head inexorably north hypnotized by the crunch of gravel, the horses' bells, the regular clop of their shoes, iron on stone. Vultures pinwheel overhead; eagles levitate on the thermals. In another month or less the river will jump its channel and roar like a hundred freight trains, off the plateau and into Nepal, and Asia will drain its sacred waters into the seas.

Ahead perhaps a mile atop a distant bluff to the west, greenery announces the valley of Tsarang, and the trail up. Laird, excited, points along the eastern flank where another side canyon drops out of the snowy range, and this one, he believes, is the mother lode of saligrams, fossils the size of Volkswagens piled in its recesses. There are no more river crossings until our final ford at the base of the trail, where we'll halt for lunch. Hearing this news from Mahendra, Jann is off her horse in an instant, and then the rest of us, wandering in a stupor through a rock hound's prolific dream.

At the ford, the clear glacial waters of the side canyon's river empty into the Kali Gandaki; the parallel currents where the two rivers blend run half transparent blues, half chocolate murk for a few hundred yards until a bow of rapids churns the two streams into a milky froth. The Sherpas cross on horseback and Mahendra brings the ponies back to us. From our side of the river, we've had ample time to study the trail rising from the opposite bank up into a ravine that appears to dead-end into a vertical three-hundred-foot cliff, and the ascent looks suicidal. No, no, Mahendra assures us, this is a well-used trail, the only route to get from the floor of the canyon to Tsarang, a thousand feet above us.

Remounted, we splash across the turquoise flow. A third of the way up the slope, where the ravine gradually attenuates into natural staircasing, Jann climbs off her horse, shaking. The trail becomes insane, more and more rugged, and we're forced to dismount and lead the ponies through a steep obstacle course of boulders. Two-thirds of the way the path flattens onto a small shelf at the base of the insurmountable cliff, and we find ourselves peering saucer-eyed up a sixty-degree chute, a cornucopia of loose, smooth, round rocks the size of grapefruits and basketballs and everything in between, a stalled tumble of rocks flowing out of the sky somewhere far above us. Just to scale the chute on hands and feet seems like an extreme act of foolishness, given the instability of the course. Except for Mahendra and the slothful Bangkokers, we're of a single incredulous mind concerning this approach—*No fucking way!* How high is it? I ask Ang Tsering, who has remained on horseback. Two ropes, he answers. Two three-hundred-foot ropes. No one's willing to bet a hundred dollars we can ride up the chute, and even Mahendra concedes it's impossible to ride *down.*

Like the horses themselves, we're balking. Cat wisely gets off; she'll walk with Jann. Mahendra admonishes us to put aside our fear, if we're afraid the horses will be afraid, be confident and go. Just then a wizened old traveler astride his pony comes up behind us from the ravine, acknowledges us with a gap-toothed smile, and whips his horse into the chute as if there were nothing to it. *"See?"* clucks Mahendra. Mike and the captain kick their horses ahead and we wrap our fists into our ponies' manes and advance. Every step tortures the animals. I haven't gone fifty feet before Jamling is exhausted, panting, lurching for solid ground as his hooves slide in the loose rocks. I try to dismount but Mahendra strongly objects; this is not the time for foreigners to quibble with Mustang's principles of sound horsemanship, because if I throw the horse off balance he'll fall before I can even pop my foot out of the stirrup.

Directly above me, Mike's horse seems about to collapse backward and roll on top of Jamling. Above Mike, the captain, indifferent to the purpose and function of reins, threatens to crush my wife into the side of the chute as she tries to scramble out of his way. And higher still, it has not slipped my notice that the old man has hopped off his pony to assault the chute's final, most radical section. Mahendra yells at me. "Just hit the horse," he urges. "Beat the horse. It will go."

Mike and Ang Tsering embrace this advice and strap their ponies mercilessly with their reins. "I left my guilt behind," Mike shouts triumphantly as his horse skitters upward, and I wonder if perhaps Mike's been in Asia too long. Myself, I kick and prod Jamling and command him forward until I imagine his lungs bursting, blood spraying from the flare of his nostrils. The rocks are too wobbly to allow him to catch his breath; he gasps and slobbers up and up, noble eyes wild from the effort. I let go of the reins and grip his mane with both hands, my head against his sweaty neck. Rocks clatter in our wake and finally he lunges up out of the earth into the opening sky and we are both, horse and rider, reborn into a world so beautiful and alive and human in its difference that the chute from which we emerge now seems purgatorial, a mythic passage between hell and heaven. One by one, the horsemen are released from the canyon and we walk across the grassy pastures of the plain of Tsarang and then remount and ride joyously into the village.

Shady, fabulous, urbane Tsarang is a balm to our senses. While camp is pitched in a backstreet corral, we wash our hair under the icy stream of a nearby public fountain, toss our pocket trash into ACAP rubbish cans, change our soiled clothes, and walk through a grove of ancient cottonwoods for a late afternoon visit to Tsarang's fairy-tale landmarks, its *dzong*—palace fortress—and monastery, both five hundred years old and unmarked by the passing centuries. Born in 1968, Tsewang, the village headman and king's nephew, accompanies us on a quick tour of these extraordinary structures, which we will return to in the morning to observe the monks' preparations for Tsarang's own Tiji ritual. The Sherpas have made their kitchen in the stable of Tsewang's family home, which is also a guesthouse, and it is there on the cushions of the tearoom, in the weak light of two overhead electric bulbs powered by the town's generator, that we have our dinner, and a long conversation with our host.

Tsewang is a Bista, the surname of most high-ranking families in Mustang, where the vestiges of feudalism linger in everyday life in the relationship between peasants and the traditional ruling class, but even so there's a solidarity between Lobas, the indigenous population of the plateau who trace their lineage to Tibet, and Thakalis, members of the more populous ethnic group south of the restricted area who dominate the political infrastructure of the entire district. Tsewang lives half the year with his wife, children, and parents in Kathmandu, returning to Tsarang in the more clement seasons to administrate the affairs of the village. It's not uncommon for any Loba with means to clear out of Mustang during the winter months rather than endure the harsh conditions. Even Mahendra takes his family to an enclave of Loba expatriates in India.

As an entrepreneur, as a functionary, as a Loba, the talk of throwing open the doors of Mustang tantalizes Tsewang, who was educated in Darjeeling and speaks fluent English. Yes, he says, right now people don't benefit much from the kingdom's limited tourism and he wants the restrictions lifted, he says, "because it will change life here for the better. A certain number of people, not wealthy people exactly but young people, have been exposed to the world; they get sponsorships to school. That's a major change here and it's been good for the people, good for the monasteries. The Lobas are pushing the government to lift the restriction," he says, "but we don't have the infrastructure to handle much of an increase, and we'd have to be able to manage it well, starting with food, because we'd have to bring it all in by mule or porter."

The strongest argument for restricted tourism, says Laird, is fuel, not just trekkers but the porters hacking up everything to cook their *dal bhat*. Tourism hasn't cut down trees here—yet.

To everyone's amazement, throughout the night it rains, and we wake up marveling at the snow line, which has dropped ever closer to our elevation at 11,000 feet. It's far too early in the monsoon season for rain in Mustang and perhaps this is a propitious omen, but Ang Tsering gazes south at the eastward-sliding storms on the Himalayas that have been stuck there for a week and we all know what he's thinking, that the hundreds of climbers on Everest are getting clobbered.

At the *dzong*, a severe, square, five-story stone tower guarding the village from marauding nomads whose bones have long turned to dust, we pass from light to darkness, feeling our way up crude, broken stairs, landing after landing, toward the bumblebee drone of chanting monks. On the cold bare floor of the fort's chapel, eight adult monks sit on cushions facing each other, four to a side, for the annual reading of the holiest of Buddhist texts, the gospel-like *Kangyur*. Rocking in the lotus position, their heads bob over the ancient rectangular manuscripts, gold-leaf script on black paper, set between brass tea bowls on the low benches in front of them. Against the back wall underneath a row of cobwebbed windows, maroon-robed novitiates—small boys with shaved heads—giggle and pinch each other and try to follow along.

Apparently this event adheres to no strict ecclesiastic regimen, and this particular bunch of holy men strike me as Shakespearean, given the earthy pleasure they take in our diversion. "Have you been drinking yet?" asks one of the monks. Of course not, we tell him. "We have," he smiles pleasantly. It's only nine thirty in the morning. A white-haired lama pats his lap and wonders if my wife would like to sit there. When I drop my pen, he snatches it up and, flashing an impish grin, slips it into the folds of his robe. What jokers, these monks of Tsarang. We leave them to pose for Laird's camera and Tsewang leads us along an interior balcony to a room unlike any other I have walked into in my life.

Pegged on the wall are medieval weapons—coats of mail, maces, battle axes, spears, scimitars, leather and metal shields, bows and arrows, all the armament any Loba might require should he need to defend Tsarang from Mongol invaders. Hanging on a rawhide thong there's an amputated human hand, black and mummified, but nobody seems to know its story.

In the center of the floor, monks and village women are making mud cones from clay and barley flour, smearing them red with berry juice, and plopping them into a basket; on the day of the Tiji festival, these cones, like Tange's fetishes, will become sin incarnate to be carried beyond the village walls and destroyed. Tsewang takes an old hand-forged key from his pocket and unlocks an elaborate cabinet in the corner. For the first time in a year, Tsarang's protector deity, Gombu, is exposed. All I can see is the gold nose of a statue poking out from an avalanche of white silk *khatas* but for the villagers in the room the occasion is momentous and they sprawl on the floor. Ang Tsering goes down too, prostrating himself three times before this god that commands his immediate devotion, and I am glad I'm there to see it happen, because my respect for Tsering bridges over to a respect for his beliefs and creates the first truly spiritual moment of our fellowship, in this land of spirits.

Too gorgeous, too comforting, too serene, Tsarang was, and no one's eager to leave, but we eat our lunch and hike down a ravine and over a footbridge behind the town to mount up for the three-hour ride to Lo Manthang. Jann and Mark take off ahead of us, fed up with life in the saddle. Captain Jack, we cannot help but notice, has been undergoing a sartorial evolution attuned to the equine ethos of Mustang and his presumed status within it, and today he's completely forsaken the Eddie Bauer look for a style that most resembles a colonial trail boss on the Burma Road—jodhpurs tucked into knee-high riding boots, linen shirt, soft leather riding gloves, topped off with a wide-brimmed felt hat and a black leather quirt perhaps formerly used to spank underage fannies in Thailand. As a fashion statement, the sensual, out-of-the-desert Lawrence of Arabia image that Michael has concocted with head scarves and lassitude seems to express the journey perfectly.

The trail becomes, by Mustang standards, a boulevard, with a hand-painted road sign pointing the way to the capital. Laird is animated, exuberant, perched atop his handsome horse, smacking and pursing his lips in anticipation. Today will be Tom's homecoming, so to speak. Today he will ride to the ancient walled city of his memory and fantasy and by nightfall be welcomed back to the palace—the prodigal son—and the aging king will ask him to sit by his side and drink yak-butter tea and talk about old times, when Laird himself was Lo Manthang's big news.

The boulevard ribbons across a mountainside; Laird and I kick our horses into a gallop and race side by side until the trail narrows back to a footpath and we are forced to trot, then forced to pull up altogether and summon our courage as the footpath dwindles to a goat path carved into a vertical slope that plummets down a thousand feet to the bottom of a boulder-strewn ravine. I feel light-headed with vertigo and can't look down to where Jamling's right front hoof falls right on the lip of the precipice, safe by a margin of inches—you could BASE jump here off the back of your horse if the winds were right.

On the other side of this hazard, the road opens up again into a desolate valley housing a lone chorten in its center and the two of us canter ahead alone into this wasteland. The horses seem to appreciate the freedom to run, and slow down only when we have crossed the valley and the slope tilts up again toward the high pass into Lo Manthang. With the slower pace, Laird and I debate what we've learned so far. The preservation aspect of restricted tourism is a success. The development aspect is a failure, which we probably should have expected since this is Nepal and the central government just keeps swallowing the money. Okay, admits Laird, there are water taps that weren't here ten years ago, but the things you would want to see change, like medical care, haven't.

"My impression so far," he says, "is the *lack* of change," but soon he'll dine bitterly on the irony of that observation.

At the top of the pass, the incessant cold wind stiffens and snaps the prayer flags strung across the road. We climb down from our saddles, tie our horses to the guy wires of the flagpoles, and crouch behind some rocks to gaze down upon the city that looks like a barge refitted as a citadel, a derelict Noah's ark run aground in a long green lake of barley fields and pastures, here on the backside of the roof of the world. "They've built outside the walls," Laird notes with regret. "It was the foreigners who didn't want them to do that." Tom, who usually expresses himself in rants, becomes reflective, soft-spoken. There below us was his home for almost a year; he had been Lo Manthang's honored guest, friend and confidant of its rulers; he had counted himself the luckiest man in the world. "I can't begin to describe the sense of melodramatic romanticism I felt the first time I stood on this pass," he says, his voice barely audible above the wind. "This was what I bought into—the fantasy, the mystery of Mustang, the young man's dream of finding the lost land. I had invested twenty years in Nepal, learning the language, courting the politicians, because this was what I wanted and it finally paid off. Now, looking at it, I think it's so barren, it's so poor. People here were really dealt a shitty hand."

Jann comes up and Tom wraps his arm around his wife's shoulder in triumph and soon the others are there too, digging into their packs for warmer clothes. As we remount our horses and descend the pass, Laird confides that in 1991 he came up this same valley in ecstasy and left a year later "crying, just crying, because I thought I had failed to really reach across the void to that other culture, to understand them and to be understood. I could never reach beyond my own cultural assumption, or theirs." But his melancholy fades as we wind up through the valley; his mood brightens and he kicks his horse ahead with Panglossian optimism. He expects things to be better now, a decade after the fact. He expects too much.

*   *   *

Down we go toward Lo Manthang, riding solemnly past the hollow carcasses of horses and other animals on the rocky slope below the city walls, furry hides sagging over skeletons, the eyes pecked out of the skulls, leering teeth naked with mortality, other garbage dumped ingloriously along the final approach to the city gates. Across the ravine are the houses of the *garas*—the blacksmiths—and the butchers, impure, low-born, forbidden to live in the city while providing it with their vital service. Everything's about to change. At the city gates we dismount into Tom Laird's personal version of hell.

Everything Changes

Across the plaza from the funky architectural wonder of the king's four-story adobe palace, the Lo Manthang Guest House cum *rakshi* faucet has all but run out of suitable lodging; *queri* have even pitched their tents on the flat roof rather than endure the last windowless dormitory space available. Laird and I follow Ang Tsering inside past a souvenir shop (Visa or MasterCard accepted) and a video parlor (twenty-five raucous preteens watching a Hindi movie from Bollywood), up two death-defying flights of stone steps, through a kitchen with weathered ladies, *didis*, squatting around a stove, along a dark corridor to an interior balcony, down two more series of ladderlike steps, through a courtyard, past a room stabling a horse and a *dzo*, and out to fresh air and a final descent of steps to a small walled corral. "This will do?" Ang Tsering asks hopefully. The city's six guesthouses are full of foreigners and Lobas come for the Tiji festival and our prospects are limited. Already I'm thinking how great it might be to be a kid in Lo Manthang, the whole massive interconnected dun-colored structure of it suggestive of something built out of the earth by generation after generation of castaway boys, a fantastic playground of dark interiors and climbing ramparts and courtyards and alleys and stairs and unexpected passageways and crannies where everyone lived as if under one roof.

All is well, all is not well. A section of the six-foot-thick ancient wall has collapsed into rubble, literally pissed down by the monks whose apartments are attached to it, their leaky plumbing undermining the wall's foundation. For their convenience, people have cut private doors into the wall to circumvent the city gates, and yes, the mayor, Pema Wangdi, a former serf, says, it's not good to build houses right outside the walls, but you know, the king sold us that land. If he didn't want us to build, he shouldn't have sold us the land. The mayor wants everybody to be a landowner, house owner, have a shop, a business, but nowadays, once you're an owner, you can't find anybody to work for you, we don't even have enough people to plow and harvest, he sighs. There's a refrain in the air, a Loba complaint: Our grandfathers created so much more than we can maintain. Fields, houses, monasteries, temples, chortens, irrigation ditches. It was much easier to keep things in shape with the serf system, of course: nothing like free labor to bring a kingdom up to speed.

Out on the jovial streets, Laird bows and hugs old friends but he can't remember names. He says he is bad with names but, married to his camera, I've rarely seen him bother. By his own admission, social skills have always been "difficult," a peccadillo that will balloon to the level of a cardinal sin before we leave Lo Manthang. We finally locate the hovel that serves as the worst police quarters in Nepal and, as we promised our liaison officer in Kagbeni, report in and are assigned a new officer to accompany us on our forays north of the city. Crime? we ask as our names are recorded in the registry. The unshaven cops look at one another, puzzled. Nobody understands the word in Mustang, nobody's seen or heard of Maoists up here. Ah, but there is one problem, a very bad problem, the police say. Mastiffs. Two policemen have been bitten in the past year, and three villagers, thus explaining why every nasty brute in town was now, thankfully, leashed.

I return to the compound with the others; Laird sets out to escort his wife on a long-awaited personal tour of the legendary city that once made her a type of war bride—a town of only one thousand people, a fifteen-minute walk end to end. We are having afternoon tea and popcorn in our dining tent when Tom bursts in: Quick, quick, he says to me, ignoring the others, we must go immediately for a brief audience with the raja and rani. We cross the plaza to the dark, litter-strewn entrance to the palace, the kind of grimy, step-out-of-sight niche where you'd expect to find junkies or working girls in a bad neighborhood in a bigger city. The king apparently is not big on upkeep either, but what are you going to do when your serfs bail out of the program? Above us on a second-floor balcony, two huge brown mastiffs bark psychotically and hurl themselves against their chains. The unlit passageways are steep, uneven, with cracked-off steps, and it's so dark you can't see the face of anyone coming the other way. On the third floor we are ushered into the main receiving room, benchlike tables fronting carpeted banquettes, ornately painted Tibetan cabinets and chests against the walls, photographs of Nepal's soon-to-be-dead monarchs framed on the wall, scuffed linoleum covering the concrete floor. A wooden rack displays an extraordinary collection of weapons—turn-of-the-century Lee Enfields, a World War II Sten gun, various musketry, and even flintlocks with pronged bayonets that fold down to allow the long rifles to be steadied and fired while riding a horse.

Ten years ago it was customary for peasants, in homage to the king, to stick out their tongues and prostrate themselves in his presence. Today power has shifted to the bureaucracies of Kathmandu, and the prostration is not so common, though villagers continue to scratch their heads in front of the king as a weird sign of respect. We pay our tribute in the form of ceremonial silk *khatas*, first to the rani, pale-faced and fine-boned and thin, elegant in her traditional gray *bukkhoo* and apron, her doe eyes beautiful but heavyhearted. She no longer attends public events, I am told: She is shy, she can't stand the dust, and most of her ladies-in-waiting have expired anyway.

In the corner along the cushions sits the taciturn seventy-year-old king, attired in a zipped blue windbreaker, a loop of prayer beads sliding through his fingers. Laird has a gift, a copy of his latest book, *The Dalai Lama's Secret Temple*, a collaboration with author Ian Baker that features Laird's photographs of the exiled Tibetan leader's private chapel in Llhasa. The king bends his attention to the murals on the page and becomes instantly absorbed, increasingly devoted in his old age to otherworldly matters. He's spacey but nonetheless kingly, a receptacle of that aura of divine composure that trickles through dynasties, but mostly the impression is of an aging monarch weary of all the nonsense he's bound to adjudicate, fatigued by the stream of not-always-distinguished guests who come petitioning his favor. From the looks of him, it would not surprise me if the king's concept of Nirvana includes retirement to the golf courses of Boca Raton. When King Jigme finally steps into that other, better world, the throne will pass to his nephew, a man fully entrenched in this one: Crown Prince Jigme S. P. Bista owns a rug factory and a trekking company in Kathmandu.

We sip lemon tea and chat about our journey, heaping praise on the agility and courage of the king's horses. The king is pleased (I think). When the topic turns to change, the king declares the Lobas are more prosperous, more educated than ten years ago. The city's a little cleaner, food's a little cheaper, and most people like the electricity introduced by ACAP, which insisted that the lines be buried underground—a difficult decision both politically and technically. As for tourism, says the king, so far so good, though he would be against an increase in the number of foreigners coming to Lo Manthang and, he adds, "the lower people don't want hotels here."

But still the villagers want more tourists, they want the restriction and the fee lifted, yes? I ask. Mm, the king softly grunts, bowing his head to the inscrutable ambiguity of his quasi-royal thoughts. His thumb caresses the beads. The audience is over.

Outside in the square, ACAP's public-address system crackles Tibetan music through the evening chill. At dinner, Laird asks the group if it's all right if we have guests for breakfast, an acquaintance from Kathmandu and the Italian specialist working on the restoration of the Thubchen temple. Later, Laird pulls me aside and confesses that perhaps he made a diplomatic faux pas in the way he had issued the invitation. He had met his friend Linda in the plaza; she was in the company of the Italian and an Englishman named John Sanday. I had noticed Sanday earlier in the day out on the streets of Lo Manthang; indeed, he was impossible to miss.

Certainly the largest *queri* in town, Sanday was hawk-nosed, pink-cheeked, and wore a wide-brimmed leather hat, navy-blue anorak, clean blue jeans, and leather boots. He seemed given to an autocratic pensiveness, a humorless brooding, and one might have imagined him to be a London film director trying to wrestle the Third World into submission. He was in fact formidable in his occupation—architect and owner of the firm Sanday Associates. His restorations were world-famous—Angkor Wat, the Hanuman Dhoka Palace in Kathmandu—and now, funded by the King Mahendra Trust and the American Himalayan Foundation, he was restoring the Thubchen Gompa, one of the architectural, artistic, and spiritual treasures of Lo Manthang. Linda and the Italian were his employees. Come for breakfast, Laird told them, but he failed to include John Sanday in the invitation, for reasons that he now could not explain. An oversight, he tells me. A tempest in a teapot, I think, only the teapot is Lo Manthang itself, and my friend Tom Laird is headed for a tutorial in contempt.

The day started in gloom and drizzle, became searing by the afternoon, and by nightfall is piercingly cold. I put on a heavier coat and join the Bangkokers in Sirendra's upstairs tearoom and nomad watering hole. The clientele might look cutthroat and unwashed, but the smiles that greet us are genuine and unceasing and the place hums with coziness, with the fellowship engendered by the hardships of the land. The captain and Mike indulge euphorically in Sirendra's home brew *rakshi*, which is not as fiery or green as others I had sampled and tastes like a watered-down version of good grappa. Tomorrow I will bear witness to a poignant moment in Sirendra's, the reunion Laird wanted, the one he foresaw, when he comes into the guesthouse bar with a copy of his Mustang book and recognizes a bashful, elfin *dropka*, a herder, sitting alone by the stove, staring with a bereaved look into a glass of milk tea. Their reunion is affectionate; Tom asks about the health of the nomad's wife. She died, says the *dropka*. But Laird photographed the two of them together ten years ago, up in the high pastures standing proudly in front of their woolen yurt. The photo is there, in the book. The man has never seen a picture of himself or his wife, but there she is, resurrected, there they are together again, and the fellow will lean over the picture misty-eyed, and for a long time he will hold his calloused fingers on the page and quietly touch his dead wife's lovely face.

Before dawn, I am unhappily introduced to the call of the hoopoe, an extravagant Southeast Asian bird that migrates north of the Himalayas during monsoon season. Unfortunately it has a persistent, monotonous threnody cry that sounds uncannily like my travel alarm clock. The sunrise is dreary, cold, threatening rain, the snow line has advanced far down the slopes of the surrounding mountains, and when I crawl from my tent to brush my teeth I find that I must walk a disconcerting gauntlet of vendors who have invaded the compound with hope, their artifacts and jewelry spread atop blankets on the ground. The Sherpas won't chase them off unless I tell them, but I won't tell them; these people are traders from across the ravine, too poor to have shops in town. I tell them if they come back later in the day, they won't be disappointed; bowing and cheerful, they retreat behind the compound walls to wait patiently for however many hours until the *queri* feel like bargaining for a yak-bone necklace or brass thunderbolt.

Linda arrives, Sanday's emissary, awkward and nervous but not unfriendly. She's sorry, she tells Laird. Breakfast won't work. Without expressly saying so, she communicates tension between her group and ours. Laird, nonplussed, chats with her about the restoration at the temple and says he'll drop by the site to see how it's going. He wants to photograph the team's work but of course Linda doesn't have the authority to commit to that. Laird and Jann remain in town while the rest of us reunite with Mahendra and the horses for a day trip north to Namgyal Monastery, the largest monastery in Mustang.

In the valleys running toward the Chinese border and the headwaters of the Kali Gandaki, the countryside's boundless solitude is muted by a scattering of villages within easy walking distance from one another, the quiltwork of pastures and wind-rippled barley fields, the ruins of an extensive system of fortresses and sanctuaries, the ghosts of sentinels perched atop every knoll and ridgeline. Yet all human endeavor here is overshadowed by vast wildness, the horseshoe of severe mountains above the cultivated plain that corral Upper Mustang, "one of the most remote, backward, and inaccessible valleys in the Nepal Himalayas," according to scholar David Jackson. Sometimes wolves prowl the fringe of the hamlets; in the higher pastures, sometimes villagers will kill a snow leopard for culling their herds. This is the home of the mythical yeti, the abominable snowman, and a bloodthirsty pantheon of local spirits; when night falls superstitious villagers bolt their doors.

My curiosity is tweaked by the captain. Ever since we've left Jomsom I've noticed he's been taking more prolific notes than I have. Insanely comprehensive, tediously meticulous notes. Now he's up here peppering Mahendra with the most esoteric queries. Why do you want to know the name of that little mountain poking out among all those big mountains? I ask him. The name of the village headman who never said a word? The name of that inconsequential stream? I'm a failed author, says the captain, and that's where we leave it.

Machiavellian Playdates

We begin our exploration of the legendary temples of the walled city, rivaled only by their larger cousins in Tibet. The great red hulk of Champa Lha-kang, dedicated to Maitreya, the future Buddha, houses a six-hundred-year-old clay statue of this same Buddha, so gigantic that it rises from the perpetual dusk of the temple's cellar through the floor of the altar room toward the structure's high-beamed ceiling and its rotted wood, a disaster in the making. In fact, the temple is in such extreme disrepair, its frescoes streaked with water damage and cracked from earthquakes, that the survival of its murals, in Laird's opinion "the world's greatest surviving collection of fifteenth-century mandalas," is in doubt. Laird, with a Sherpa in tow lugging his gear, photographs like a madman, groaning at the ten-year advance of decay throughout the once luminous paintings. The raja, however, is waiting to judge the success of the Sanday team and the American Himalayan Foundation in their restoration of the Thubchen temple before allowing them to rescue Champa. "What do you think?" the king asks Laird later in the day. "Are they doing a good job over there?"

Tomorrow we will see for ourselves, but we spend the remainder of the morning inside the chapel of the palace with Tashi Tenzing, the head lama of Lo, inhaling thick clouds of juniper incense while the monks of Chyodi Monastery immerse themselves in the *puja* ritual with which the Tiji festival commences. Above the drone of their chanting, cymbals crash, drums rumble, horns shriek and blare—the short *kagyling,* the twelve-foot-long copper *dunchens,* squealing double-reeded trumpets—and what seems most remarkable about this sacred music is that, like Mustang's architecture, the instruments express a perfect interpretation of the land—the stormy monsoons, goats bleating, the drawling bellow of yaks, the river's roar—and the unceasing thresh of man's endurance.

The more profane vicissitudes of Lo lurk just around the corner the next day at the colossal, brilliantly pillared Thubchen temple, which a camera-laden Laird and I enter, stepping across mounds of construction debris. Directly inside, on the wall opposite the altar, a crew of local workers sits on scaffolding under the blaze of floodlights, delicately swabbing clean an area of murals. Virtually nothing is known outside Mustang of Lo Manthang's temples, masterpieces of fifteenth- and sixteenth-century Inner Asian culture. They are incomprehensible achievements, their murals painted in the glow of butter lamps, their wooden beams and massive pillars hauled by yak from the southern slopes of India, their statues cast by ancient Lo's own metallurgists. To my untrained eye, John Sanday's team has performed miracles—the roof replaced and waterproofed, the original banked skylight allowing sunbeams to bathe the altar rebuilt—and in comparison to the soot-darkened, stained, and cracked frescoes yet to be addressed, the opulence of the restored murals stuns the senses. The paintings gleam from the walls like sheets of jewels.

But no sooner do we enter the great hall than the floodlights go out and the crew of young Lobas up on the scaffolding climbs down and leaves. A foreman advises Sanday, an imposing figure standing amidst the forest of pillars, that the generator has broken. I approach Sanday, hoping he can tell me about the technique for cleaning frescoes. "Ask the boss," he growls, ill-tempered and enigmatic. "I don't know who the boss is, except you," I say. "It's not a trick question." Sanday, exhaling hostility, refuses to engage even in polite conversation, and my impression of him is neither kind nor, at the moment, informed. I haven't a clue what's going on here, this sudden turn of bad manners, unchecked scorn. Also, I'm perplexed by Laird's behavior, his audacious insistence on standing fast—he *will* take pictures of the restoration, he *will* wait for the generator to be fixed. Sanday ignores him; the rest of us leave.

I meet up with Laird hours later; he tells me the generator won't be fixed until tomorrow, when he has scheduled an hour-long shoot, for which, he adds, he has shelled out a hundred bucks, not to Sanday but to the mayor, Pema Wangdi. In the afternoon, we watch the king's men unfurl another of the city's treasures down the length of the square's south wall, a three-story-high appliqué *thangka,* Tibetan-made and antique, the backdrop for the upcoming festivities. A few minutes later, returning from the mayor's house, Laird and I run into John Sanday and Linda on the street; the encounter escalates directly to ugliness. Tom begins by asking about the generator and offering a reasonable explanation of his motive—compiling a before-and-after portfolio—for photographing the restoration.

"The locals are very distressed about you," Sanday tells Laird. "We've worked very hard for four years to establish trust here with everybody, and you have a bad reputation from ten years ago."

"I've heard you have a bad reputation too," says Laird, ambushed. A stranger to the art of discretion, he wants to mouth a counteraccusation but wisely doesn't.

"Who's telling you this?" says Sanday.

"Who's telling *you?*" says Laird.

"Well . . ." says Sanday, hesitating. And then, pushed onstage by a trickster spirit, the premier witness for the prosecution happens to walk by. "This guy," says Sanday, motioning over the dour-faced fellow. "This guy Tashi says you owe him twelve thousand rupees from ten years ago." Laird and Tashi fold themselves into a heated discussion. Sanday and Linda back away and leave.

The amount is roughly $200, overpayment for some rope, six wool bags, and rental on a tent. Laird has no recollection of the debt. Tashi, as everyone knows, had worked for Laird regularly, earning many tens of thousands of rupees. There's not much Laird can do—of course he'll pay. "There's plenty of room for this to have happened," Laird tells me after the fellow storms away, "plenty of room. I'm not saying Tashi invented this. He kept saying, 'I was like your child,' you know, this whole feudal thing, and I was his father, and he trusted me completely. And what am I supposed to say to John when he says people are saying bad things about me from ten years ago?"

The dispute is only the tip of the Machiavellian iceberg lodged deep in Mustang, Nepal, Third World development, cross-cultural interaction, human nature. Who's got dibs on what? Who *owes*? Who *controls*? Standing on the street, Laird feels the anguish, as anybody would, of accusation.

There is at least one other person besides Tashi both Laird and I know Sanday might have named: Brot Coburn, a former Peace Corps volunteer in Nepal occasionally employed by the American Himalayan Foundation. Coburn is the embodiment of the My Village syndrome common to Western aid workers in the Third World, jealous of any incursions onto his turf, and from personal experience I know that Brot, impulsive and sanctimonious, can't restrain himself from committing gratuitous acts of cruelty and malice. Laird and Coburn had known each other for many years and the relationship was always, from Tom's point of view, antagonistic. Still, they were expats in the Himalayas and sometimes found themselves relying on each other's magnanimity. The year Laird lived in Mustang, Brot and adventurer Stan Armington arrived in Lo Manthang just before Tiji; Laird allowed Brot to share his quarters, as Tom himself had stayed at Brot's house a few years earlier in Tengboche, where Coburn was wiring the monastery for the American Himalayan Foundation.

Falling asleep talking in Lo Manthang, Laird mentioned the trail the flood had cleared through the upper gorge. What, no Westerners have ever traveled the river route through the gorge? Brot wants to go; Laird can't bear the thought of being one-upped by a rival so he accompanied Brot and Stan. He left them at Chele and rode back up to Lo Manthang. Brot and Stan continued down to Jomsom. That summer and at least for the next two years, until Tom confronted him, Brot began rumormongering in Kathmandu, suggesting to people that Tom Laird was up in Mustang stealing art and smuggling out animal parts (the skin of Matthiessen's alleged yeti?). John Sanday would have had to plug his ears not to hear some version of Brot's gossip, and it's difficult now to believe that the temple's generator broke down just as we entered the temple.

"You begin to understand," says Laird as we walk back to Sirendra's, "the people leveling the accusations believe it, they believe it. Then what can you do, especially if you can't have a logical conversation about it? How can you appease them?" How do you appease them and, in the end, appease the gods? The story gets better, or worse, depending on your loyalties. To quote Brot Coburn long ago quoting Dharma teachings to chasten me: *Karma ripens.*

That evening a velvet couch is carried out into the square for the king to watch the ACAP-sponsored song festival, the intent of which seems to be to assert Nepali culture in Mustang. The mastiffs bark hellishly from the balcony of the palace while Thakali women perform a traditional Nepalese dance, and teenagers in the audience scribble on the appliqué *thangka* with laser penlights. And yet ACAP fills the void left by the central government, and the NGO's contributions to the quality of life in Mustang are real, even as the *rongbas*, the people from "below," assume an ever-greater presence in the affairs of Lo Manthang.

The following day, when the appointed hour arrives, Tom enlists a Sherpa to help him with his gear and the three of us walk over to the Thubchen temple. The generator's working, the floodlights burn onto the walls, the crew is on the scaffolding, and Laird, resolute, sets up his tripod. Sanday, resigned to Laird's tenacity, engages me in an amicable discussion about the restoration. The project is in many ways a model worth replicating, a transfer of knowledge and skill into the communities: Sanday and his experts are training twenty-six young

Lobas from villages throughout Mustang in wall-painting conservation. Four more trainees are carpenters; five others are being instructed in masonry repair.

Given my first impression of him the previous day, I think I misjudged Sanday, and when I ask about the generator, I believe him when he says he was told it had broken and doesn't know otherwise; if it was sabotaged, he doesn't know about it. But as we talk, one of the young Loba trainees pulls the switch on the floodlights, the workers monkey down from the scaffolding—this time, nobody bothers with the ruse of a broken generator. Sanday seems genuinely surprised. These trainees, all of them teenagers, twentysomethings, are a new breed of Loba, products of the opening, of democratic verities and illusions, a generation molded by forces they have mounted but will never conquer without being conquered in return. Now an anger has stirred them, seized their emotions. They are striking because of Laird, and the charges fly. Sanday translates the gist of it to me: The kids venerate these paintings and think Tom desecrated them.

In Lo Manthang, the central cleavage on the Tom issue was religious conservatism, exacerbated by the vestiges of feudalism—whether somebody was a noble or had been a serf—and, incredibly, the drought of 1992. And money, naturally—people were convinced he made a fortune on the Matthiessen book. When Laird first arrived in 1991, the villagers were vehemently opposed to his attempts to photograph the massive wall paintings in the temples, but the king had given his blessing, and Laird was willing to suffer social opprobrium to record the works, because he believed then, and remains firm in the belief, that artwork is protected once you photograph it. But the Lobas hold the conviction, also very strong, that photography angers the gods and invites stealing. In 1992, the year Laird photographed the temples, the rains were late, and he was blamed, forced to choke on the difference between the supernatural and the absurd, between East and West. Then one day three wandering yogis came to town, the rains followed, and Laird packed up his gear and was gone.

Not that Laird didn't make mistakes in Mustang. He was dumb enough to start a my-guys-don't-like-your-guys feud, never clearly explained to me, with the Crown Prince. One day he scaled a chorten with his camera and the king himself warned Laird that this was taboo. On a trek up to the northwest highlands to photograph Chudzong, the legendary water fort, over Laird's strong objections his liaison officer took a rifle along to shoot endangered argali sheep, which caused a great furor back in the walled city, people claiming he was terrorizing the countryside and breaking into temples. It was always rumors, and always depressing.

Ten years ago in the temples, Laird would yell at Tashi and his other helpers: Don't touch a ladder unless I'm there; if these paintings get damaged I'll be blamed. Now the trainees have mobbed around Laird in the Thubchen temple to echo his words back to him: You damaged paintings with your ladders, you stood with your legs spread over deities on the floor, you're a bad man, and nothing you can say will change our opinion. Laird is appalled, despairing—he loved the paintings and felt compelled to show them to the world. The Lobas can't see his heart throbbing for the art, never understood his passion; they thought it was about money. Tom came and treated us like animals, one of the young workers tells me. How old were you then? I ask him. Seven.

Sanday won't intercede and I can't really fault him—he has a future here and Laird doesn't. Laird pleads for his friend Linda to defend him and, halfheartedly, she tries, but to no avail and, overcome by the certitude of his detractors, understanding that it never mattered to them if any of his crimes were true or not, Tom weeps. Beyond embarrassment, the tableau spews forth enormous pathos. The last thing Tom Laird could ever have imagined for his life had come true—he was the Ugly American. In the eyes of the Lobas, he had caused a fucking drought. What could be uglier than that? And now ten years later he could still see it in their faces—he was the Ugly American who came and caused the drought. Symbiotic fantasies of paternalism and gratitude exploded like terrorists' bombs and healing is not possible.

In obvious pain, Tom listens to the feelings coming out of these kids, knowing that many of their fathers said the same things ten years ago. But back then it was local, a sizable difference, and now it's spread out into the larger community of foreigners and institutes and you could see his shoulders slump under the weight, see the stress in his legs, struggling to hold himself upright.

Yet regardless of Laird's peccadilloes and shortcomings, I empathized deeply with his predicament, and this is why you're hearing this story, because he is no more innocent and no more guilty than any Westerner working in the Third World, where even the purest heart becomes quickly entangled in profound and ancient conflicts that elude resolution or reconciliation. ACAP's mantra, printed in big red letters at its Lo Manthang office on the square, is a pretty thought, a seductive lie: *Nepal is here to change you, not for you to change Nepal.* More true are the words of Lo Manthang's new *amji*, the royal physician, who carries forward his revered father's dream of a school for Tibetan medicine. A year after his father died, the school was built by outside sponsorship. "Only foreigners," the *amji* believes, "can make real change up here."

A legion of Tom Lairds roams the planet's hinterlands. They're always out there, autodidacts, loners, freelancers, info-hustlers, image hounds, students of adventure dedicated to exotic histories and enigmatic cultures, surviving by their wits, altruistic or not, imperfect but devoted, dilettantes and professionals bearing witness, brave and arrogant, exasperating and unprotected and chronically misunderstood and underappreciated, skirting convention, working without a safety net but not without a value system, not without scruples, not without, for lack of a better word, a calling. Yes, karma ripens . . . and vindicates. The Lairds of the world are a catalyst, part of a trigger mechanism certainly; they come and they go, and then it's up to the locals themselves, like the Lobas, to close the gap between the past and the future. Or not.

Listen, there had been other episodes in the temples of Lo Manthang—film crews chased off, cameras damaged, film destroyed, liaisons intimidated, endless misunderstanding. Every great achievement comes packaged in some variety of hurt and nightmare. Sanday is not paranoid, he had to choose sides, and for the trainees, John Sanday is a gold mine. But for Laird, this is nothing but water-cooler politics played out in a cultural quicksand, with no objective place to stand and fight. Tenzing, the project's cultural liaison, steps into the fray to calm everybody down. The past is past, he tells the workers; now you have to create a new relationship with Mustang and the people, he says to Laird.

So what should I do? Tom asks the workers. You should support the American Himalayan Foundation, they say. Next time work with the community, a young woman says, the implication being, *not with the king.*

Support the American Himalayan Foundation! For Laird it was like hearing the oracle speak and telling yourself, No, *that* can't be true. In a sense, their loyalty had been bought, just as when they were serfs to the king. The gods were now out of the picture, along with the raja, the mayor, the head lama, who approved of Laird's work in Mustang. What remained was the American Himalayan Foundation, an organization that Laird felt had shunned and denigrated him. This is all Laird needs to hear to collect himself and resume his obstinacy. He looks at his wristwatch and tells John Sanday he has twenty-seven paid minutes left in the shoot. My allegiance is waning in the face of Tom's stubbornness; I try to pull him out of there but he won't budge.

Go up, Sanday tells the trainees, pointing to the scaffolding. Let them do it. If they make a bad story . . . (he grabs a kid and twists a fist toward his face). Was that supposed to be sarcastic? Tom asks me later. Yes, I think, just a little joke, but I remember Tenzing had pulled me aside to say we should thank the king before we leave Lo Manthang, because if we didn't have a connection with the king, we'd have "big trouble." Back at his tripod, Laird squints into his camera's viewfinder and snaps a picture. "One picture—100,000 rupees," says one of the trainees gathered around him. The shutter clicks again. "Two pictures—200,000 rupees," says another young Loba. "Look at how much money he's already made," they jeer. From atop the scaffolding, the workers pelt him with paint-soaked cotton balls.

"John's his own worst enemy," Laird says when we're back on the street. "He's just like me."

On the first hot, bright, clear day since we rode out of the canyon, Laird and I ladder up through somebody's roof to walk the eastern wall of the city. From our vantage point we can see that most of Lo Manthang's houses have solar panels, some have solar water heaters, one has what you're going to find anywhere in the world these days—a satellite dish. Directly below us, a field is overtaken by the construction of a new boarding school for monks. Laird is hugely melancholic. The people are gone, he says, the people who cared about you, the people who just wanted to be better. They died. The *amji*, the Kempo. They possessed human qualities Laird wanted to emulate. Even the fantasy of the Good King had receded into history, and with it the peasants who still believed in the Divine Right of Kings. Ah, but what exactly is Laird's regret? The insularity, some might say the purity, of Lo Manthang has been contaminated by the modern world, by time itself, an inevitable fate, and not the tragedy that Westerners might assume. I think Laird understands that, and understands that in fundamental ways Mustang is less changeable than Death Valley, than the bottom of the ocean, than the moon.

"The first thing people expressed ten years ago was hopelessness," says Laird. "'We're living here like dung beetles, eating on the carcass. We're so poor we can't even take care of the things our fathers left us. Why do you want to come here? We work with dust and eat dust. You work with light and eat light. Why are you here eating all this *doolah*— dust?' They were my grandparents on the farm in Mississippi."

The passage of those ten years has made the world of the Loba no longer simple or static, and I remember Mahendra telling me that "life wasn't confusing until the *queri* came—*you* made it confusing."

Not just Tom Laird—everybody. Laird inhales heavily and sighs; not self-pity, I think, but grief. "I love the paintings," he says. "I love these paintings so much, and if I had just walked away from it things would be different for me up here now, it would be so much easier." Any role he had to play in the history of Mustang is over, kaput. His legacy here, despite the emotions, fabrications, distortions, despite his own cynicism, is positive, life-affirming. He was a forerunner of change, a not insignificant particle in the convergence of forces—democracy, tourism, economic reform in China—that lifted the veil from the Lost Kingdom of Lo. However embittering, that it's not ending well for him is perhaps irrelevant, and the real cost to Laird is internal, he has lost the dream, the young man's dream of hidden kingdoms. A year from now, after photographing terror and civil war and massacres, Laird will move from Kathmandu to New Orleans; after thirty years he is too tired to stay.

The groan of horns in the palace square ends our conversation. Tiji, the annual cleansing ritual, has begun. As they have for centuries, the lamas in their magnificent costumes will perform their legendary slow-footed dance. The courtyard will twist with incense and dust as the good spirits, the better spirits, pull mankind back from the brink of darkness. The demon—the tattered skin of a Bengal tiger—will be symbolically stabbed and defeated. In the crush of spectators will be Mustang's own version of mall girls, flirting unabashedly with a posse of Loba hipsters in Chinese jeans, Chinese jackets, Chinese running shoes, looking very much like any group of suave young men on any street of any city in Asia—the generation who will shape Mustang's future, or abandon it to the wind. The new will battle the old and win at best a synthesis of tradition and opportunity, and at least this is certain: the next generation has already adapted to the process.

The horns will wail and bleat throughout the evening. A year's worth of malignancy will be paraded beyond the ancient walls and destroyed. The elders in their white robes will discharge their matchlocks into the air, children will bowl firecrackers at each other's feet.

Returning from a meeting where he has cleared his debt with Tashi—"I now have an enemy with twelve thousand rupees"—Laird will be accosted by townswomen, who have just finished with their civic duty, who will grab him, paw at his sleeve. "We watered the street," they will nag. "Pay us," they'll demand, a more overt version of the Lo Manthang shakedown. Life will be renewed, absolution dispensed sparingly, but nothing will be forgiven, and in the morning Mahendra and Tomay will bring the horses and we will leave.

Where are you going?

Tula—below. What Lobas call Nepal.

PART FOUR

Knowledge and Pain

(2001, 1997, 1991, 1994)

We all move on the fringes of eternity and are sometimes granted vistas through the fabric of illusion.

—*Ansel Adams*

The Fabric of Illusion

Mahendra: *Kale phe.* Go slowly. If you slip . . .

Tom: I know, we're gonna die.

We ride out of Lo Manthang over the pass, along a terrifying cliff-side where I close my eyes sometimes not so much in fear as in resignation, Jamling's hooves striking the soft lip of the edge of the nothingness we will fly into should one rock dislodge or the earth shift downward a few inches from our weight, and I slip my boots out of the stirrups thinking I might have a chance to save myself but probably not. Jamling stumbles, dropping his head, and I float above him for a moment, an awful feeling of disconnection, my feet scrambling in the air to find the stirrups again. The roof of the world, and we are riding along its window ledges, reeling with adrenaline. Behind me, I hear Mahendra laughing— "Oh, you caused me so much problems when you didn't know how to ride. Now everything is better." I suppose it's true, we wouldn't have been so foolish to stay mounted on such a dangerous path in the early days of our horsemanship.

We are happy to be moving again, trying to reclaim the robust momentum we had established coming up the canyon, the energy taken out of us by Lo Manthang's constant furtive press of traders determined to sell us carpets, turquoise, temple bells, antiques, the family jewels, by the city's fog of intrigue, by the melodrama at the temple. No one would argue that we had overstayed our visit, and

I feel a great sense of regret for Tom and Jann, the reversals of this, their long-deferred adventure together to the Forbidden Kingdom, and cannot shake the irony out of my mind, the image-spool of Jann as she left the walled city forever in a smoldering rage at the injustice dumped on her husband like a pail of foul dishwater.

Past Tsarang, our day's final destination isn't far, the village of Ghami, three hours by foot. Four of us decide to walk the distance; Laird, the Captain, and Mike will ride, but not before napping through the heat of the afternoon on the cushions of Tsewang's tearoom. Jann and Mark are the most intrepid striders, a blessing in disguise, for my wife and I soon find ourselves alone on the trail together, enjoying a day made sublime by the singular pace that is us. Tsarang La, the second-highest pass we will walk over on the expedition, at 12,836 feet, rises ahead of us, and with each ten steps we take up the incline, another panel of the view unfolds, until we are standing on the col awestruck by the full panorama of the Himal, snow peaks as far as the eye can see. I rummage in my pack for the last roll of prayer flags I've carried with me to Mustang and climb the cairn, thousands of small rocks to mark the gratitude of the pilgrims who have passed this way throughout the ages, and tie one end of the string to the pole on the summit, its shaft swathed in wind-shredded flags. My wife of twenty-five years grabs the other end and we stretch our prayers across the narrow gap of the col, where they speak more eloquently than any other religious symbol of the beauty and sorrow of the world, of life's fragility and lost souls and remembrance and the eternity that we fall back into. The wind lifts the flags and we hold each other dearly. Except when someone has died, we have never cried together. She has never seen the Himalayas, but she has carried the ache of their ineffability inside since the morning I stood without her in Darjeeling, waiting for the sun to rise . . . well, I have a roundabout explanation.

Ten years ago, while Tom Laird was on his way up-canyon to Mustang and the first President Bush was marshaling coalition forces against nearby Iraq, I stood atop Nemrut Dagi in eastern Turkey, sniffing the air for windblown chemicals and waiting for the sun to float up over Persia and bathe the Euphrates River valley in rosy light, and it was there I first encountered a disturbing trend among sunrises: that, like celebrities, some are so well attended that they never have a moment's peace, and their fame churns up a hungry cloud of avarice—of both sybaritic and sacred varieties—in its wake. Which is to say, sunrises as cottage industries are peculiarly irreverent events, eclipsed by a motorized army of famous-sunrise worshippers followed close by the entrepreneurial tribes: the famous-sunrise postcard vendors, the famous-sunrise fake archaeological treasure hucksters, the famous-sunrise Polaroid artists, and the famous-sunrise tea merchants, toting large thermoses—all of which Lo Manthang can look forward to. In Turkey at least, the majority of celebrants were not outsiders but national tourists, welcoming their world-renowned sunrise with the robustness of soccer fans, singing patriotic songs, loudly reporting the progress and possibilities of the forthcoming show, and blowing snot out of each nostril onto the cold ground. As the darkness ended and the landscape brightened into silhouettes, flashbulbs popped like sniper fire. Every few minutes the horde of pilgrims reached a shivery consensus and warmed up with calisthenics. Forget meditative repose, the precious silence of dawn. Think of a virgin theme inseminated with an embryonic park, though no one in particular—not even a Disney—is to blame for the vulgarization of this ancient site, acclaimed by Alexander the Great.

I mention all this so you will be sympathetic, perhaps, to the skepticism and jaded sense of déjà vu with which I approached my second famous sunrise three years later, standing atop Tiger Hill, above the former colonial hill resort of Darjeeling in northeastern India. I was on my way to Sikkim, the Himalayan mountain-state which, I had read, "Tibetans have long regarded as a mysterious hidden sanctuary resembling the fictional Shangri-la." The government of India had just opened Sikkim's northern district to foreigners for the first time in a generation, and I had stopped for several days in Darjeeling to begin acclimating myself to the altitude, which is not so easy to do at sea level in Florida, where I live.

The spectacle of Tiger Hill had been playing for at least a century, since the carriages of the British raj were drawn up its severe slopes to deposit their cargo of tea planters and memsahibs on its bracing crown. Like all famous sunrises, the attraction was double-headed—the sun shared the bill with what its rising revealed. In the case of Tiger Hill, spectators gathered to divide their attention between the eastern and northern views. To the east, the sun mounted the endless corrugations of southwestern China and burst forth over another formerly forbidden and still restricted kingdom, Bhutan. As it did so, however, it cast an unforgettable kaleidoscope of color, light, and shadow upon one of the planet's most stunning panoramas, a mammoth uplift of the earth's crust culminating in the five summits of the world's third-highest mountain, and most sacred of its fourteen 28,000-foot peaks, Kangchenjunga.

I had been in this part of Asia only once before—a short but ambitious side trip out of Hong Kong, where I was teaching, to visit old friends in Kathmandu. A week later I had returned to the States with two staggeringly vivid images imprinted on my memory and, for lack of any other word to say this, ever-present in my soul. (One wonders, however, as a product of a post-religious society, how I came to have a soul, and what is to be done with it?)

Pashupatinath, the temple compound on the banks of Nepal's holiest river, was an engine of surreality, emitting a steady exhaust of details both hellish and transcendent. Here the dying and dead were brought for their final earthbound performance, to be set afire on the stone and concrete platforms—ghats—lining the bankside, their ashes picked through by monkeys, then broomed into the filthy water and slowly drained molecule by molecule into the Ganges. Crossing a footbridge, I saw a sight that penetrated the intense calm of Pashupatinath, its otherworldly and pitiless absence of sorrow. Where the bridge joined the stone embankment, a pyre had burned sufficiently to require tending, tidying. In its case of flames, a skull radiated with heat, on the verge of transparency, and at the center of the ghat, the furious transformation was complete; no trace of human being was evident among the coals. But at the end nearest me, a set of white-hot discs that were knees were still attached to blackened shanks, each tapering to a perfectly good feminine foot sticking out of the blaze, the gauze shroud burned away without effect and the manicured toes pointed skyward. I stopped to stare, horrified, because these blister-less, youthful, and indeed healthy-looking feet seemed to contain a heart-rending surplus of untraveled miles. As I watched, an attendant ambled forward. With his pole, he tucked the disembodied pair under a golden blanket of flame where her womb would be, and finally I turned away, self-absorbed, obviously, by mortality. They made chilling metaphoric sense to me, these feet—the reluctance of flesh to follow spirit and step away from life. But in Nepal, and later in Sikkim, I learned that it is quite possible, though never as easy as it looks, to walk right out of the world.

All I knew before arriving in Kathmandu that first time was that the mountains lay somewhere north of the city, shielded by intervening hills and the last days of monsoon season. I had resigned myself to the expectation that any pleasure I got from the Himalayas would derive simply from being in the neighborhood, like visiting the home of a Hollywood star who won't come out of her room. It hardly strained my senses, though, to feel them out there, titans looming behind the clouds: Annapurna, Everest, Kangchenjunga.

Frustration got the better of me and on my last day in Kathmandu I borrowed my host's mountain bike and pushed out into the murder-ous morning traffic, headed for the medieval city of Bhaktapur, en route to Nagarkot, a hilltop village on the northeastern rim where, with any luck, the legendary snow peaks would expose themselves wholesale. Sixty klicks up and back but a dream-easy ride through time more than space, despite a four-thousand-foot rise in elevation. The day was bright with sunshine and, on the wooded slopes and free of diesel fumes, exhilaratingly fresh. I topped the ridge by late morn-ing and found myself at the end of the road, a barrier and guard post announcing the perimeter of a military zone.

Dismounting, I walked the bike down a footpath traversing the northern face of the ridge, scouting for an isolated spot to perch in solitude and look out upon the roof of the world, first with great antici- pation but then with a mild sense of disappointment. I rationalized that a landscape so painted in awe-inspired rhetoric as the Himalayas was likely to be a few degrees overrated. The midland range that helped shape the bowl of Kathmandu rolled down into another terraced valley, then hopped up again to another ridgeline, then another and another, an ocean of crests, each successively higher and steeper and ultimately capped by a froth of clouds. Showers still roamed the vista during these last days of September, although the overcast was beginning to tear up and scatter.

I peered into those clouds, their perceptible flux, disappointed but not crushed: not seeing the Himalayas was not, after all, the equiva- lent of life passing you by. And, if somewhere concealed within the impenetrability of the clouds lay an answer, an epiphany, a step in the direction of truth or enlightenment, I had, without regrets, become middle-aged without that answer, and probably would be stumped about how to use it anyway. My good fortune, however circumscribed, would consist of being where I was, on a ridge above Kathmandu, on a beautiful day, with hope in my heart. That should have been enough.

After several minutes I saw a hawk plunge, swooping down into the inner valley. It stalled and seemed to change its mind, wings expanding to release itself back into the updraft above the wheat-colored paddies. I watched as the bird climbed above the layered ridges until it was level with, and then higher than, the mountainous horizon. From my perspective, it appeared to ascend above the clouds into smears of blue atmosphere, and I tracked its flight until my mouth gaped and I shook my head, disbelieving. In the high air, where nothing belonged or ever existed for me, forms shifted, crystallized, spilled vapor, like humpback whales knifing straight up through the surface. What I saw I felt was inconceivable—another world embedded in the stratosphere, exactly where I gazed a minute ago, seeing emptiness, dismissing any other possibility. Sometimes you have to look at something many times, physicists are fond of saying, before you see it once.

They were there, wrote the Scottish mountaineer W. H. Murray, describing his first sight of the Himalayan snow peaks. *An arctic continent of the heavens, far above the earth and its girdling clouds: divorced wholly from this planet.*

"A mountain, especially a Himalaya, especially Everest," Salman Rushdie wrote in *The Satanic Verses*, "is land's attempt to metamorphose into sky; it is grounded flight, the earth mutated—nearly—into air, and become, in the true sense, exalted."

What should have been a cerulean void was stacked magnificently with dazzling snow-streaked fantasies—veiled, unveiling, veiled again, ducked behind their screen of mists, there for an ephemeral moment but ever-elusive, a trait I have come to associate with the Himalayas (and, I suppose, consciousness, insight, truth, meaning). The moon had crashed here, cracking into a half-dozen colossal, icy pieces. I've never been so surprised by geography nor so thunderstruck by the generous scale of reality. What I mean is this:

My eyes played upon the divine. Framed. Lucid. Like before and after pictures from the Hubble telescope. Feeling fucked is an appropriate first response. The ridge above Kathmandu seemed to place me right on the edge of godly disclosure—not the most comfortable feeling, metaphysically speaking. Nor, I suppose, should it be. At moments like this, perhaps the first goal of enlightenment is to resist the compulsion to begin bargaining for your life and the way you've been living it, or pissing it away. I bargained for a single blessing: the opportunity to return to the Himalayas, to find the third image that was the synthesis between a pair of feet in flames and a celestial graph of sacred peaks.

I pedaled back to the ridgetop village to buy a cold soda from a tea shop. On an adjoining patio, a group of Nepalese students, young men, beckoned me over. One of them was struggling to compose a love letter to his sweetheart down in the valley, hoping to impress her with his command of English, and asked for my help. After several trial lines, he made his intentions, and stylistic requirements, clear to me, and I began in earnest on the sentimental greeting card he handed me: *My Dearest Darling—I count the minutes and the hours until we are together again, dreaming of your devastating beauty.* What does this word mean, *devastating*? the student asked. It's the greatest form of beauty, I told him. The most sublime. It was as if we had connected to share a common cause, each addicted to his own inescapable desire.

Three years later I found myself in the back of a Jeep, in the pitch of night, freezing, thrown about as the driver muscled the wheel into another hairpin turn. Steeling herself against nausea, Christine, a British tourist I had met at the airport in Bagdogra, down on the steamy plains of West Bengal, rode shotgun, trying not to vomit. We left the roller-coaster streets of Darjeeling below us and soon fell in line with a sluggish caravan of fellow sightseers, our chain of headlights sweeping the mountainside as we plowed up Tiger Hill. My mood soured as I realized that the summit would be as crowded, commercialized, and philistine as the scene I had once observed on Nemrut Dagi.

There's so little left of the world where men and women live their lives in the luminous presence—and ominous throb—of its physical sacredness, and I had to wonder, riding up Tiger Hill, if any place remained where the sublime continued to exist unviolated; where, with some assurance, a person could invest his or her spirit in the world without battling the adulterations. For me, nature wasn't a metaphor or a myth informing a system of worship, but a pure interpretation of the mind of God, or, to say this another way, the force of intelligence within creation. But was this force best acknowledged in solitude, or queued up in noisy fellowship, like angels on the head of a pin?

On the other hand, how could such a thing matter? Back on the ridge above Kathmandu, the sensation that I looked upon divinity had been immediate and, at the time, in complete ignorance of the cultures and theological traditions of the Himalayas. But, *what then?*

Celebrate? Propitiate? Prostrate? All my life, either growing up in a zealous Catholic household, or later as an agnostic, contemptuous of the great religions, either God was shouting in my face or God was dead on arrival, a prop for the powerful vanities of man. Perhaps the best angle on God was indifference—the hell with God. Who cares? God never seemed able to exercise a working knowledge of compassion, it seemed, when it came to human affairs, or seemed to have a proper place to be—except, of course, in nature. Yet even nature's literalness could be obscured by narrative device, outrageous symbolism, and illusion. Sometimes it was easiest to believe that the divine could only be adequately approached in the nuclear lab, counting quarks. Still, when it wasn't trying to kill you with the fury of an absolute truth, nature could always be relied upon to provide glimmerings, intimations, whiffs of hyperconsciousness—bursts of sensory phrasings that seemed freighted with meaning, but nothing too articulate, nothing that could be explicated or deconstructed into understanding. In a small boat far away from land, or walking across flat desert, or lying on your back under a night sky salted with stars, you got pretty strong clues about the character of infinity, but still they were only clues. Nothing to take to the cosmic bank.

We passed through Tiger Gate, then maneuvered our way through the observatory's busy parking lot to a space at the north rampart, where the world dipped away from Tiger Hill and then heaved itself, fifty miles off in the distance, up into the solar system. It was 5:30 a.m.; the viewing area swarmed with people, mostly Indian tourists. A continuous stream of Land Rovers disgorged passengers into a cul-de-sac of fumes. Unlike the daylight hours, the predawn sky was pristine, clear, inky blue except for a faint scarlet thread of light in the east. When we had picked up Christine at her hotel, she was drinking tea in the lobby with an Australian couple, also heading up Tiger Hill, and they had asked me about the weather. Excellent, I told them. "Good thing," said the man. "I didn't come all this way to see clouds." Sometimes that's *exactly* what you come all this way for,

I felt the urge to say to him, but he was a bit of an ass, and I think he would have misunderstood me.

Christine and I unfolded ourselves from the Jeep, walked the few steps to the wall, and stood there, focusing, the cold snapping us alert. There was a half-moon, and in its light we could make out the ghostly shape of the mountain, almost opalescent, floating on clouds bivouacked throughout the valleys. Beyond Kangchenjunga, the white nose cone of Everest thrust upward, another apparition. Unlike a hurricane, which you can only experience in fragments of its sum, immensity has never been more consummately packaged than it is in the massifs and peaks of the Himalayas—never more revealed, and never more approachable. Where we stood, the elevation was about 8,000 feet, high enough, actually, if we were in, say, the Colorado Rockies, but Kangchenjunga rose another 20,000 feet above us, incredibly, into the heavens.

In less than ten seconds since we left the vehicle, something extraordinary happened. As we stood and tried to comprehend the mountain—our first true sight of it—a shooting star blazed down, remarkable in itself, but more remarkable was the fact that the star began to burn *below* Kangchenjunga's summit, streaking down at a diagonal right to left, perhaps another five thousand feet, before it extinguished. Christine and I were dumbstruck for a moment, and then I blurted out, without forethought, a line that wholly surprised me. "That was about my child," I said. I had no idea what I meant, but I had left behind me in the States a wife pregnant, after many torturous years of trying, with our first kid, the only time I was ever able to knock her up.

In fragments the mountain allowed itself to be defined, sharpened by contrasts of light and shadow. The clouds sank and melted into grayish flannel swaddling the base of Kangchenjunga, and directly below the observation platform I began to see a score of lines emerge from the darkness, strung with hundreds of prayer flags, all intersecting toward the mountain. As dawn broke, the flags gently absorbed their hues, transformed from colorless charcoal to the most vivid saffrons, burgundies, whites, and blues. Twenty minutes before sunrise, Kangchenjunga was as pale and delicate as porcelain, and it was easier to imagine men walking on the moon than actually scaling this colossus. Its slopes pinkened, and then right before sunrise the clouds became restless and began to levitate out of the valleys. Their interplay with the five summits was astonishingly, teasingly mystical and I preferred this hide-and-seek game, since the Himalayas seemed to belong more to the universe than to humanity. Minute by minute the clouds devoured Kangchenjunga, opening and closing windows, here a marble throne room, etched in gilt and bronze; here a sudden glistening crag of summit that makes no visual sense, a shard of earth broken free. Then it's gone and it is easy not to believe it was ever there.

"That's it," the Australian complained to his wife. "It's ruined, absolutely ruined."

The sun rose, the snow peaks disappeared except for a few lost islands off toward Tibet, jutting from a sea of hazy clouds. The crowd dashed for transport, each driver jockeying for position, and we all descended Tiger Hill in a single roar, back to the lively city, where I fixed myself a hot bath and then packed my bags for a four-hour road trip to Gangtok, the capital of Sikkim. I was happy, waiting for my ride under a sky filled with children's kites, remembering the falling star, the enigma of its message, the sudden supernatural energy that jerked the length of my spine, the magnetic pull of a nameless passion that lightens the weight of your heart. My wife had insisted that the right to name our child was hers alone (since I'd been the one to name our dogs), but that morning I made a queer and surely ludicrous decision that the kid's middle name should be the tongue-bending, mind-twisting name of this mountain, Kangchenjunga. In the days ahead I would tell the story of the shooting star to new friends in Sikkim, and they would congratulate me on the gift of such an auspicious omen. A month later I would receive letters from them at my home in Florida, prayers that all was well with the child, that my firstborn would be a son, but by then

I already knew that the very hour I had seen the star smear across the face of Kangchenjunga, halfway around the world the fetus had died, a shadow-child forever lost in the cosmic mail, and my wife was in the midst of a miscarriage.

And so years later alone together on the pass in Mustang, we raise our flags and hold each other, brushing the sting from our eyes, and then move on.

There would be no other child than the one that lived as a star, and fell.

Down to the World

If you let your imagination run to paradise, what shall you find on its balmy shores and arcadian glades, what do you need there, if you're willing to at least forgo the suicide bomber's pedophiliac dream of virgin cherry-picking? What's the proper frame of mind to complement the psychic necessity? I don't know why I've never adorned my vision with extravagances: water, if you're dry; shade, if you're hot; soup, if you're hungry; mineral springs, if you're sore; peace, if peace has eluded you; love, if you've somehow lost it. All my wayward dogs come home. Leafy simplicity and small abundance seem splendid enough, and never incongruous with the paradisiacal, but in truth I've never felt an overwhelming need for paradise, and the ones I've known have not fared well against the stealthy creep of progress.

Like hobbits we descend through an oversize and infernal landscape, hypnotized by the barrenness until we come to the top of an austere bluff and look down upon a village wedged into a high glacial-fed valley, so beautiful and so green, that my wife is satisfied we have found it—paradise, Shangri-la, some place blessed but not too holy. We hike joyfully down and wearily up, down, up, through a series of earth-cracked ravines and, as we lose altitude, increasingly fragrant layers of water-scent and plant aroma begin to pamper our senses—it's always better to be walking where things grow. Down to the crusty valley floor, past a side canyon blooming red with Sedona-like cliffs and chromatically garish fanglike formations, we trudge past a head-high wall of prayer-carved *mani* stones reputed to be the longest in the world.

Atop a mesa separated from the village itself by a deep final slice of ravine, we absorb completely the fairy-tale wonder of Ghami and meet its sorcerer—an eighty-year-old chain-smoking Japanese horticulturalist named Kondo, charismatic and jolly as Santa Claus, his chest draped with the long white wispy beard of a Kurosawa hermit. "I have devoted my life to poverty," Kondo says, lowering his kiln-dried body onto one of the two chairs his village staff have carried outside the mud walls of the compound where we find him. "Very honorable." I take the other chair, on his left side, and feel the odd impulse to lift his gnarled saintly hand in mine and hold it. Honorable, yes, my god, yes—I want to ask what crimes of nationalism he is paying off tenfold, beyond the ones obvious to his generation, but I would shame myself, doubting the purity of this old man's generosity. Four decades ago he annulled his tenure at the National University of Japan and invested the next twenty-five years in the hinterlands of Nepal, the last three in Ghami, where he has laid almost four miles of four-inch irrigation pipe, planted fifteen thousand apple trees, dug carp ponds, built greenhouses for winter vegetables, is growing rice at the highest elevation in the world, and has conjured a hundred-hectare farm out of the desert badlands. As if that weren't enough, the old man built a hospital for the village, convinced a doctor to staff it, and muled in an X-ray machine that runs off solar power. Life's better than ten years ago, exalts the village headman, but it's not because of the tourists, it's because of Kondo. Kondo the Magnificent, and I am daunted by the fact that he is so unlike anyone I've ever met in the dense, busy, self-congratulatory world of altruistic industry, bureaucratic charity, deluded idealism, where money flushes endlessly back to its source, air-kissing the globe's poor as it passes over the haplessness of their lives. Not a redistribution of wealth, but a contained distribution of influence and power. Sometimes, not often, a Samaritan like Kondo steps out of the system and into grace.

"Because the government does nothing to help them," Kondo ho-hos after a meaningful silence, when I ask why he's here. He wants ten years more from life to single-handedly whip Nepal into an agricultural nirvana. "This is my dream. Many Japanese people help me, God helps me. In the future I will make a forest here. For me"—Kondo smiles impishly, his black eyes radiating intelligence and purpose—"it's very easy." What makes him so different from the rest of us, the Christlike magnitude of his love hardwired into the residual imperial impulse to *get things done*, seems prototypically utopian—Kondo is what human-kind was meant to be, if only humankind could ever be trusted to set aside its venality. Probably most villages in the Third World would benefit from a low-key Buddhist sugar daddy like this octogenarian; unlike serene Ghami, probably many of them would drive him away, or crucify him, within a year.

The horsemen arrive dusty and sore and still nap-headed, their eyes dull from the heat of the ride, and we follow them across the ravine to the village center, where Jan and Mark lay asleep like lambs in the soft grass along the tree-lined riverbank. Water gushes everywhere through Ghami, and its music enters me like a narcotic, emptying my mind, petting my bones.

Mahendra and Tomay unsaddle the ponies and feed them a mix-ture of wheat from his own fields and Chinese peas. Our campsite is a former threshing floor attached to a rustic roadhouse where a beau-tiful young mother perpetually feeds a stove, making butter tea and porridge for travelers. A puppy plays at her feet; the family dog, her husband says, was eaten by a monster last winter. They never saw the beast, just heard the terrible growling and snapping outside in the dark, and in the morning, the dog was gone without a trace. After dinner we stand watching a lightning barrage behind Annapurna, thankful that the monsoon has receded back to the south slopes and left us, if you could forget the wind, with ideal weather. Having walked the entire day, I roll into my tent with barely enough energy to remove my boots, shaking with chills.

According to the map in the morning, five passes, including the col above Geling—Nyi La, the highest of the trip at over 13,000 feet— separate us from our next camp at Samar. Although we bypass Geling, Laird remembers it well, if not fondly. Ten years ago coming through Kagbeni, the monks at the temple wouldn't have anything to do with Laird and his cameras but Kagbeni wasn't Lo, so he paid no attention to their resistance. But Geling was the first place he really tried to document the heritage of Mustang, and the first place he heard the disheartening message to go fuck himself. Visiting Geling's monastery, he noticed a voluminous pile of fourteenth- and fifteenth-century *thangkas* of tremendous value gathering dust in a corner, but the lama would not consent to let Tom photograph them for fear they'd be stolen, which they were anyway—stolen—five months later. Laird felt great relief he hadn't photographed them, then great sadness that they were gone forever. Without the documented means to identify them, the *thangkas* could go direct to Sotheby's with no questions asked, and there was no way to ever get them back—a tragedy, because the layers of history in Lo had mostly evaporated except in the art and architecture of the last five hundred years, wafting away into obscurity with successive generations, and once the artisans were gone, the Lobas sank back into a subsistence primitivism, that place we all seem headed for, after the next world war.

The day unfolds immediately into a hair-raising series of verticals, descents too steep to ride, ascents so extreme that the trail has been stepped with flagstones, the horses clattering up staircases in the middle of this strange prehistoric wilderness, our knees clamped to their ribs, our bloodless fingers wrapped in their manes, Mahendra and Tomay leading the frightened women, yanking the horses up to the high passes. The route seems impossible, it seems blaringly lethal, but although there have been accidents here, no one's died on horseback in at least ten years, or so Mahendra assures us. We cross a side river on a high suspension bridge, my wife channeling Helen Keller, sightless and deaf and mute in her not fully suppressed hysteria. On the approach to Samar, the incline is angled so radically that my saddle slips straight back on Jamling's haunches, causing me to yank the steel bit so hard into his mouth that the horse surely thinks I'm trying to rip his jaw away, and he jigs and skitters wildly on the precipice until I can fling myself off to the ground, my blood hammering in my ears.

We camp that night in a wet, grassy apple orchard in Samar and awaken at dawn with our water bottles half-frozen, the lot of us groaning and grousing, wanting our warm beds, getting too old and unresilient and psychologically arthritic for this shit, given the demoralizing reception we ran into up north. Laird keeps scheming out loud at mealtimes about moving with Jann back to Florida to nest in the semi-bourgeois life he chucked in 1972.

Later, when we step inside the village headman's house for a cup of tea, it seems his family and friends have been working on a version of the same idea. The older women wear traditional *bukkhoos*, but the younger ones wear tracksuits, and except for the lumps of turquoise planted in their earlobes, the guys are dressed like caddies on a golf course in Seattle. World music plays on a cassette player. Out comes the salt butter tea, out come the photos of vaguely prosperous grown children in America, Japan, one of twenty-year-old Jigme, working at a hotel in New York City—Laird photographed him as a boy helping thresh the village harvest. "Ten years ago we hadn't been to the West," says Tara, a sexy young woman in sweatpants and emerald fingernail polish who is one of seven Lobas out of twenty-four staffers who work for ACAP in Mustang. A good job taking her nowhere. "Yeah, it's hard work [overseas] but take me. I'll wash dishes, I'll cook, clean floors. I'll clean toilets. I'll go make money and come back." Sure, you want to tell her, let's go, indenture yourself to that other world where your own fantasies reside, send money home, but don't ever expect to come back to Mustang except in your dreams.

The father, the village chief, knows. His son hasn't written him in three years. "When they go to foreign countries," he laments, "it's a lot of pain."

"Tom," I had heard Pema Wangdi, the mayor of Lo Manthang, say happily, "have you noticed how much we've changed? We're richer now," and that was in part because of trade with China, but mostly because Lobas were going abroad, creating their own modest diaspora around the world. Tourism as an agent of change wasn't even on the mayor's list.

Meanwhile, the deadly descent between Samar and Kagbeni is standing in the way of the safe completion of our journey. "The horses cannot be ridden down," announces Mahendra, nursing a *rakshi* hangover. The skin on my face, deep-fried by two days of ultraviolet sun and dry cold wind, needs tending to, my wife decides unilaterally, and she thinks she's doing me a favor by slathering jojoba oil onto my forehead, then smearing a layer of sunscreen over the moisturizer. By the afternoon we will both have cause to regret her well-meant doctoring.

Higher up on the slopes above us, juniper and birch forests have inserted themselves into Mustang's lifeless ecology. First with gusto, then with increasing caution, finally with abject fear, we begin going down, the path nothing more than a groove along a sheer wall that drops a thousand feet to the floor of a side canyon tumbling out of the mountains to the roiling Kali Gandaki. At the trail's most frightful narrowings, my wife clutches my hand and makes me stop until she can open the flue on her vertigo and clear out necessary headroom, and even a whiff of her internal spinning sends a whirlwind jolt of imbalance sloshing through my own viscera, a sudden loss of one's primary sense of gravitational force. Oh shit, the body thinks, I can fly. We press ourselves against the overhang of upside wall to let a mule train pass, our nostrils filled with the beastly smell of foaming sweat, dumb acceptance ready to ignite with panic. Halfway down the mountainside, in the welcome stretches when it's safe to glance around and not focus with such obsession on our feet, we look eye level out into space at vultures auguring the air, corkscrewing out of sight below us as others, as if on counterweights, pop up back into a holding pattern. There's a reason for this activity and my suspicion is confirmed a hundred yards down the path, where a mule has lost its footing and Brodyed over the side, its carcass visible far far below on a talus slope, where the birds peck and tear at its mangled body.

At Chele we are free of the greater heights, no longer obliged to shuffle like penitents, our heads bowed, our eyes downcast, reduced to measuring the world one fiercely planted step at a time, knowing that one pays for even the smallest mistake with the ultimate price. We clamber down the last escarpment to the Kali Gandaki riverbed and its promenade of crushed cobble, pausing to gaze knowingly, a final time, into the throat of the upper gorge before the hike to Chuksang to rendezvous with the horsemen.

Yet this freedom from fear is only temporary, and we have reinherited the wind, so demonically violent beyond Chuksang—forty, fifty miles per hour—that it staggers the horses as we ride them through a blizzard of dust and grit. Mouths and noses hide behind bandannas. We strap hats on with scarves knotted beneath our chins, pull the bands down upon our brows, and ride slit-eyed, leaning over the necks of our ponies, like gut-shot renegades. Captain wears goggles; Mike's a Bedouin manqué. Abandoning Submarine in Lo Manthang, Mark hasn't been on a horse since and now he's somewhere ahead of us high on the cliffs with the indomitable Sherpas, wings on his feet along a trail only a foot wide, interspersed with shale slides. Without the Sherpas to shadow, he would have stopped to second-guess himself, monkeyed back down to the floodplain where we clop onward with our horses, because more than once the path would lead him around a corner only to be slammed by a wicked gust and he'd think, *Fuck, if another gust hit me right now I'd pitch off.*

Sand blows under my sunglasses and into my eyes, burrowing into my scalp, my vision already blurred by floating oil slicks that have melted off my forehead, and I can barely see through the dancing blobs. Mahendra, however, has developed enough confidence in my horsemanship to let me lead, to judge the fords by myself, and so I get way out front with the captain, Michael, and Ang Tsering (on the revitalized Submarine, who appears to have had a sex change, female to male, in Lo Manthang); we canter up to the river crossings and splash across and keep going, determined to have this over with. To the west, we pass another side canyon, a confluence spurting coffee-colored melt from the snowpack. Laird gallops up with word from Mahendra to halt: The river is high and too dangerous to ford at the next crossing. We are forced over to the cliffs, but where the trail leaves the floodplain we all stare at its extraordinary narrowness and steepness and edginess, wishing for a funicular. We've taken the horses far past what we once believed were our limits, human and equine, and became, had to become, master horsemen, and fearless, instantly. Mahendra says its possible to ride the path but in the wind, now blowing fifty, punching the horses backward as they stand, we all share a rare moment of collective sanity and refuse.

The king's men struggle ahead with the horses, far enough beyond us so we don't have to fret about rocks dislodged onto our skulls or, the ultimate bad day in Mustang, slowing the impact of a horse with your body as it cartwheels into you off the equivalent of a twelve-story building. Sometimes on hands and knees, the group then claws its way up and out onto the wall but I stop, a desperate attempt to clear my vision, and Cat and I fall behind. The two-hundred-foot climb up to the traverse isn't terribly rigorous, but the traverse itself is my wife's worst-case fever dream, a scenario I know she has spent her entire waking life avoiding. The ledge dissolves into a scree slide of pulverized shale, billions of flecks of shale slowly tinkling downward like the sound track for a spritz of fairy dust. The slide contains not a footprint, not a hoofprint, no sign that anyone has passed this way since before Noah's flood. I look over the side to the river straight below, to assure myself the entire expedition isn't heaped at the bottom.

I'm comforted by the good news, that the slide is roughly three paces across and no more, but where you place/misplace your foot inevitably has dire consequences. I move out onto this geological wound, horrified that I can't get a firm footing, step gingerly across to solid ground, and turn back for my wife, trying to focus my eyes, but I see her only in watery patches. She is understandably mortified, sick with vertigo; sinusitis has skewed her equilibrium, the wind is knocking her around, and, just looking at her, I know she's seconds away from being immobilized by terror. I reach out my hand and feel the bones near breaking as she vises on and I pull her across. "I don't ever want to do that again," she says, her teeth chattering. For a second I have to hold her up because her knees want to buckle. If I knew I wouldn't tell her: She has to do it twice more, and the slides are worse. If we were alone I would turn us back, but the fact that the group has crossed ahead of us preempts such a decision. We wait for even the slightest lull of wind and cross the second slide without incident, both of us gasping for air, as if we had been afraid to breathe, as if breathing would have put the tiny chips of shale in motion. When we reach the third and widest slide, Ang Tsering, recognizing the peril, waits for us on the other side, his hand extended, pummeled by the brutal wind.

Ang Tsering was on Everest with a team of Yugoslavians that fatal spring of 1996. At 2:00 p.m. on May 9, five hundred feet from the summit, the weather was turning, the hour was late: He made the decision to turn his climbers around, saving their lives. On May 10 . . . well, everybody on the planet knows what happened that day. At this kill-zone level of hazard on a glacier, the three of us would be roped up, and what's awful, what's unthinkable, is our total lack of margin, no backup, no fail-safes, the wall is bare, conditions are suicidal, maximum exposure without handholds or bracings, and no space for adjustment, an extra step to regain your balance and composure. If my wife slips, she'll pull me over and with me Ang Tsering, unless I let go of her, or let go of him. He, I know, will not let go. Even thinking about it doesn't matter, because even if she starts to fall, and even if I start to let her go, the velocity of disaster will suck us over the edge as one, like tightrope walkers.

I step out into the middle of the third slide, this nascent avalanche, trying to wedge and plant my feet into the scree and the whole mass, billions of shale splinters, shifts a few centimeters and buries my boots to the ankles. Below me, shale sprinkles straight down into the river. Behind me, my wife is petrified, repeating my name in a way that unnerves me, and the cruel thought zings across my mind, that I am destined to kill her, or she is destined to kill me, here on our twenty-fifth anniversary, on the Lairds' belated, rotten honeymoon. Crouching forward, Ang Tsering leans as far over the slide as he humanly can, we link our fates together, and I remember Laird's admonition—Sherpas put their lives in your hands for your fantasies; every other trek a Sherpa would literally be saving a client's life. Okay. I don't care whose is the operative fantasy here, reality has checkmated all motivations, frivolous and grand. I reach back for my wife and have to shout at her to give me her hand before a gust or another ooze in the slide makes this whole exercise moot, and when she completes the trinity Ang Tsering pulls and I pull and the shale pours over the lip ledge like jackpot nickels and the feeling is so clear and irreversible that Tsering and I have yanked my wife out of the rabbit hole, disconnected her, disconnected ourselves, from the spell of Mustang and plugged back into the lower world, which in these times was no less surreal.

Ahead I could see the rest of the group huddled into each other's backs along the goat path, what people instinctively do when subjected to gunfire or bombardment, clutching boulders to keep the wind from blowing them off to Jerusalem. Jann is sobbing into Tom's shoulder, and my wife would weep too, I suspect, if she wasn't at the moment predisposed to trauma, but who among us would exchange this day for nine-to-five and an evening in front of the television? That's what the Lobas want, newborn to modernity, but we've had enough of it for a while. The role reversal doesn't have to make sense, and fairness, so much a part of the swing of every life, is not a part of this. Lucky, we are all so lucky.

Together we crawl against the howling back down to the riverbed, to our horses, and ride to the sanctuary of Kagbeni.

At the Red House Inn, Mark, Mahendra, and I send our brains dog-paddling through a pool of silky *tongba*—homemade millet beer—while the jolly proprietress massages Michael's fleshy pectorals, squeezing them into the shape of pubescent breasts, a sight so absurd her daughters think this could well be the funniest thing they have ever seen. When we were similarly in our cups in Lo Manthang, administering to ourselves therapeutic doses of *rakshi* to ease the city's intrigues, we somehow let slip our ability to count the calendar. At lunch in Tsarang, we suddenly discovered a missing day, an extra, and tried to figure how to spend it to our benefit. Laird and I had mulled the practicality of a forced-march side trip to the fabled cave of Luri, which our colleagues greeted with universal apathy, having met their quota of monasteries for the year. Well, Laird ventured, there's always Marfa . . . sort of a Zen-Swiss hybrid (without the Swiss) an hour's walk below Jomsom into the lower gorge where you can get burritos, hard apple cider, clean beds, *hot showers.*

This is how the journey ends, as most do in the Himalayas, with a willful embrace of comfort and debauchery, a giddy upwelling of relief. *More* chhang *for my men and horses.* The next night in Marfa, I sit with the freshly spoiled crew drinking hard cider, indulging in a mood that swings between celebration and dismay, perturbed that I could never get a tonal fix, let alone metaphysical coordinates, on our travel through Mustang. One by one, the group peels off for showers and bed until I find myself alone with the Bangkok Bachelors, abusing our constitutions with local brandy, stripping the last guarded inhibition out of our windburned, raw-assed hides. The discourse is nonstop but random, this, that, proclamations out of the blue, fragments of Thai-pussy nostalgia, jungle war stories, not really a conversation, without segue or logic. In fact, our stream of language is mostly idiotic, in equal parts, so there exists no real diplomatic line to cross when I ask the captain, snockered, beaming, ever-the-hail-fellow-well-met, our Jack, if he had worked for the CIA in Laos, directing the secret war in that country, during Vietnam.

"Not for them, *with them*. I worked for the air force. There's a difference."

"And Captain, what's with the prolific notes? Are you filing a report with the agency on Mustang?"

"Well," says this Cold War cowboy who had never seriously entertained the thought of abandoning the wallow of Southeast Asia for a life in the States, his moment of veritas, "probably not with the agency. It'll probably just go to the DOD." Oh, just the Pentagon. Why? I ask him. Why the fuck?

He plays the patriot card with a spike of sobriety; in twenty years, believes the captain, America was going to be at war with China, in twenty years boys from Kansas would be marching up the Kali Gandaki to retake Llhasa, or something like that, and his pretend mission was to recon the route. Apparently the captain doesn't understand that his service has been rendered archaic by satellites and drones. It's hard to shed the game when the game is so awfully fucking self-aggrandizing.

"Are you out of your mind? Jesus, Laird's got enough troubles without the stigma of guilt by association with the likes of you."

No one will ever know, suggests the captain, unless I told them, not even Laird. I stumbled back to my room in the Paradise Guest House and dove onto my bed, biting my pillow to keep from waking my wife, but my snickering turned to gales of laughter and the laughter wouldn't stop, this type of laughter that was a raging fever, a demonic possession. I tried drinking water but the laughter gurgled through it, unfiltered wicked laughter, so contagious that my wife started chuckling too, saying, What is it? What is it? And what the hell was I going to tell her—that, on our charade of discovery, we had been toting along this farcical relic of the glory days of espionage, that we had unthinkingly borne, in many guises, the prodigious sins of the world with us into the lost-and-found kingdom of Mustang?

What was I going to tell anybody?

He who gathers knowledge, it is written in Ecclesiastes, gathers pain. And when you romance a dream to death, what remains is a dry residue of absurdity that will mock your passions for all eternity.

On May 29 we fly from Jomsom to Pokhara to Kathmandu and into the midst of a national strike, ferried from the terminal to our hotel in a Volkswagen bus pasted with big signs informing demonstrators we are tourists and not worth killing. Ambulance drivers have not been so fortunate. On the morning of Thursday, the thirty-first, the day we are leaving Nepal, I take my wife and Mark to Pashupatinath, where we watch a son place a torch to his father's mouth, the shrouded corpse atop a stack of sandalwood on the cremation ghats beside the Bagmati River. History speeds up, history crackles through the present. By the weekend, the river will reflect the blaze of royal pyres, the sparks of Nepal's past sucked away into the celestial darkness of midnight.

All readers yearn for meaning, all travelers, all pilgrims. But where is the joy in understanding? History speeds up, the future implodes into the present. Sometimes quietly, sometimes not. Kingdoms open, kingdoms close, kingdoms . . . disappear. Tongues of flame speak riddles from the lips of a monarch, the heads of dying gods radiate heat and light like a row of setting suns, a king's heart turns to ash as cold as the dust on the moon. A prince dreams of love and wakes up bathed in hatred. A rich man dreams of revolution and justice and murders his shoeless cousin, his penniless neighbor. A husband and wife dream of a child who will come no closer to their lives than a shooting star, vanishing back into the unknowable night of nothingness. A young man dreams the most spiritually fertile of dreams; he dreams of Shangri-la and wakes up old, disillusioned. Meaning is not understanding. And for a moment, this moment, Nepal has slipped past both.

The monsoon arrives in force. Something to count on.

Afterword

The night of June 1, 2001, our flight to New Delhi was delayed and delayed again and we sat in the terminal of Kathmandu's airport, grumbling and weary, not knowing that back inside the central city at the Narayanhiti Royal Palace, Nepal's greatest modern tragedy was unfolding in blood and horrific carnage, and that this other journey, a kingdom's journey and its centuries-old dynasty, was also inexorably drawing toward its end. Even as we queried the agent at the departure gate, the deranged Crown Prince Dipendra pointed his assault rifle from mother to father, from sister to cousin, methodically massacring a beloved king and queen and seven other members of the royal family. Eventually, late in the evening, he turned his regicidal fury on himself, he who would be king, were he ever able to restrain his earthly desire and transcend his rabid self-regard. Eventually, late in the evening, our plane boarded and ascended into Kathmandu's bowl of darkness below the stars and, at that moment, we had no idea what madness we were inadvertently fleeing, the airport closing behind us for the foreseeable and unknown future, Nepal itself shutting its doors and windows, locked down and quaking in a state of emergency, and it was impossible to understand then what today, more than ten years later, still seems incomprehensible, that the forward-looking summer of 2001 was a harbinger of darker days to come, a summoning of global demons on the eve of ten continuous years of unleashed hatreds, unimaginable suffering, knee-buckling loss, and explosive change, not just for the nation of Nepal but for much of the world.

"The lost decade," the writer Timothy Egan has called those first years, the aughts, the double zeros, of the new millennium, and it's impossible to whisper that phrase to myself and not feel the painful truth of it sink its sorrow into my heart.

Toward the end of that summer, back home in the States, I received an e-mail from Tom Laird, attached with his censored series of photographs of the royal family's cremation on the ghats at Pashupatinath, the pyres set ablaze at the base of Lord Shiva's temple, Shiva regarded as the guardian deity of Nepal, fallen asleep perhaps at his post, and I could not help but stare in grim fascination at their terrible beauty. The images clearly captured and expressed a sacredness that had fallen away from grace in modernity, an event ceremonially ancient and catastrophically divine—timeless spirituality the trademark of the forces Westerners find so compelling, and seek out, in the Himalayas. The flames soared, the fires burned, the ashes cooled, and from their mound rose a new king, an existentially cold king, and not beloved, who mounted a tiger and charged to war, an absolute fool who seized absolute power in the name of gods who themselves were on the cusp of dethronement.

Along with the pictures came a note from Tom in which he mentioned his new bad journo-habit, hopping aboard helicopter gunships and riding out to the western regions with the Nepalese army to photograph the government's merciless battles with the Maoists.

Be careful out there, I told him, as I would tell anyone, an automatic ecumenical prayer for my friends in the press or the military. Since the early 1990s, Nepal has lived with a particular stain on its soul, devolving into a nation where journalists who feel obligated to step into the political mix find themselves quickly only one more perilous misstep away from their worst nightmares. Today the danger in Nepal is even greater for the media than it was twenty years ago, a nation where "impunity seems institutionalized," laments the *Hindustan Times*, and the Committee to Protect Journalists has annually judged Nepal's malfeasance seventh-worst in the world, a country where journalists are regularly murdered and their killers go free. It seems fantastical, it defies belief in the culture of *Namaste*, but which nations did Nepal outrank on the committee's Ten Most Deadly Countries list a few years ago? Ready? Mexico, Russia, and Pakistan.

Nepal's decadelong civil war ground to a halt in 2006, the path to a shaky conditional peace littered with twelve thousand corpses, uncounted wounded, and seventy thousand displaced persons. The government and the Maoists (official name, the Communist Party of Nepal/Maoist, to distinguish itself from one of its prime adversaries, the Communist Party of Nepal/Unified Marxist-Leninist) fought themselves into a stalemate, mass pro-democracy demonstrations paralyzed the country, and cynical, if not wiser, heads prevailed. That spring of 2006, the accidental king, King Gyanendra, found himself stalemated by the rage of his people, his hapless subjects exhausted by the atrocities of war and the dignity-robbing abuses of megalomania.

The wheels of parliamentary government, chock-blocked by the royal palace for more than a year, began to turn again, and by May, a newly reinstated House of Representatives unanimously voted to sideline the king and reinvent the nation through the agency of an indelible irony, dismantling Nepal's identity as a Hindu kingdom and proclaiming the nation a secular state, bucking one of the twenty-first century's most volatile global trends. While Islamists pretended to accept ideology, exploiting democratic means for theocratic ends, Nepal, a state acknowledged universally for its pervasive enlightened religiosity, seemed to spin on its heels in the opposite direction, favoring politicians over divine representatives in order to coronate ideology as its supreme god, not an unworkable approach at all until you consider there is no such creature as an ideology in Nepal with a track record for justice, human rights, and development. Capitalist or Communist, populist or patriarchal, ideology in Nepal is a parlor trick of ruling-class elites, a ruse to accumulate power, whether for the warlord or the businessman, and all the ideologies spoken in Nepal's governmental scrum share the same implicit vocabulary of greed and arrogance.

Which is to say, Nepal's transition from monarchy to democratic republic has been ugly, as such transitions often prove to be, once again underscoring the maxim, *It's not the revolution that counts, it's what you make of it.* Nepal's travails are disappointing but they are not unique (although the US government continued to designate the enfranchised Maoists as "global terrorists," which strikes me as a singular absurdity). But reincarnation, like any elevator, cosmic or commonplace, can transport its cargo in more than one direction. Since 2008, the country and its leaders and the mobs behind those leaders have displayed a dismal talent for sliding downhill on their collective backside. Prime ministers keep resigning, a new constitution continues to elude its drafting, law and order dissemble into abstractions, the stink of burning tires from protests and strikes rivals the fragrance of incense burning from within the shrines, political unrest competes with the tranquillity of spiritual engagement in the cultural ethos—an ethos that, despite its recent gloss of democracy and its religious motifs, remains fundamentally unchanged in a society that remains fundamentally feudal.

One quarter of Nepal's population of thirty million, doubled since 1981, lives below a radically deep poverty line, 46 percent of the nation is unemployed, almost half are illiterate, the median age is an unappeasable twenty-one, life expectancy less than sixty years, and deforestation of the countryside, Nepal's greatest resource, is endemic. In a country under such socioeconomic pressures, the potential for spontaneous violence seems no greater or less than the prospect for lasting peace.

In Kathmandu itself, its 1.5 million residents in the metropolitan area have submitted to the daily rhythms of humiliation and frustration—electrical outages, spotty phone service, unrelenting gridlock, rising crime, and unpredictable curfews—and throughout the decade the city's increasing untenability could be easily tracked by the decline and abandonment of its most legendary subculture, the Rock and Roll Raj, expiring of old age or simply packing up and getting out, retreating to The Place Formerly Known as Home, bummed out by disillusionment, stressed out by instability. It was the death of the era of enchantment for the erstwhile travelers of the Silk Road, its second-most-famous terminus, Goa, going to hell as well, the hipster pilgrims in Kathmandu replaced by a much less freewheeling community of expatriates and salaried wallahs, NGO do-gooders, and multinational corporate do-badders. And of course the adventurecrats. The Lairds themselves joined the exodus, moving first to Florida and then to New Orleans, just in time to be creamed by Hurricane Katrina in 2005.

As for the extraordinary kingdom of Lo—Mustang and Upper Mustang and the fabled walled city of Lo Manthang—the perspective of a second ten years of openness and access offers both reassurance and concern. In 2008, the king of Mustang, Raja Jigme Dorje Palbar Bista, was himself sucked into the monarch-cleansing vortex of Kathmandu politics and was forced to abdicate his title, if not his funky dilapidated palace or his people's recognition, still esteemed today by many Mustang residents for his lineage and his piety. Despite the difficulty in just getting there, foreign trekkers continue to visit the region at the rate of over a thousand each year—over two thousand in 2008 alone—each paying his or her fifty-dollar-per-day permit fee and collectively creating a reliable seasonal trickle of hand-to-hand revenue into the local economy.

I take it as a fact of human nature that affluent, intrepid Westerners will damage the internal stability—the deep social metabolism—of a far-flung place like Mustang, infecting the medieval status quo with aspirations and dreams, the very presence of outsiders and their sensibilities evidence that a more comfortable, less oppressive life, a life a bit more prosperous and hopeful, less weighted by endless hardship, exists and is not impossible to attain. Aliens alighting in your world, no matter how benign, are bound to have an effect. The most overt result has been a major out-migration of Mustang's young people in the past ten years, not only to Nepal's cities, according to anthropologist Sienna Craig, but abroad to New Delhi, Seoul, Tokyo, and New York City in search of work and a better life.

But the real change in Mustang is not the inevitable result of visitors throwing gum wrappers on the ground or inflating the price of eggs (although everything counts). Bigger, more intractable forces are at play, with Mustang on the front lines of a geopolitical Great Game conducted between India and China over influence in Nepal and, sorry, China doesn't give a shit about the indigenous culture of anywhere and anybody. China presents a macro-example of a Faustian bargain between a people's soul and a people's progress, and in that sense it is simply a high-definition mirror for every other nation and its own compromises between past and future.

The once restricted border between the Tibet Autonomous Region—less euphemistically known as Chinese-occupied Tibet— has been breached by a nearly completed road bisecting Mustang from top to bottom and continuing southward through the depth of Nepal to the tropical plains of India, thus creating only the second (and lowest-altitude) drivable corridor from the Tibetan Plateau through the once almighty barrier of the Himalayas. As of 2012 only five and a half miles of the route remain unbuilt, the section scheduled for completion within the next few years, when it would not be unreasonable to expect Mustang's horse culture to be utterly wiped out by the region's hyperactive highway culture, considering that the road is but a leveling and paving of the millennia-old salt-trading route between the lands north of the snow peaks and the lands to the south.

What can be said about this astronomical alteration to Mustang's insularity? I doubt you could find a foreigner who has hiked or ridden a pony into Mustang who approves of it. And yet the cultures the trekkers represent, willingly or not, have paid rarely more than lip service to preserving traditional ways of life if those traditions ever stood in the way of a bulldozer: Out with the old and up with the new. The Buddhist appreciation for impermanence has many layers, and many of those layers resonate with the dynamics of Western development. Double standards breed in shallow waters, and you can't be a credible emissary from the modern world devoted to a type of nostalgia that depends on other people remaining shackled to their destitution.

Opportunity is a human right, and the people of Mustang have an appetite for it as much as any other people. Education, health care, clean water, ample food, freedom from oppression—you know the drill. So it shouldn't have surprised anyone when the Upper Mustang Youth Society threatened that, as of October 1, 2010, it would do everything in its power to ban foreign tourists from coming to the restricted area of Upper Mustang. The issue was not cultural contamination, or environmental pressure, or anything at all implying a negative impact from Mustang's modest industry as an exotic travel destination. The issue was money, Mustang's promised 60 percent cut of permit fees, millions of dollars in revenue for local development and services that never found its way out of Kathmandu.

A central government stealing blatantly from local and regional governments, however, doesn't qualify as breaking news anywhere in the world. Wealth distribution and resource allocation are, in practice, what they are—platforms for corruption and injustice. The issue is under discussion, permanently, and everywhere.

In the meantime, trekkers still embark on the arduous spectacular journey to the walled city of Lo Manthang. This will always be, even if they must trudge on the shoulder of a trans-Himalayan highway. Farther to the east, the climbers will arrive from every corner of the earth to summit—and perish—on Everest. This will always be. When the cremation fires have died and cooled, the monkeys of Pashupatinath will scurry onto ghats to scavenge the ashy crumbs of our kings and our queens, and this will always be. The suffering and the joy, the awe of life and the fear of death, this will always be, as will be the holy man's, or the crazy man's, detachment from it all.

Nepal's eternal magic, born under the lakes of the snake gods and atop the peaks of the thunder gods, these days seems shriven and diluted by mankind's vanities and negligence, but this too will always be, onward into the infinitude of being, which has no response to *Cannot be* until nature's reckoning itself answers, *Done.*

(2012)

Something Wild
in the Blood

Hurricane Darby had broken up, humbled by shearing winds into a tropical depression, trailing a steady, bracing suck of breeze that stretched east from Cuba all the way back to the Turks and Caicos Islands, where, on Providenciales, a young islander in swim trunks helped me lug a mountain of gear from my Turtle Cove hotel to his pickup truck. I asked the driver if he was the boatman, too, and he said yes, he was Captain Newman Gray.

"Good. You can tell me where we're going."

"East Bay Cay."

Twenty years ago, when I first came to Providenciales aboard the *South Wind*, a derelict ninety-eight-foot tramp freighter captained by Tay Maltsberger and his wife, Linda, the forty-nine Turks and Caicos were tiny, arid, sunbaked, and mostly useless outposts of the British Crown, still virgin turf for sportsmen, drug runners, and real estate pioneers.

Now I was looking out the window of Captain Newman's truck at the resorts and casinos crowding Grace Bay, remembering when there was nothing on its austere sweep of beach, when Providenciales did not have a jetport or a store, only an islander-run rice-and-peas shop at its dusty main crossroads and a warehouse stocked with booze, frozen steaks, and a thin collection of building supplies. Nobody was around on the bay then except Tay and Linda and my wife and me. We'd swim from shore to a nearby reef and spear lobsters, perform ballet with eagle rays and sea turtles, and slowly retreat from the tiger shark, big as a sports car, that regularly prowled the formation. At the end of the day, we'd walk carefully back through the thorny island scrub to where Tay and Linda had anchored themselves and were attempting an unlikely enterprise for professional seafarers: Provo's first nursery and landscaping business.

"I know that place," I said to Newman, pointing to the new parking lot and retail office of Sunshine Nursery. I told him there had been a time on Provo when everybody—blacks and whites, and the West Indians especially—knew and loved the couple who started that nursery. But the captain had never heard of my friends the Maltsbergers and made only the smallest grunt of acknowledgment. My memories were beside the point to young Newman, who had migrated from his home on North Caicos to Providenciales to take advantage of the recent economic boom. I was simply the latest job, an American who wanted to be dropped off for ten days on some ideal island, the only criterion being that the place had no people, no nothing, except flora under which I could escape the sun.

Within an hour we were aboard the captain's twenty-four-foot cat-hulled reef cruiser, flying toward East Bay Cay, a skinny sidecar that hugs North Caicos's windward edge, separated from the mother island by a half-mile-wide channel. I had provisioned myself modestly with rice, beans, fresh vegetables, onions and limes for conch salad, beer, a bottle of rum. Otherwise I planned to fish and dive for my food, which is what one does, happily, on a deserted island in these latitudes.

Captain Newman jutted out his chin to direct my attention to a narrow cut, which I could not yet demarcate, behind a glistening bar mouth between the big island and the cay. "This is the road in," he announced, pointing to a slight taint of turquoise indicating deeper water—perhaps six inches deeper.

We came aground about a hundred feet off a rocky point, the terminus of the shaded white-sand beach I had been watching unwind for twenty minutes. We waded the gear ashore through transparent water, the two of us together hauling the heavy coolers and my main duffel bag, and finally it was done. I saluted the captain good-bye and then turned my back on him and (I hoped) every other human being on the planet for the next ten days.

As his boat receded into the distance, I pulled a celebratory beer from my cooler and sat down to engage myself in what could have been a most illumining conversation about the liberties we finesse for ourselves, but my mind went stone-blank with euphoria and I could only stare at the opulence of color—the blue of jewels, eyes, ice, glass—and the glowing white towers of late-summer cumulus clouds queuing across the wind-tossed horizon.

I was alone, as sooner or later we are all meant to be.

Texas, three days earlier.

More than a few years had passed since I last bunked with Captain Tay, and this was by far the largest space we had shared: an expansive bed in a dim apartment annexed to the house in San Antonio that had once been his father's and was now his son's.

The captain's one-room apartment had the ambience of an exhibit in some provincial museum—the Explorer's Room—its walls hung with crossed spears, shark jaws, barnacled fragments of sunken ships, intricately carved wooden paddles, yellowed newspaper clippings, and glossy photographs of adventure.

I opened my eyes to stare at the ceiling, the morning sunlight a radiant border around the two makeshift curtains pinned over the windows, and finally called the old captain's name. No answer, and when I nudged him, no response. Captain Tay was a self-proclaimed dying man, an arthritic and half-blind silverback awaiting winter in his bone-strewn lair, and I thought, *Well, that's it for him.* Apparently he had slipped away in the night, fulfilling his chosen destiny by dying in the same bed his wife, Linda, had died in thirteen years earlier.

The night before, the captain had shown me a sketch on a legal pad: the outlines of a human body, front and back views, with twenty-eight red Xs drawing the viewer's attention to a catalog of the physical indignities Tay had suffered over the years: stitches, concussions, animal bites, punctures, cracked ribs, broken bones, and a shrapnel wound he had sustained from a mortar round in the jungles of Colombia while tagging along with his blood brother, a commander in the National Police, on a 1973 raid against guerrillas. Not indicated on the drawing were the recent, less visible assaults: a bad heart, diabetes, clogged lungs, an exhausted spirit. He had also handed me—one of his designated undertakers—his self-composed obituary, the last line of which read, "He will be buried at sea in the Turks and Caicos," and his desire was that the burial take place over the *South Wind*, the ship his wife's ashes had been scattered over in 1987. As I would be leaving for the archipelago after my stopover in San Antonio, I thought it was damned decent of the captain to die with my convenience in mind.

But when I came out of the bathroom a few minutes later, Lazarus was sitting up, pawing the nightstand for his glasses and cigarettes. He was already dressed because he'd slept with his clothes on. As far as I know he had always done so, ready to leap up at a moment's notice into the god-awful fray.

"I thought you were dead."

"Any day now," said the captain with a spark in his hazel eyes, lying back down to smoke, his shoulders and head propped up with stale pillows. He'd been lying there for six or seven years, a veteran recluse, the lone survivor of all that he had loved, shipwrecked here on this rumpled king-size mattress.

I offered him a respite from the soul-heavy inertia of his retirement, as I'd done annually since he had hunkered down. "Come with me, Tay. Ten days on an uninhabited island. The sort of thing you and Linda used to love. What the hell are you doing lounging around here, waiting to croak?"

This was a bit more irreverence than the captain was accustomed to, and I could hear the growl form in his throat. "I'm seventy-one years old, I'm an alcoholic, my legs are going out, I've buried all my lovers, and I've done everything a man can do down there where you're going," he barked. "Get it through your head. I want to die."

I tried to imagine him as he had been four decades earlier: a thirty-one-year-old man carrying a briefcase and an umbrella, dressed in a Brooks Brothers suit, stepping aboard the commuter train in Westport, Connecticut, riding to Manhattan in the glummest of moods, believing he had traded his "real" life for a halfhearted commitment to virtues that read like a checklist of the American Dream—social status, upward mobility, material comfort—but were somehow entering his system tilted, knocking him off balance. He had married Barbara Rolf, a lithe, sensual blonde from the Ford Modeling Agency, a woman whose face was radiating from the covers of *Life* and *Paris Match* and who had borne him a son named Mark. Tay was natty, lean, dashingly handsome, husband of one of the world's original supermodels, and the father of a towheaded three-year-old boy—all this, and yet he was still a despondent man riding a commuter train from Westport into the city. It wasn't another company job he was hunting for, but a resurrection, some kind of life in which he could breathe freely again.

He had had that freedom, had pursued it with Hemingwayesque flair—Golden Gloves boxer, three years with the Eleventh Airborne Division during the Korean War, the big man on campus at the University of the Americas in Mexico City, twice elected student body president. In Mexico City he had operated his own gymnasium, teaching boxing, judo, bodybuilding. Exciting opportunities had knocked relentlessly at his door. While doing graduate work in industrial psychology, he had led a group of scientists into unexplored regions of British Guiana, Venezuela, and Brazil. There was something wild in his blood that wasn't going to be tamed, no matter how much he muffled it beneath button-down oxfords and dry martinis. Being Texan was likely part of it, he figured. His family had come to Texas just before the Alamo fell, and his great-grandfather had been a civilian scout for the Mormons on their trek to Utah. On both sides, his family lines were heavily saturated with footloose visionaries and hell-raisers and uncontainable spirits.

Stepping off that train in Manhattan, he crossed the platform and caught the next train back to Connecticut. Off came the suit, the brief-case landed in the trash, and he hired on as first mate on a sailboat out of Westport that carried tourists around Long Island Sound. And then he was gone.

"All right, come die in the islands," I told him. "Save me the sorrow of carrying you back there in an urn."

"I'm not moving," the captain snapped, but then he shifted himself upright and his voice became sonorous with care. "You have a good knife?" he asked. "Something that will hold an edge?" He eased up off the bed to rummage around in his moldy piles of gear. "Here, take this knife. I want you to have it."

Ever since I had met Tay and Linda in Colombia in the early seventies—I was fresh out of college, a twenty-two-year-old tadpole who had decided to see the world—the Maltsbergers had seemed intent on teaching me how to take care of myself. I took the knife, just as three months earlier I'd reluctantly taken the pistol he'd been trying to give me for years.

"Any advice, Captain?"

"Keep your matches dry."

Then I held him—the man who had taught me the vocabulary of freedom, schooled me in how it could be seized and harvested and lost, who had made his world so big and then made it as small as you can have it outside of a coffin—and said good-bye to him. For all that, I could see that his inner world had never really changed, and that for those of high spirit, a life wish can at times bear a terrifying resemblance to a death wish, and a certain degree of metaphysical disorientation is bound to seep into the program. It was only that the seep had become a flood. You could walk on its banks all day long, throwing lines into the current, but the captain was indifferent to rescue, not dissatisfied with being swept along toward a promise he had made to Linda decades ago.

I will not leave you alone in the sea.

It was January 1971.

Meteorologists call the type of storm that slammed into Tay and Linda in the Bay of Biscay, off the northern coast of Spain, an extra-tropical Atlantic cyclone—an out-of-season, out-of-place hurricane. Trapped in the storm's cataclysmic center, the ten people aboard their boat, the *Sea Raven*, watched in awe and horror for seventy-two hours as the fury doubled and then tripled in intensity. Their efforts to reach port were cruelly defeated by straight-on winds, with the tops of the massive waves humping green over the bow. Force 6 became Force 8 became Force 10. The mainsail blew out, and the captain, unable to steer, ordered the crew to chop the mizzen sail off its mast to bring the ship under control. The pummeling wind and pounding swells vibrated the caulking out of the boards beneath the engine housing, and the ship lost power.

They issued a Mayday, but the answer from the Spanish Navy only increased their sense of helplessness and doom. They were going to have to wait in line; ships were in desperate straits throughout the bay, and resources were fully deployed and floundering. Not far from the *Sea Raven*'s position, a tanker's castle toppled into the water, taking sixteen men with it. Thirty people were rescued off an American freighter that was going down nearby. A boat put out from the port of La Coruna to respond to the *Raven*'s Mayday but had to turn back, heavily damaged. Linda watched the water rise up the hatchway steps as the *Raven* sank lower and lower into the colossal waves.

One summer night eight years before, she'd pulled up in front of Slug's Saloon, an infamous bar and jazz club in Greenwich Village, in a green Porsche coupe. Linda Johnson, a bony doctoral candidate in experimental psychology at NYU, was working in the lab at Albert

Einstein College of Medicine. She also was a girl who'd been stuck too long in the convent of her education, and she was beelining from Mary Washington College to Manhattan, the center of the universe, partying like nobody's business and collecting so many speeding tickets in the city that she'd have to sell her beautiful car. She took a seat at the bar at Slug's, where Tay, back after a year in the islands, was running the food concession.

Glamour-wise, Linda was the antithesis of Barbara Rolf. She was a big-toothed, stringy-haired blonde who talked with a cornpone drawl and a skeptically raised eyebrow. The daughter of a Virginia state senator, she looked like an egghead, her blue eyes blinking behind thick kitty-cat glasses she was always terrified of losing. What Tay saw when he came out of the kitchen that night was . . . brains, an irresistible, exotic quality, given the women he'd been dating. They talked just long enough to recognize themselves in each other: two dreamers in a barely subdued fever of restlessness, possessed with a great need to be on the move away from an ordinary life. She showed up the next night at a party at his loft, and they started seeing each other. She had finally connected with the man who would open the door to the controlling passion of her life: the ocean. When her mother suddenly died in 1965 and left her $20,000 and a Volkswagen, she and Tay hit the road.

"I have left New York—it's true," Linda crowed to a childhood friend four months later in a letter sent from Isla Mujeres, off the coast of the Yucatán. "With only two chapters left to write on my dissertation, eye to eye with a goal that has teased me through sixteen, seventeen, eighteen years of training, I pulled the reins on my job, my Ph.D., my career, all for a little taste of fantasy. After cooping up my spirit for so long in stiff-paged textbooks and overcrowded seminars, when it finally broke free it shook my whole foundation, like waking up with a dream intact, or falling through a keyhole you never thought existed. . . ." She promised her friends and family that she'd be back in several months, but that would never happen. Her jaunt, her waking dream, her infatuation with the questing beast, would last for almost twenty years.

And what exactly was that trip? A very old story, a myth, the type of tale humans have been telling one another for thousands of years: two enchanted lovers, a magical boat called the *Bon Voyage*, harrowing misadventures, a pot of gold—in this case sunken galleons in Cartagena Bay, off the coast of Colombia. They'd been together for five years when in the autumn of 1968 Tay got word that his ex-wife, Barbara, was dying of leukemia; back in the States, ten-year-old Mark needed him. By this time, Linda had fallen in love with Tay to the extent that she could no longer imagine a life without him, and their next few months were a whirlwind of sorrow and happiness. They were married in November, Barbara was dead by January, and before the winter was out, Tay and Linda and Mark were living together in Dallas, where a network of friends had helped Tay secure a job as foreman of a highway construction crew. But as soon as the three of them had reached a level of comfort as a family, the shared lust for adventure churned back into focus. Their recurring dream: to get a bigger, better sailboat and return to Colombia. Linda took classes with the Coast Guard and earned her license as a full navigator, Tay began to cultivate investors, and together they constructed a castle in the air called Sea Raven Enterprises, printed stationery and business cards (CHARTER SERVICE—SEAFARINGS—UNDERWATER PHOTOGRAPHY—SALVAGE—CRUISING—MOVIES—TREASURE), and sold shares of stock.

Linda had found the *Sea Raven* in Denmark, frozen solid into a fjord: a 99-ton, 110-foot, gaff-rigged-topsail ketch, a classic Baltic trader built in 1920, as beautiful as any ship ever put to sail. She purchased it for $13,000, and soon Tay and Mark followed her to the Danish coast. The three of them lived on the ship at first, out on the ice; then, when the harbor began to thaw, they set up house in a nearby shipyard and hauled the boat to dry-dock for a year of extensive refurbishing.

And then, having sent Mark back to his grandparents in Texas and having welcomed aboard as their captain a former Dutch naval officer named Jaap Stengs, his movie-actress girlfriend (who had never been to sea before), and a crew of six free spirits, they were finally setting sail across the Atlantic, passing first through the Bay of Biscay.

By the fourth day of the storm, the *Sea Raven* was drifting aimlessly in sixty-foot seas and Force 12 winds. The ship's main pumps had ceased to function, and two hundred tons of water had risen four feet above the bilge line. The nearness of death was like a dull pressure somewhere behind the freezing weight of Linda's adrenaline-wracked fatigue, and it translated into a specific dread, which she expressed to Tay: With the *Raven* about to go under, Linda feared they would be separated, and she couldn't bear the terrifying thought of being alone in the sea. Prodding her up the slopes of panic was the image of being tossed around—alone and drowning, with her eyeglasses slapped from her face by the waves, cruelly blinded at the one moment when clear vision, and thus a clear head, might provide her with one small hope for survival. How could she swim to Tay if she couldn't even see him? He calmed her nerves as best he could by roping her to him with an umbilical cord of sheetline. Come what may, he promised, they would be together.

They waited for the ship to sink or for help to arrive, whichever came first. At last out of the howling gloom a Spanish tanker appeared. With superhuman effort a line was made fast, and the *Raven* was towed into the harbor of Gijon, where, according to the official record of the Spanish port authority, "after having moored the *Raven* and put new pumps on board, Captain Jaap Stengs burst out weeping and was not to be calmed down within fifteen minutes. Then he fell asleep."

For five months Tay and Linda remained in Gijon, overseeing the repairs to the storm-mauled ship, but back in Texas the corporation Tay had started was imploding, riddled by infighting and embezzlement. The Maltsbergers' shipyard account was suddenly cut off. To lose a ship in a hurricane was no injustice, but to lose a ship to crooks and double-crossers was an unbearable, and time-honored, betrayal.

There's a Jimi Hendrix lyric that poses what perhaps is the only question worth asking: *Are you prepared to be free?* Not free from responsibility, necessarily, but free from external oppression and internal fear. In everyone's life, it seems, there is a season in which this question is addressed or withdrawn, one's habits changed or calcified, one's dreams realized or rejected.

When I was coming of age in the 1960s, in the suburbs of Washington, D.C., my mother took to calling me, disapprovingly, a wandering Jew, implying that I was infected by some disease of waywardness that had the potential to undermine my future and land me in serious trouble. When I graduated from college in the spring of 1973, the gate finally opened on the mystique of other places, other cultures, *otherness* itself, and four months later, instead of securing an entry-level position in my expected career as a journalist, I boarded a flight from Miami to South America. My mother's suspicion was confirmed: At age twenty-two, I was declaring myself a type of hobo, falling from middle-class life into a pit of daily uncertainty.

Flying toward the San Andrés archipelago in the southwestern Caribbean, the cheapest destination available that was technically in Latin America, I was unaware that there were other people like me, people who might think of their urge to travel as an acceptable characteristic of a bona fide lifestyle. Romantics, to be sure; fools, possibly; escapists, probably. Dreamers who pursued irregular but nonetheless intrepid dreams of dubious value to the social order, their minds flaring with extravagant narratives. That's who Tay and Linda were, the first adults I befriended who had decided to step off the well-marked path and keep going.

"I surge into the waves of time, fascinated by the billowing soul of man," Linda wrote a few days before she died, composing her own epilogue. "What imponderable excess baggage we travel with on this trip bound for old bones and flaccid skin. Why ever let it be boring?"

I was grateful for the way she lived; she was the boldest person I ever knew. A life of bravery begins almost by default when you first find yourself oppressed by a low and unforgiving threshold for being bored. The only deliverance for the neurotic, the explorer, and the traveler alike is to throw herself off a cliff into the boiling waters of crisis. And then, to the best of his ability, to have fun.

"You know what's funny about our adventures all those years?" Tay mused as we lay back down together in his bed, smoking cigarettes and watching the Weather Channel play a mindless loop of Hurricane Darby footage. "We never had any money."

A friend, hearing in the Maltsbergers' sad tale a raw need to move beyond the agony of the *Sea Raven*, mentioned he knew an old gringo in Colombia who had a gold mine high up in the Andes and was looking for help. Never especially pragmatic until they were already immersed in challenge or folly, Tay and Linda went off to live in a bone-chilling tamped-earth hut at 11,500 feet, above the jungles of Bucaramanga. Tay and the old man struggled to refine a process for filtering gold out of the large heaps of tailings left centuries earlier by the Spanish conquistadors. They collected seven or eight ounces a week, but it wasn't enough.

After a year and a half the Maltsbergers packed their sea chests and descended the mountains all the way to the coast and beyond, to the San Andrés archipelago, where they had previously charted out the *Bon Voyage*. This time, they homesteaded on remote Isla de Providencia, its barrier reefs dotted with the seduction of shipwrecks and the promise of treasure. On the edge of Providencia's central town they rented a two-story clapboard building called Lookout House and opened a four-table restaurant, the only thing they knew to do to make a living while they engaged in their treasure hunt. Mark, by then fourteen years old, joined them; he was being homeschooled by Linda and living like a kid in *The Swiss Family Robinson*, every day a boyhood novel of adventures.

The first time I met them I was a customer in their restaurant, having sat next to one of their partners in fantasy, Howard Kahn, a diving instructor from Chicago, on the flight from Miami to San Andrés. After a fabulous dinner of baked red snapper, Linda offered us drinks on the house and sat down with us, her only customers. I had planned to stay on Providencia for a week, but before the month was out Howard and I had rented a house together down the beach. Soon I was strapping scuba tanks on my back to claw through the ballast stones of the wrecks that Kahn and the Maltsbergers were working, inconceivably, by hand, the salvage operation ill-equipped for recovering anything more noteworthy than a few copper spikes and coral-encrusted potsherds lying half-exposed on the bottom. At dinner each evening, Tay and Linda would open their mouths and it was like popping the cork on a magnum of rich stories. A year passed before I tore myself away.

Lookout House was sold out from under them, and they moved to Bottom House, the poorest village on the island, sent Mark back to family and to public school in Texas, and lived on the beach in a hut they had nailed together out of hatch covers from a shipwrecked freighter. One day a pre-cartel entrepreneur plying the trade routes between Colombia and Florida sailed his sloop into the island, and the Maltsbergers sailed away with him to the Bahamas, passing through the Turks and Caicos, which looked to Tay and Linda like their kind of archipelago.

On Grand Turk, they opened a restaurant, only to have the newly elected government fire the sole airline that brought tourists to the island. They took to the sea again, with Tay as captain and Linda as first mate of the *Blue Cloud*, a five-hundred-ton freighter that sailed from South Florida to ports throughout the northern Caribbean. But after a year of offering themselves up to every petty bureaucrat in every customs house on the trade routes—imagine bringing a shipload of anything into the wharves of Port-au-Prince and you get the picture— they bought a few acres of scrubland on Providenciales and jumped ship, their long love affair with life on the sea having ripened and burst. I think they meant to start another restaurant on Provo, not a nursery, but they inherited a truckload of pots and potting soil from a bankrupt hotel and that was that. In their fifties, the Maltsbergers finally retired their quest for gold, more emblematic than real anyway, and returned to the fold of property-owning, tax-paying citizens.

My wife and I visited Tay and Linda in Provo whenever we found the time and money, and the last time the four of us drove the road between town and Sunshine Nursery, we stumbled out of the bar at Turtle Cove into the star-smeared island midnight. As we walked toward the nursery's muffler-less old Chevy pickup, Linda tripped on a rock—the roads were unpaved then—and in falling to her hands and knees she lost her glasses, which we promptly found and placed back on her face. The four of us squeezed into the timeworn cab of the truck, Linda behind the wheel. "My God," she exclaimed a few hundred yards down the road, "Bob, you're going to have to drive." She slammed on the brakes. "Tay," she said fiercely in her molasses twang, "I've drunk myself blind. I can't see a fucking thing."

In the morning we solved the mystery of Linda's sudden blindness: When she tripped coming out of the bar, the lenses had popped out of their frames, and they were still there in the dirt when Tay drove back to look for them. But on the road that night, her worst fear had finally materialized: She had lost her precious sight, the ability to see and navigate the world. She and I had climbed out of the truck in total blackness, not a light to be seen anywhere but from a canopy of diamond-bright stars above, with one big one blazing down as we passed each other around the front of the Chevy.

"God damn," she said. "I may be blind, but I saw *that*. Beautiful."

Seven years earlier, after a radical mastectomy, the doctors had given Linda six months to live, and she had lit into them, calling them frauds and swearing she would prove them and their voodoo wrong. She and Tay had been running the *Blue Cloud* then, and Linda had started visiting an experimental cancer-treatment center in Freeport and injecting herself daily with a controversial immunological serum she carried everywhere in a dry-ice-filled thermos. Her cancer had been in remission ever since, but she could sense it was coming back, and it wasn't very long after that night together on the road that they would sell the nursery, which was prospering as the island developed, and Tay would take Linda to the States to die. He brought her ashes back to spread over the wreck of the *South Wind*, which had proved so unseaworthy that it had been sunk by its owner, a Provo entrepreneur, off the reefs of the island, to be enjoyed forever after by scuba divers.

After the star fell and we started down the road again, Linda, staring blankly into the darkness, surprised us by asking whether we believed in life after death. If there was life after death, Linda wisecracked, Tay had better watch out: Her ghost would come a-chaperoning his liaisons with other women.

But there would never be other women, because grief, too, is blindness, sight fading inward toward memory, and the captain was too heartsick ever to care to begin again.

"Last chance," I said to Tay as I rose up from his bed. "You coming with me?"

No, he wasn't, not today and never again.

On East Bay Cay I savored the exquisite waste of time, time that other people were using to benefit from the world in some measurable way, time forged by others into progress and still others into dreams. I dove for lobster and conch, speared snapper, fly-fished for barracuda just for the violence of the hookup. Down in the sand I walked for miles, beachcombing in a daze. I scribbled dry observations in my journal as if it were a ship's log, and I slept soundly every night, lulled by the constant noise of nature: the far-off thunder of waves on the reef, the persistent hiss and flutter of wind, the lap and sigh of shorebreak. For ten days I did precisely what I wanted: I read. Great books have made me unemployable; I can't pick one up without shutting down my daily life. In this respect Linda's influence continues to inform my days, for it was she who introduced me to Gabriel García Márquez (who we sometimes saw on Isla de Providencia at the cockfights), she who gave me my first copies of Peter Matthiessen's *Far Tortuga*, Joshua Slocum's *Sailing Alone on the World*, Graham Greene's *The Comedians*.

I knew what I was doing here on this far-off island—I knew how to take care of myself, how to enjoy myself—but I couldn't quite explain to myself why I had come, what I was looking for. Perhaps it was only a rehearsal for my final voyage with the captain. Or maybe it was an act akin to a transmission overhaul, lubricating the machinery damaged by life's inevitable grinding down of the romantic dream.

I thought of Captain Tay, back there on the king-size island of his isolation, about his influence on how I'd lived my life, and about how I might measure the difference between us. Technically, at least, we were two of the most cut-loose people on earth: Americans, white males, sometimes penniless but possessed of the skills and tenacity that would always stick enough money in our pockets to get by, with a powerful and abiding sense of self-reliance and self-sufficiency. We were doing what suited us and what often made us happy. But Tay's obstinate disconnection from a world he had formerly possessed with such ferocious energy had unsettled me. Perhaps I saw myself doing just that: disconnecting. What is it that finally conquers your appetite for the world? Fear? Exhaustion? Cynicism? The formerly wild places now sardined with stockbrokers on tour? Paralyzing nostalgia for the way it was? Age and health? Self-pity? Sorrow?

The epiphany of my relationship with Tay and Linda Maltsberger, the revelation that had become as clear and guiding as the North Star, still struck me as the larger truth: Whatever your resources, the world was yours to the exact degree to which you summoned the fortitude and faith to step away from convention and orthodoxy and invent your own life. Tay and Linda knew better than most that there's never a good reason to make your world small.

An image presents itself from aboard the *South Wind*, an abominable vessel with a tawdry history as a drug runner, eventually rehabilitated to run fuel between Provo and the Dominican Republic. In 1980, her owner coaxed the Maltsbergers into bringing the freighter down from a Florida boatyard. They hired me on as ship's carpenter to enclose the toilet on the stern of the boat—Linda never did get much privacy in her life with Tay—and to help them deliver the *South Wind* to Provo.

On the fourth day out from Fort Lauderdale we entered an armada of vicious squalls in the channel off the Exuma Cays. At midnight I took the helm from Tay, and for the next three wretched hours I fought alone in the darkness to keep the ship on course, waves breaking over the bow and foaming down the deck, lightning strikes bracketing us on all sides, white rain pelting horizontally into the glass of the wheelhouse. Toward the end of my watch Linda awoke, stepped over to the radar screen, and proclaimed that she didn't know where we were, but from the looks of it I had steered too far west and we were about to crash into unseen rocks. Terrified, I changed course twenty degrees, and Linda, storm sibyl, as always so transcendently composed, walked out into the tempest. Sometimes I had to shake my head clear to see her properly. Her physical self, her sense of style—the clothes, the cut of her lank hair, the clunky eyeglasses—seemed so retrograde, so bolted down to the Camelot sixties, as if she still was and always would be some bookish chick from NYU who couldn't quite finish her dissertation on the urban insane.

After the ship's mechanic crawled up out of the engine room to relieve me at the wheel, I went looking for Linda and found her back at the stern. The worst of the storm had passed, and she stood in the cone of illumination under the pole that held our running light, her body swarmed by hundreds of shrieking birds that had sought refuge with us, swirling like snowflakes past the fingertips of her outstretched arms, landing on her shoulders, her head. It seemed for a moment they might carry her away. There was a look of extreme delight on her rain-streaked face, and she turned toward me and nodded as if to say, *How marvelous! How miraculous! The world is full of wonders.* And then she retreated to the wheelhouse to chart our position and bring us men safely through the night.

(2000)

Here the Bear and
the Mafia Roam

In the central Siberian city of Tomsk, children play a game called Dead Telephone, whispering a sentence around a circle until someone fails to repeat the original wording accurately, and for the child who gets the sentence wrong, the penalty is "you must go live in Kamchatka." Meaning that the loser has been imaginatively banished from the relative comforts of Siberia to the very end of the earth. Kamchatka, perhaps Russia's most famous nowhere, the wild east of the Russian and Soviet empires, nine time zones and over six thousand miles distant from Moscow.

Tundra. Shimmering twilight. A slow, high-banked river the color of tea, as if it flowed from the spigot of a samovar.

Where I should have been was on a vodka-clear, rock-bottomed river, fast and wild, somewhere to the north and farther inland with a phantom cadre of biologists, fly-fishing for salmon specimens on the Kamchatka peninsula. Where I'd ended up was about three klicks inland from the Sea of Okhotsk, on an estuarine section of another river that I'd been advised, by the self-proclaimed criminals who deposited me here, to forget about, or else.

We had come from the end of the road, three hours across tundra and beach, atop my host's—let's call him Misha—GTT, a large, blunt-snouted all-terrain vehicle that came into his possession when the Soviet military began to disintegrate in 1991. Despite Misha's earlier assurances, not only were we not going to the river I'd traveled thousands of miles to fish, in hopes of seeing what I'd never seen before—the phenomenon of a massive salmon run—but we'd be leaving in the morning, a day earlier than I thought had been agreed upon. Misha, who looked like a blond-haired, cornhusking quarterback, had Brandoesque mannerisms; waiting for my tantrum to subside, he tilted his head back and cocked it coolly, peering down the nascent beefiness of his ruddy face, and then chided me in the hushed cadence of the ever-reasonable gangster.

"Robert," he said, "I'm Mafiya, Mafiya, Mafiya—not a tour agent."

Then he wrapped his hands around his throat, as if to strangle himself, and said he would, if I wanted, take care of my inept outfitter back in Petropavlovsk-Kamchatsky (P-K), and for a moment I thought, Nice guy!

At the Mafiya's oceanside fish camp, when I explained that, to salvage something out of the trip, I wanted to be ferried across the lagoon to spend the night upriver, Misha considered this desire stupid and pointless, but mostly he considered it dangerous. Bears were as thick as gooseberries over there, he said, and I didn't have a gun, but when I persisted he ordered his boatman to take me across. Rinat, my half-Tatar, half-Russian interpreter/driver, was coming with me. Sergei, our wilderness guide, said he'd rather not.

Now, standing on a tiny tide-swept island in waist-high grass at the end of this remarkably strange day, I cast futilely for silver salmon with my spinning rod, the strong wind sailing the lure within inches of a sandy patch of beach jutting out below the opposite shore. On the steep bank ten feet above me, Rinat had his nose in the food bag, tossing spoiled provisions out onto the ground.

"Rinat! Are you mad? Throw that food in the river."

Kamchatka is said to have more and larger grizzly bears per square mile than any place on earth, but Rinat was churlishly indifferent to their presence. A city boy, born and raised in P-K, the peninsula's largest metropolis, he was employed by a local tourist company trying to bluff its way into the wilderness biz. His employer—my outfitter—let him come out into the ever-perilous, grizzly-roamed outback without a proper food container, without even a tent (I'd brought my own). Earlier in the summer, we'd done soberingly foolish things together, taken risks that Rinat never seemed to recognize—traversed glaciers in our tennis shoes where one slip would send you plummeting into oblivion; edged ourselves out onto melting ice bridges; stood on the fragile crater floor of the belching Mutnovsky volcano, our lungs seared by sulfurous gases. How, I often wondered, was this puckish, hardworking fellow ever going to survive his occupation, here in one of the last great wild places left on earth?

"Sushi," Rinat giggled irreverently, pitching stale bread and moldy cheese into the river, making a reference to Michiko Honido, the renowned bear photographer, who was eaten by his Kamchatkan subjects last year.

A minute later I hooked up with a good-size silver salmon, which cheered me deeply, here in the land called the Serengeti of Salmon, where I had been consistently thwarted in my (apparently not) simple quest to savor a fine day of fishing. The fish made its freedom run, keeping me well occupied, and when I looked up again, Rinat, the imp, had set the tundra on fire.

I landed the fish, put my rod down, hopped back to the mainland, and began hauling pots of water while Rinat slapped at the rapidly spreading flames with a fiber sack. Though I'd just reeled in the first salmon of my life, the experience had been akin to losing one's virginity while your little brother's in the room, playing with a loaded pistol.

Later, as I planked one of the fillets for smoking, Rinat cut the other into steaks for the cook pot. We lolled around the campfire, uncommonly taciturn, because Rinat had found it politic to give away our last bottle of vodka to the boyos.

"Here we are with the criminals," he said, shaking his head morosely. "Here we are with the bears."

Imagine an Alaska sealed tight for fifty years, suspended in isolation, inaccessible to all outsiders until 1990, when the sanctum's doors ease slowly open to the capitalists on the threshold, the carpetbaggers, the tycoon sportsmen, and, of course, the gangsters. Unworldly Kamchatka, with a not-quite-propitious swing of history's horrible pendulum, is called upon to reinvent itself, and not for the first time.

As gold had once inspired the conquest of the New World, the lust for fur—beaver in North America, sable in Russia—accelerated the exploration of two continents and the spread of two empires. Russia's eastward expansion very much mirrored America's westward expansion—the genocidal subjugation of native peoples in the pursuit of natural riches and trade routes. White guys on the move.

Annexed for the czars by a Cossack expedition in 1697, Kamchatka provided Peter the Great with a global monopoly on the fabulously valuable sable. Within forty years, the ruthless, plundering Cossacks had decimated the coastal-oriented Itelmen and reindeer-herding Koryaks, the likely descendants of indigenous people who had crossed the Bering Strait to North America. A native rebellion in 1731 resulted in a mass suicide, and before long 150,000 tribal people had been reduced to 10,000, their number today, barely 2.5 percent of Kamchatka's population. Racially and culturally, Kamchatka is as Eurocentric as a bottle of Perrier.

In 1725, Peter the Great sent Captain Vitus Bering on an unsuccessful mission to determine the relation of eastern Siberia to the American continent. Bering was recommissioned by Peter's successor, and his Great Northern Expedition, which took years to plan and execute and eventually involved three thousand people, is rightfully remembered as one of the greatest voyages of discovery. Bering sailed his two packets, the *St. Peter* and the *St. Paul*, into Avachinsky Bay in 1740 and founded the town of Petropavlovsk, named after his ships. The following spring he set sail for the coast of North America, sighting land in July—Kayak Island off the Alaskan coast—and throughout the summer and fall he mapped the Aleutians, charted the Alaskan shoreline, and then turned back toward Kamchatka, discovering the Commander Islands. His efforts had irrevocably opened the Russian Far East and Russian America for development and trade—in particular the fur trade, which continued to dominate the peninsula's economy until 1912, the year St. Petersburg banned the trapping of sable for three years to restore the species' population.

Surprisingly, no one showed much interest in the more available resource—salmon—until 1896, when the first fish processing plant, sponsored by the Japanese, was established at the mouth of the Kamchatka River, once the site of the peninsula's most prolific run. By the time the last Japanese left the peninsula thirty-one years later, Kamchatka had been thoroughly incorporated into the Soviet system, and both the salmon fishery and the sable trade were transformed into state monopolies. Kamchatkans were free to harvest as much salmon as they wanted until 1930, when the state's imposition of limits radically affected subsistence fishing, and by 1960 the official allowance, 132 pounds a year, was barely sufficient to keep a sled dog from starving. Meanwhile the commercial fishery was booming, and by 1990 Kamchatka's total annual salmon catch had increased from 30,000 tons to 1.5 million tons. As in Alaska, the fishery began to develop dry holes—a river here, a bay there, under severe pressure.

As Kamchatka receded behind the curtain of official xenophobia after World War II, Moscow rapidly developed the area's defenses—a submarine base in Avachinsky Bay; intercontinental ballistic missile launch sites, satellite tracking stations, military outposts up and down its coastlines—and expected in return "gross output." Not just salmon and sable; now everything was up for grabs. By the late '80s, central Kamchatka's primary forests, 60 percent old-growth larch, were decimated; the Soviets had managed to annihilate Kamchatka's herring spawning grounds as well. Today, in a debauchery of joint ventures with foreign companies, Moscow has taken aim at the crab and pollack fisheries, at risk to suffer the same fate as the larch, the sable, the herring. Nor has the end of communism spelled anything but crisis for Kamchatka's legendary brown bears. By 1997, the peninsula's Cold War population of grizzlies, an estimated twenty thousand bears, had been halved by poachers and trophy hunters. At the rate things are going, says Boris Kopylov, the vice-director of Kamchatka's State Environmental Protection Committee, the most powerful federal agency mandated to preserve the peninsula's natural resources, "In the next five years all the endangered species will be at a critical level, the sea otters and bears especially." This year, the agency's staff was halved: Conservation law enforcement in remote areas vanished as helicopter patrols were reduced from three hundred flying hours to zero, and the system, as Kopylov lamented, didn't work anymore. "If you want to save Kamchatka," said Robert Moiseev, one of the peninsula's leading environmental scientists, "you're welcome to pay for it."

Shortly after dawn, the criminals returned to collect us, a humorless sense of urgency in their manner. The chiefs were mightily vexed, they told us, having last night discovered that thieves had spirited away twelve hundred kilos—more than one ton—of caviar the gang had cached on the beach.

"Check Rinat's knapsack," I said. The criminals smiled uneasily—heh-heh—and we loaded our gear into the skiff. I'd come to Kamchatka, twice, to fish, and so far I'd been allowed to do damn little of it. In July, a rafting trip on the Kamchatka River quickly devolved into some awful hybrid of absurdity—Samuel Beckett meets Jack London. The rafts were dry-rotted, the river had been dead for ten years, the mosquitoes were nightmarish, our fishing "guide" was actually a hawk-eyed tayozhnik, a taiga woodsman, who had given his stern heart to hunting and horses but had probably never seen a sportfisherman in his life.

On my second expedition to Kamchatka, the day I arrived in P-K from Anchorage an Mi-2 helicopter crashed, killing everyone aboard, and I no longer had a ride to the mythical river up north. My local outfitter hadn't considered a Plan B. The only alternative, untested, that the outfitter could offer was for Rinat and me to head out to the coast and try to beg a lift across the tundra with anybody we could find in possession of a GTT—the acronym translated as "Tracks Vehicle: Heavy."

First we drove in Rinat's truck to a village south of P-K to collect Sergei, the wilderness guide, a Russian version of Bubba, attired in camouflage fatigues, who was an erstwhile law-enforcement officer for RIVOD, the peninsula's fish regulatory board. He was now employed as a fieldworker by TINRO—the Pacific Scientific Research Institute of Fisheries and Oceanography, a state agency operating in association with the Russian Academy of Sciences but in cahoots with commercial interests. From 1990 to 1996, hard currency gushed in as TINRO became a clearinghouse for the avaricious flow of foreign investment into Kamchatka's fisheries. "Everybody in the institute got very rich. There was so much money they didn't know what to do with it," a TINRO scientist had told me. "The bosses built big dachas, bought expensive cars." The institute's sudden wealth finally attracted the attention of Moscow, which began sucking up 90 percent of the institute's revenues and controlling quotas.

Sergei, as a quasi-scientific government employee, was our insurance, along for the ride not only to steer us clear of official trouble but to legitimize whatever it was we might end up doing that was a bit too *diki*—wild, independent—for the apparatchiks.

At the last town before the windswept barrenness of the coast, we turned down a dirt road toward a pre-Soviet Dogpatch, a cluster of clapboard and tar-papered houses, stopping in front of the first one we saw with a GTT in its yard. There on the wooden stoop was Misha, barefoot, wearing camouflage bib overalls, one of his forearms intricately tattooed. He could have been any midwestern hayseed waiting for the glory of team sport. Sergei hopped out, explained our mission, and offered to hire Misha and his machine.

"Nyet," insisted Misha. Money, he explained, was nothing to him; therefore, yes, he would take us up the coast, but as his guests. I had no way of measuring the offer and began to ask predictable questions, anticipating predictable answers. The house wasn't his, he said; he came here on the weekends from P-K with his friends to relax.

"What do you do in the city?"

"We are criminals," he replied. "Even the FBI knows about us."

"What'd you do," I joked naively, "sell missiles to Iran?"

Misha narrowed his eyes and demanded to know why I asked such a question. I swore I was only kidding around, and he studied me hard for a good long minute before his demeanor changed and, clapping me on the back, he decided, I suppose, that I was good entertainment out here in the hinterlands—an American writer dropped into his lap.

"Robert, you will write your story about me, you will put me on the cover of your magazine, you will tell the truth," he declared matter-of-factly, an extravagant display of hubris.

The truth, as I understood it, went something like this: Years ago Misha had committed a crime, the nature of which he refused to explain except obscurely. The old system—the Commies, I suppose—threw him in jail in Siberia for "not fitting in," where he fell in with like-minded troublemakers sharing grandiose, if not exactly morally based, ambitions for a better life. Most significantly, he connected with his fierce partner—let's call him Viktor, and then let's forget that we ever called him anything.

Gorbachev, perestroika, freedom, the implosion of the USSR, crony economics, the democracy scam—Misha and his Siberian Mafiya crew moved to Kamchatka and became underworld oligarchs. These were the days, the early '90s, of the *diki* Mafiya: no rules, every man for himself, and bodies in the streets. As best I could determine, Misha and friends privatized—seized—a huge tract of state property on the coast, an expansive fiefdom containing four or five rivers plus a processing plant, and went into the caviar business. Eventually the Mafiya and the government realized they had to coexist, so now, after massive greasing, the Mafiya had all the requisite documents and licenses they needed in order to legally do what they were doing—harvesting and processing an astonishing thirty tons of caviar a season to ship to their associates in Moscow.

"The Mafiya," explained Misha, "is a state within a state," and perhaps it was destined to morph into the state itself, because if the government ever tries to recover the properties and companies and concerns the Mafiya had sunk its claws into, "there will be a coup d'état," said Misha emphatically, "and there will be a civil war." Which was exactly the sort of dire prediction I'd been hearing from every upright citizen in Kamchatka throughout the week.

We went inside the austere little house, where Misha sat me down at the kitchen table and smothered me in hospitality, happily watching me shovel down the grub he set out—pasta with minced pork and silver salmon dumplings. Someone appeared with a large bowl of fresh curds and whey. Bonbons? asked Misha, sticking a box of chocolates in my face. Out came a bottle of Armenian brandy. The cross-cultural we-are-all-brothers stuff proceeded splendidly until I made the mistake of cussing.

"Robert," Misha objected, "don't hurt my ears with bad words. Real men," he admonished in his lullaby voice, "don't need to talk to each other this way."

In the morning, Misha double-checked the tide chart he carried folded in his wallet. "Robert, let's have one for the road," he said. What he meant was, Let's have one bottle for the beginning of the road. Aspirin and vodka, the breakfast of criminals. Afterward we mounted the GTT and crawled headfirst through the hatch covers into the cavernous interior. We bucked and roared out of town, across the east-west highway and onto the much-scarred tundra, stopping long enough for Misha, Rinat, and myself to climb up on the roof, where we each wrapped a hand around safety ropes and held on as the driver slammed the beast into gear and we slopped our way forward through the bogs.

An hour later we arrived at the coast, littered with the shabby sprawl of a government fish operation. We churned onward through the pebbly sand, the blue Sea of Okhotsk to our left, huge slabs of tundra peat eroding from coastal bluffs on our right. Misha, surveying his kingdom, took delight in pointing out the sights—white-tailed eagles swooping down out of the moody heavens, flocks of berry-fat ptarmigans tumbling clumsily out of the scrub, a pod of all-white beluga whales, scores of sea otters bobbing in the waves off a river mouth. We crossed another without a hitch and Misha happily announced that we were entering private property—his.

We saluted the first brigade of his workers, a motley crew of caviar cowboys. They looked like—and perhaps might someday soon be— partisan rebels in their black rubber waders, filthy overcoats, stubbled faces. We cracked open another bottle of vodka, ate lunch, and Misha wanted pictures, group pictures, buddy pictures, and I took out my camera. We went on, conferring with another survivalist cell of workers farther up the coast, always a guy with a rifle or shotgun standing nearby.

By now Misha had become a bit nervous, his bonhomie turned brittle. Somewhere up ahead was his jack-booted partner Viktor, who had outlawed alcohol in the camps. If you signed onto a brigade, if you were lucky enough to be asked, you came to work, worked yourself to numbing exhaustion, but after a twelve-day cycle of setting nets, pulling nets, tearing the roe out of thousands of now-worthless salmon, and processing the eggs into caviar, you went home with a small fortune—$1,500 a man. Then, and only then, you could drink your Russian self blind, for all Viktor cared.

Twenty minutes later, we came to a pair of Ural trucks ahead on the beach. "No pictures!" Misha warned as I followed him to the dune line, toward a storm-built village of wooden-hulled shipwrecks. At this moment I had to be honest with myself about Misha's character flaws relevant specifically to my presence there on the beach: His pride— he wanted to boast. His gregariousness—he wanted to be liked and appreciated. His generosity—he wanted everyone to understand he was a big man who looked after his own. Viktor, Misha's partner but apparently the first among equals, had no such flaws.

"Here is Viktor," said Misha. It wasn't an introduction. I glanced toward Viktor, who looked at me steadily, his round face and Asian eyes, icy with menace, and I immediately turned and walked away, careful not to acknowledge him, as he was so clearly offended by my existence. Misha had erred in bringing me here with my retinue, playing games when there was serious work to be done, caviar to salt, traitors to whack, and now he vied for Viktor's forbearance of this cardinal sin. When we rendezvoused with Misha back at the GTT, he was singing the same tune of camaraderie, but in a different key.

Which brings everything back to this lagoon behind the Mafiya's northernmost outpost, where I stood that morning after my night out on the tundra with Rinat, not caring so much about how the treachery of the stolen caviar might somehow come crashing down on us when we reunited with Misha and Viktor at low tide, but instead far more concerned with my new belief that I was destined never to have a solid day of good fishing here in the angler's paradise of Kamchatka.

When Misha had dropped us here the previous afternoon, we'd spent a moment discussing the nature of things, fishwise. His men had gawked at me, the sportfisherman. Not a one had ever brought in a fish unless he had gaffed, gigged, netted, snagged, or somehow scooped it out of the water like a bear. When Misha finally understood the style of fishing I was intent on doing, he frowned.

"Nyet, nyet, nyet," he said. "Don't bring that here. We don't want catch-and-release here." We argued: If he kept harvesting the roe at such a pace, where would the fish be for his children, his grandchildren? "Robert," Misha smiled, "you and I alone are not going to solve this problem."

And then, too quick, always too quick, it was time to go. Back in Misha's orbit, the criminals actually were in high spirits. It had been a good season so far, the silvers were starting to arrive, and the interior of the GTT was packed solid with wooden casks of precious caviar.

"I don't like to catch fish," Misha said breezily. "I like to catch money."

Kamchatka's exploitation was both an old and a new story, but so was the campaign to preserve its wealth of resources. In 1996 Russia bequeathed more than one-fourth of Kamchatkan territory to the UN Development Programme. A stunning gift to mankind—a World Heritage site that includes the Kronotsky State Biosphere Nature Preserve, 2.5 million acres of some of the most spectacular landscape on earth. The Kronotsky Preserve contains a geyser field that is second only to Yellowstone's, and the Uzon Caldera, filled with steam vents, smoking lakes, mud cauldrons, and dozens of hot springs. It also is home to three times as many grizzlies as in the entire Yellowstone ecosystem, plus the greatest known populations of Pacific and white-tailed eagles. The park has twenty-two volcanoes, including the Fuji-like Klyuchevskaya, 15,584 feet of elegant cone, the tallest active volcano in Asia and Europe.

Many Kamchatkans fear that, as the economy plummets and the country opens itself to the unchecked appetites of the free market, the peninsula's natural resources will be raided and areas like Kronotsky overrun by tourists. When I spoke with Boris Sinchenko, vice governor of the Kamchatka region administration and one of the men at the helm of Kamchatka's future, he told me, "In five to ten years, we expect to host five to ten million tourists annually and to have built the infrastructure to accommodate them. The territory is so large, we can easily lose ten million people in its vastness."

Many Kamchatkans also harbor a corollary fear. The peninsula's total population is less than five hundred thousand, three-quarters of which lives in or around P-K. An environmental scientist told me with a shrug, "When there's no electricity, the people say, 'We don't care about nature, give us heat!'" One day, Rinat had slapped an orange sticker on the front of my notebook, given to him by his ex-wife, who worked for a Canadian gold-mining conglomerate: HUNGRY, HOMELESS, NEED A JOB? CALL THE SIERRA CLUB, ASK ABOUT THEIR NO GROWTH POLICY. Only the most arrogant conservationist would demand that Kamchatkans remain impoverished in order to preserve their wonderland for a future less hopeless and bleak than the present. Talking with Sinchenko, however, I sensed there was something a bit cynical about signing over a quarter of the peninsula to the enviros at the UN, as if now that it had proved its enlightenment, the state had earned carte blanche to do what it pleased with the rest of its resources.

There were precedents for such cynicism. Twice, in the '60s and the '80s, the Soviets began to erect power plants on swift-flowing rivers inside or near the reserve, destroying spawning grounds and wasting millions of rubles. Nevertheless, a large hydroelectric project is under construction on the Tolmachevo River, and the gorgeous, fish-rich Bystraya River flowing through the village of Esso was stuck with a dam and power station. Sitting below the areas around Esso are some of the richest unmined gold deposits in the world. When I spoke with Boris Kopylov of the State Environmental Protection Committee, he mentioned that his agency had been successful in stopping exploratory drilling on west coast oil deposits and halting placer mining for gold near the mouth of the Kamchatka River, but it was clear that sooner or later the oil was going to be drilled and the Esso gold deposits were going to be extracted, ultimately endangering spawning grounds in central Kamchatka. "In previous years all the [environmental] agencies were completely against all exploration for gas, oil, and gold," said Kopylov. "Now our position is to change a little."

In the salmon fishery, the magnitude of greed, multiplied in many instances by a struggle for survival, was mind-boggling. "Illegal fishing out of Kamchatka yields $2 billion a year," David La Roche, a consultant for the UN's environmental mission to Kamchatka, told me over beers in a P-K café as we talked about the local flowchart for corruption. "The legal fisheries are yielding not as much."

The economic pressures that confront the ordinary Kamchatkan were made viscerally clear to me in July when I met Vladimir Anisimov, the headman of Apacha, a sprawling collective farm about ninety-three miles due west of P-K. A prosperous dairy farm until Gorbachev presided over the nation's demise, Apacha's ability to survive had seriously corroded, its herds whittled away by the state from four thousand to four hundred head, its buildings in sad disrepair. In desperation, the Apacha villagers had signed an experimental one-year contract with the Japanese to collect mushrooms, herbs, and fiddlehead ferns from the surrounding forest. And then, like almost every other collective in Kamchatka, Apacha had gone into the fishing business.

Everyone was waiting, waiting, for the fish to start their run, but when I returned to Apacha in September, I learned that, as in much of Alaska this summer, it never happened—the July run of salmon never really came in from the sea. Nobody in the village had been paid a wage in recent memory. Vladimir was at a loss; the collective hadn't netted half its quota of twelve hundred tons when, if truth be told, it had counted on netting its legal quota and then doubling it with another thousand tons off the books, as is the common practice. Apacha was rotting on the hoof, the central government gnawing away at the resources that the people had struggled fifty years to create. Since the middle of August, the ruble had lost two-thirds of its value, and the last day I saw Vladimir, shops were empty of basic foodstuffs and Apacha was without electricity because there wasn't any fuel to run its generator. Even in such dire straits, the kindness and generosity that all Kamchatkans had shown me did not abandon Vladimir, and he embarrassed me by siphoning gas out of his own vehicle so that I could go fishing.

Sergei, heretofore simply along for the ride, suddenly awoke to the idea that it was time to take control of our half-baked expedition, now that we had parted with the Mafiya and exhausted every option in our one and only plan to head north to that never-fished river. Pointing for Rinat to take a turnoff up ahead on the east-west road, Sergei allowed that if all I truly wanted to do was fish, then he had an idea that might finally relieve me of my obsession.

Sergei disappeared down a path. I sat in Rinat's diesel truck, praying that something good might come of this. Rinat wouldn't look at me, and I could hardly blame him. His country was falling apart around him, and he was stuck chauffeuring a sport-crazed American, one of the nominal victors in an ugly game we had all been forced to play. All he could do was resign himself to an even uglier truth—foreigners equal money equals hope: Drive on.

Sergei reemerged from the trees, beaming. He had a pal, the local tayozhnik, who owned a skiff and was caretaker of a hunting cabin about a half hour's cruise downriver at the base of the mountains, at the mouth of a tributary as thick with char and *mikisha* (rainbows) as the main river itself was obscenely packed with the season's final run of pink salmon. The tayozhnik would be willing to take us there.

"But there's a problem," said Sergei, wincing. "No gasoline for the outboard motor."

Okay, that was a problem—there was only one gas station within sixty miles, and it was closed. We drove to a shack atop the bluff above an invisible river and picked up the tayozhnik, an unshaven backwoods gnome we might have roused from an Appalachian hollow, and together we traveled a half hour to Apacha, where Vladimir, the destitute head-man of his destitute people, came to our rescue with the siphoned gas. Two hours later, back on the bluff, while I repacked my gear for the boat, Sergei and the woodsman suddenly took off to run unspecified errands.

Rinat and I broke out the medicine and resigned ourselves to further delay. Then began the cirque surreal. First to wander across the clearing was a lugubrious old man who stood gaping at me with wet eyes, as if I were the Statue of Liberty. I passed him the bottle of vodka so that he might cheer up. Then a group of hooligans from Apacha screamed up in their battered sedan, disco blasting, apparently convinced we had come to the river to party. Obligingly, I passed around another bottle. Another hour ticked off the clock.

Sergei and the tayozhnik returned, followed in short order by a carload of RIVOD inspectors, blue lights flashing, replaced only a few minutes later by the militia, who sprang from their car patting their sidearms. Again, we passed the bottle.

Night was quickly falling. Just as I bent to hoist my duffel bag, a van rolled into the clearing and out flew a not unattractive woman in a tracksuit and designer eyeglasses. "I heard there was an American here!" she shouted breathlessly and, zeroing in, almost tackled me in her excitement. She dragged me back to the van and shoved me inside, where her three companions rolled their eyes with chagrin, handed me a plastic cup, and apologetically filled it with vodka. My abductor—Marguerite—knelt in front of me, her hands on my knees, babbling flirtatiously.

"What gives?" I said, utterly bewildered. She slipped a business card into my shirt pocket and pleaded that I allow her to represent me, refusing to hear my explanation that there was nothing to "represent." Okay, she said, let's do joint venture.

"Robert?" I heard Sergei calling me. They were ready to go, no more endless dicking around.

I tried to get up, but Marguerite pushed me back in my seat. I grabbed her hands, looked her in the eyes, and firmly declared, "I have to go fishing."

I lurched for the door, but she had me wrapped up. This couldn't be more bizarre, I told myself—until Marguerite began stuffing six-ounce cans of caviar into the pockets of my slicker. Okay, I said, if you want to come, fine, but I'm going fishing now. Marguerite relaxed just long enough for me to bolt out of the van, but there she was again, welded to my arm, attached to me in some frightening, unknowable way.

There was a quick, sharp exchange between her and the gnome, and the next I knew I was threading my way, alone and free, down the bluff through the darkening slope of stone birches. The air was warm, but when you inhaled it was the river you breathed, its mountain coldness, and I felt transcendently refreshed. Then we were all in the boat, sans Marguerite, shoving off into the main current of this perfect river, the Plotnikova, clean and fast and wild enough for any harried soul.

We were carried forward on a swift flow of silver light, stars brightening in the deep blue overhead. Then the light died on the river too, just as the tayozhnik beached the bow on the top end of a long gravel bar, bellying out into the stream. It was too late, too dark, to forge on to the hunter's camp, and I said fine. Sergei begged off again, said he'd be back to pick us up tomorrow, and I said fine to that too. Rinat and I threw our gear ashore, and I pushed the skiff back into the current and then stood there, the black cold water swirling around my waders, singing praise on high for the incredible fact of my deliverance. This river made noise; this river sang.

We dug out our flashlights and dragged our packs about a hundred yards up from the water's edge to the trunk of a huge tree ripped from the riverbank and washed onto the bar. Rinat collected wood for a campfire, and soon we squatted in a private dome of firelight, watching a pot of water boil for tea. I hadn't eaten all day, and my stomach growled.

"Rinat, where's the food?"

He cleared his throat and confessed he'd given everything to the Mafiya, mumbling some ridiculous explanation about the code of the wilderness.

"Where's my candy?"

"I gave it to the criminals."

"You gave the Mafiya my candy! They had their own candy."

"It was the least we could do," said Rinat, "since, you know, they didn't kill us when you hurt their ears with bad words."

We rocked into each other with laughter, howling at the absurdities we had endured together. Our assorted adventures, supernaturally screwed up and filled with hazard, were over but for one true and honest day of fishing, out on the sheer edge of a magnificent world, in a nation going to hell. I patted my pocket for cigarettes and discovered a tin of Marguerite's caviar, Rinat produced a hunk of brown bread, and we ate. He rolled out his sleeping mat and bag and tucked himself under the tree trunk. "Let me apologize in advance," I said, "if the bears come to eat you."

And in the morning, the fish—like the trees and the gravel bar, like the screaming birds and humming bottle flies, like the sun and its

187

petticoat of mists and everything else to be found in its rightful place—the fish were there. I had never seen anything remotely like it, the last days of an immense salmon run. What first struck me, as it hadn't last night, was the profound stench. The gravel island was carpeted with the carcasses of pink salmon—humpbacks—from the height of the run, one of the most concentrated runs in recent years, as if so many fish within its banks had made the river overflow. Now the slightest low spot on the island was pooled with rotting eggs where fish had spawned. Maggots were everywhere, a sprinkle of filthy snow across the rocks and mud and weeds, and dead fish everywhere, rimed with a crust of maggots. I slipped into my waders, walked down to the river through shoals of decomposing fish, and entered the water. Humpback salmon nosed my boots as they struggled wearily upstream; like the prows of sinking ships, the gasping jaws of debilitated male humpies poked out of the water as the fish drifted by, their milt spent, their energy spent, the last glimmer of life fading into the sweep of current. In the shallows, gulls sat atop spawned but still-living fish, tearing holes into the rosy flesh. Fish still fresh with purpose threw themselves into the air, I don't know why, but what I did know was that the salmon were bringing the infinite energy of the sea upriver, an intravenous delivery of nutrients funneling into the land, the animals, the insects and birdlife and the very trees.

Here, in a salmon, nature compressed the full breath of its expression, the terrible magnificence of its assault, and I stood in the current, mesmerized. On the far bank at the mouth of a tributary there were poachers. At first glance it seemed that they had built low bonfires on the opposite shore, the red flames licking and twisting, but where was the smoke? I wondered, and as I looked more deliberately I saw my mistake: The writhing flames were actually fish. One poacher worked at the base of the tall bank, poised like a heron above the stream, using a long staff to gaff salmon—females, hens—as they swam past and then flipping the fish overhead to a pile on the top of the bank, where his partner crouched, gutting out the roe.

When the spell broke, I sat down on a log and finally accomplished the one thing I had passionately desired to do for days, months, all my life: I rigged my fly rod for salmon fishing.

I decided to head down the bar to where the currents rejoined at the rapids below its downstream point, an eddy splitting off to create slack water. The island was probed by wayward, dead-end channels, trickling into basins where the sand had flooded out, and as I waded through the biggest pool scores of humpback salmon, coalesced into orgies of spawning, scurried before me in the foot-deep shallows like finned rats. In the deeper holes the season's last reds cruised lethargically in their scarlet and olive-green "wedding dresses," as the Kamchatkans call a fish's spawning colors. I sloshed onward to dry land, the fish gasping, the birds screaming, and everywhere the reek of creation.

On the tail of the bar I planted my feet in the muck and cast into a deep turquoise body of water that resembled nothing so much as an aquarium, waiting for the connection, that singular, ineffable tug that hooks a fisherman's hungry heart into whatever you want to call it—the spirit of the fish, the bigness of life or even the smallness, the euphoric, crazed brutality of existence, or simply a fight: the drama of the battle between man and his world. Not every cast, but most, ended with a fish on my hook, a glorious humpback, three to five pounds each, the hens painted in swaths of mulberry, green, and rose, the males beautifully grotesque with keel-like dorsal humps and hooked jaws like the beak of a raptor.

A day of humpies landed on flies here on this grand river was enough to quench my deepest craving for the sport, but then my rod bent from the pressure, the reel sang its lovely shrill song as the line escaped, and here came the silvers, big and angry, like bolts of electricity, filled with the power of the sea. Rinat finally joined me in this dance, and by the late afternoon, when Sergei and the tayozhnik returned, we had two fish apiece, the limit, silvers as long and fat as our thighs.

We gathered more wood, Rinat started the fire, and Sergei brought his cook pot from the boat. "I'm going to show you how to make a poachers' *ukhž*," said Sergei, cutting off the salmon heads and tails and sliding them into the boiling pot with diced potatoes and onion and dill. I had caught dozens of pinks but kept only one, a female, and Sergei slit her belly to make instant caviar, unsacking the eggs into a bowl of heavily salted water.

We sat in the gravel with our backs propped against the fallen tree and gazed lazily out at the fast blue dazzle of the river, slurping our fish soup. A raft floated down from around the bend, paddled by two RIVOD officers. The poachers on the opposite shore vanished into the forest, the wardens paddled furiously into the tributary, and we listened as the crack of gunshots resonated over the river, here in the Wild East.

Sergei, waxing philosophical, quoted a poet: "It's impossible to understand Russia, only to believe in it." Then he lifted a spoon of caviar to my lips, and I recalled the last fish I had caught that day, a hen, which had no business hitting my fly, ripe as she was. When I brought her from the water she sprayed a stream of roe, an arc in the air like a chain of ruby moons, splashing over my feet onto this most eternal, unsettled world of the river.

(1998)

Huevos Fritos

This is a small story, inhumanly cruel, and it ends with a terrible howl.

It takes place in a dark forest on the Kamchatka Peninsula in the Russian Far East, a place where parents in St. Petersburg threaten to send children if they misbehave, an inhospitable place known for exploding volcanoes, mosquitoes that swarm like hornets, and, most fearsomely, its bears. The story itself contains a cosmonaut, more grizzlies than anywhere else on earth, a criminally amused wife, and the unimaginable horror that befell its narrator, a hapless, pitiable soul named *Poor me*.

So. Let's get it over with.

I would make two long trips to Kamchatka to connect with the Russian mafia, who had, in their ever-inspiring entrepreneurial spirit, begun stealing entire rivers, netting runs of wild salmon, shipping tons of illegal caviar back to their associates in Moscow. Anyway, I took my wife along on the first trip though not the second. She was obsessed with catching one of Kamchatka's legendary monster rainbow trouts, something in the twenty-two-pound range. Which she did, a bona fide Grade Two worst-case scenario, which is why she was forbidden to go along with me on the second trip. Too much bragging.

She and I and Rinat, our local fixer, had an idle day before our expedition launched into the distant wild, so we decided to pile into Rinat's pickup truck for a day trip about an hour's ride north of

Petropavlovsk, the capital city, to a national park at the base of the Mount Fuji–like volcano that towered above the city. We had read about this park in a government-produced tourist brochure I had been given at the airport.

The road ended at a small cluster of clapboard dachas along the banks of a frothing river. The park headquarters, clearly marked on the brochure's map, did not exist, and the park itself, on the far side of the river, was what it had always been—a vast, dense spruce and birch forest, accessed by a shabby cable-and-plank footbridge or a shallow crossing for four-wheel-drive vehicles. Across the river we could see a few mushroom hunters prowling among the trees.

"Let's cross over and go for a hike," I suggested and my wife said sure and Rinat said absolutely not.

"We will absolutely be eaten by bears," Rinat declared, and settled into the truck to await the eventual recovery of our chewed-upon corpses.

Because this story also contains a six-ounce can of pepper spray stuffed into the left-front pocket of my jeans, I felt it was not irrational to be respectfully nonchalant about the bears.

My wife and I clambered across the rickety bridge and followed a path past a group of picnickers until we came to a primitive road leading deep into the sun-dappled forest. We hiked ahead, alone in the woods, enjoying the pristine solitude, until suddenly a rusty blue Soviet-era van appeared on the track behind us and stopped as it came alongside. The driver, a lean, blond-haired man, wagged his head at us, frowning, and said something in Russian that had the tone of an admonition. His wife and teenage son nodded their heads gravely, confirming the seriousness of whatever the man was saying.

We don't speak Russian, I said, shrugging, and the man switched to English.

Go back, he said. What are you doing here? Are you crazy? The bears will absolutely eat you. You cannot walk here without big gun, eh?

It's okay, I said. I have pepper spray.

You have pepper spray? he snorted. What for? To make bear cry before he absolutely eat you? Turn back now.

Thanks for the advice, I said, waving good-bye as they drove out of sight, shaking their heads in disbelief at our stupidity. Ten minutes later we came upon them again, parked in a glade off the side of the track, each with a carbine strapped on their shoulders, each carrying a bucket. The family stared at us as if we were the most foolish people they had ever had the misfortune to behold. Again, a lecture from the driver about our recklessness. Then he sighed and said, Okay, as long as you are here, come with us. They were cutting through the woods, crossing a river, then climbing up a short rise to a meadow where they were going to pick berries.

From this place, the driver said, you have excellent nice good view of volcano. I asked him where he learned English and he revealed he was a cosmonaut on vacation with his family.

We followed them through the forest for a few minutes until we came to a raging river spanned by a fallen tree, its wet trunk just wide enough to walk across, slowly, carefully, single-file. My wife looked at the white-water rapids below the log and said she wasn't doing it. The cosmonaut said, Come on, just up the top of bank you can see volcano. I said to my wife that I'd be right back.

On the opposite shore, I scrambled fifteen feet up the bank to a treeless plateau overgrown with brush so high it was impossible to see anything at all. Just ten more minutes, said the cosmonaut, but I knew I couldn't abandon my defenseless wife back on the other side of the river. I thanked the cosmonaut and his family for their hospitality and started back down the steep bank, checking my speed to keep from tumbling into the water. When I took a couple of steps out onto the log, I felt off balance and instinctively crouched to use my hands to steady myself. I have a permanent visual image branded into my memory that accompanies what happened next—my wife waiting for me on the far bank, her quizzical expression turning to wide-eyed, jaw-dropping astonishment as she watched me, poised above the river, rear up from my crouch in a roar, digging frantically into my pants pocket, pulling out an object that resembled a smoke grenade, and hurling it into the rapids.

Bending down to gain my balance as I had stepped onto the log, I had triggered the can of pepper spray in my pocket, its aerosol blast locked into an open position aimed direct at my crotch. Imagine a tiny jet engine in your boxer shorts. Imagine that engine throttled up to its white-hot after-burn. How to minister to such a grievous, potentially life-altering injury, how to relieve the suffering? Only the kindest, most generous and selfless nurse would have a clue.

When I finally stopped howling, my wife had trouble keeping a straight face, eyeing my wincing, bow-legged gait back through the forest. Perhaps something about watching a guy self-immolate his nuts brings out the mirth in women. I felt like I had just ridden a rhino bare-assed for thirty miles. My wife kept reminding me that the after-scent of pepper spray, once its stinging properties have faded, is a bear attractant, smelling much like an order from Taco Bell.

That would be one overcooked burrito with a side of huevos fritos.

(2010)

Greetings from
the Big Pineapple

Beyond the rooftops of the mansions of Miramar—once an aristocratic neighborhood and still an elite address—storm clouds scrape low over Havana. Columns of purple rain march through silenced barrios. Banks of steam erupt from the streets, wisps like puffs of smoke snagging in the treetops. It's the end of May, Cuba's rainy season has begun, and the ribs are showing on the emaciated body of the island's not-yet-middle-aged revolution. From the balcony of my hotel room, the first impression is hard to shake: Havana is a city at war, a city on a dire countdown, a city that understands it's about to be invaded.

Of course, it isn't, and won't be, not really—armed conflict is a chimera employed to focus the attention of revolution's children. But there are other kinds of invasions. Forsaken by his sugar daddy, the Soviet Union, Fidel Castro has singled out tourism for no-holds-barred development, dispatching a fun-in-the-sun strike force to bandage Cuba's hemorrhaging economy with hard currency stripped from a relatively toxic source: Western consumerist culture. WE DEFEND SOCIALISM BY DEVELOPING TOURISM, say the billboards. We need a miracle, says *El Jefe*, but what is he thinking, rolling out the red carpet for the capitalist hordes?

Even before we boarded the Ilyushin-18 in Cancún, I was experiencing a mild case of apprehension not entirely associated with being lifted into the air by a Soviet hand-me-down. Miami's Cuban-expatriate community had led us to expect the very worst: a cowed and sullen population, suspicious of one another, their lips glued by fear. An infrastructure in accelerating collapse. Overt loathing for yanqui imperialists, who had used the Gulf War as a dress rehearsal for satisfying Washington's longest-running grudge, the Cuba problem. Since the first of January, more than six hundred men and women had flung themselves into the Gulf Stream off Cuba's northern coast on inner tubes and makeshift rafts, the largest exodus of refugees since the Mariel boatlift in 1980. Word on the street in Havana had it that only one out of every hundred who attempted this desperate adventure made it to the shopping malls of southern Florida alive. The Cuban word for these people was *escoria*, "scum."

Cuba, always forced by its two-crop economy of sugar and tobacco to export everything it produced, could no longer afford to import the basics. The twenty-eight-year-old US trade embargo was squeezing the island harder than ever, causing already short supplies of food and medicine to dwindle. In Miami, scholars who had traveled to Havana for an academic conference advised me to pack soap and coffee as gifts. Don't plan on renting a car, they warned—the gas pumps had run dry, and Fidel had proclaimed 1991 the Year of the Bicycle. As dictated by the US State Department in its paradoxical wisdom, American tourists were free to travel to Cuba, but spending money while there was illegal, good for a $250,000 fine and up to twelve repentant years in jail.

Cuba, the Big Pineapple, seemed a Dantesque hellhole, and I couldn't imagine what sort of reception awaited us at Havana's José Martí International Airport, especially considering that we—the Professor, Caputo the paparazzo, and I—had tired of waiting for Havana to grant us proper visas and decided to slip into the country by way of the back door, Mexico. The State Department would no doubt have taken exception to our plan, but there was no time to waste. We were on our way to observe the forty-first Ernest Hemingway International Billfish Tournament—one of the oldest billfishing competitions in the world. North American anglers, for the first time in years, had found a way to participate in this most prestigious event, dropping bait into the socialist sea. We figured to wet a line, then travel the length of the island from Havana eastward to the beaches and freshly painted facades of the *turista* archipelago of the north coast, then to the mountains, the Sierra Maestra, where it had all started, where a young university student/gang member/lawyer/baseball pitcher had decided that it was time to take paradise off the market, choosing instead the course of ultimate adventure, the Everest of political endeavor, revolution.

So it was that the day before the tournament was to end, we boarded an Air Cubana flight out of Cancún sobered by the caveat of the agent behind the counter. Protect yourself from your government, she advised; don't have your passports stamped in Havana. After a seemingly endless delay our flight was called, and we were bused to an isolated corner of the tarmac to board an ancient Soviet-made flying steam-bath. The cabin thundered with the noise of the Ilyushin's four propellers. Minutes later we listened in dread as the engines were cut one by one, delivering us into a terrible silence. The flight crew abandoned the cockpit, mopping cascades of sweat from their brows, muttering about electrical failure.

Sitting in front of us, a trio of extremely merry Mexicans, undaunted by the drama, appointed themselves social directors. "Don't worry," the most extroverted muchacho declared grandiosely. "Everything's under control." They passed around a calming bottle of tequila. "We are making a study of Cuban girls," explained their point man. His two companions nodded wolfishly. "We are very concerned about our addiction to these girls, and have decided to analyze the situation further." This news cheered the Professor, who admired their academic spirit. By and by the electrical failure was repaired, the brave pilots returned, the engines cranked over, and we began to lumber down the runway. "Go, go, go," chanted the muchachos, rocking in their seats as if we were puttering up the hill in a Volkswagen.

"Well," observed the Professor, plumbing the bright side of the delay, "at least we got a sauna out of it." As we reached altitude, it began to snow inside the plane, icy flakes blowing out of the air vent onto Caputo, who took the change of weather in stride. Cuba, after all, was the home of magical realism.

Once on the ground, we queued in front of the immigration booths, anxious and humble, and advanced together like three lost lambs. The official who examined our passports unsettled us profoundly: I can't say we ever quite recovered. She was young and lovely, and she flirted with us—sweet chat and welcoming smiles. We cleared customs without the agents displaying the slightest interest in our gear.

"This siege mentality," said the Professor, "is going to wear us down fast."

How clever of these die-hard Marxist-Leninists, I thought, to lull us like that, but surely the charade would end once they were confronted with the boys from Mexico City, three horny, half-drunk, and totally irreverent specimens of the type border guards love to turn away. If Cuba accepted the muchachos, then the place was wide open.

We pushed through the terminal doors into a muggy, overcast afternoon. There were the Mexicans. Their leader ambled over to us, all mischievous eyes and conspiratorial grin, wagging his finger as if we were the naughty ones.

"Sooner or later," he crowed, "we knew you were going to come." Someone had just told him we were North American tourists.

In the beginning was the word, and the word was Ernesto himself, the progenitor of the marlin tournament, and an honorary god in the Cuban pantheon of machismo. Off and on throughout the 1930s, Hemingway leased room 511 at the Hotel Ambos Mundos, conveniently around the corner from La Bodeguita del Medio—a bar crazy enough to let writers drink on credit—and a ten-minute wobble from a more sophisticated watering hole, El Floridita. Papa found Cuba a resourceful environment to pursue his three addictions—writing, billfishing, and boozing—and he immortalized each pursuit. His alcohol-infused wisdom still adorns the wall above the bar in La B del M—MY MOJITO [a rum-based mint julep] EN LA BODEGUITA, MY DAIQUIRI EN EL FLORIDITA.

In 1934 Hemingway commissioned a Brooklyn boatyard to build the *Pilar*, his legendary thirty-eight-foot marlin hunter. Five years later, a fifteen-acre farm south of Havana caught the eye of Hemingway's third wife; they rented the Finca Vigía, and Hemingway spent much of the next two decades there, purchasing the place in 1940 with his first royalty check from *For Whom the Bell Tolls*. By 1950 Hemingway's own ascent to fame paralleled Havana's burgeoning notoriety as the New World's most decadent amusement park, a saturnalia orchestrated by Cuba's corrupt military dictator, Fulgencio Batista. Batista's Babylon offered a standard buffet of sin—prostitutes, drugs, gambling at mafia-owned casinos, live sex shows at the seedier nightclubs, and a more restrained extravaganza of tits and ass at the dazzling Tropicana—and well-heeled tourists poured onto the island to be thrilled by the wicked ambience. Down at the Finca Vigía, Hemingway finally figured out what to do with all of his wealthy friends, the celebrities and playboys, the hunting buddies and would-be heroes who kept circling through Havana. He herded them into a bona fide fishing tournament.

There's a fascinating photograph, shot from the bridge of a sport-fishing boat on the event's tenth anniversary in May 1960: a young Fidel Castro is hunkered over Che Guevara, who sits in the fighting chair; two lines are in the water, but Che's legs are stretched out, his booted feet rest on the transom, and he's reading a book. Hemingway had invited Castro as his guest of honor, hoping to convince the charismatic warrior, who seemed permanently attired in olive fatigues and combat boots, to present the winner's trophy. But Castro himself, the luckiest man in Cuban history, won the tournament, hooking and boating the largest marlin.

There's a second photograph: Hemingway and Fidel, *macho a macho*, beaming, Papa surrendering the trophy: two men who helped define their times. They had never met before and never would again. That day Hemingway rode the *Pilar* out into the Gulf Stream for the last time; soon he would leave Cuba for good and go to Idaho, where a year later he would commit suicide. That same year, 1961, his tournament disappeared behind an iron curtain of ill will manufactured by uncompromising ideologies. There were far worse casualties, to be sure, but once Hemingway came ashore off the *Pilar*, no other North American boat would participate in his tournament for three decades. Not until a good-natured, tenacious, fish-crazed, egomaniacal heart surgeon from New Jersey chutzpahed his way onto the scene.

"The Americans are in a position to win this tournament," Dr. David Bregman proclaims as we breakfast with him on Saturday, the final day of the competition. The Cubans at the table suppress laughter. The US team—three boats from New Jersey, two from Florida, one from Maryland—have managed a paltry two fish between them even though the action has been hot thus far. Naturally, since the Cubans know the fishing grounds, a Cuban boat is in first place, and two Mexican boats are not far behind. But in the end, the Hemingway tournament is no more Cuban than an international bankers' convention in Miami Beach. The theme is Cuban, the stage set is neo-Floridian, and far below the surface creak the worn-down gears of everyday Cuban life. But the tournament unravels somewhere else.

Over eggs, the Professor, Caputo, and I receive our sailing orders. The three of us will ride out with Doc aboard his forty-eight-foot Viking, the *Heart Mender*. We will observe to our hearts' content, but Doc will attend to any fishing—after all, he reminds us, it's his boat. As the last Cubans drift out of the dining room, Doc snatches a platter of sliced pineapple off the serving table and foists it upon the Professor.

"Quick," Doc urges, "don't let them see you." He requisitions two more platters—cold cuts and watermelon—and, chuckling, he and the Professor make a mad dash for the rental car. Clearly, Doc and his crew are having a splendid time.

"My Spanish is great," explains Doc as we rocket past the police checkpoint at the landward entrance to the marina, barreling toward a gas pump at the back of a gravel lot. We slide to a halt just before we hit the attendant. "I took a couple of years in school and—it's amazing—it's all coming back to me. *'Donde is el gasoline?'*" he queries the pump jockey, who shrugs his shoulders, and off we speed at an alarming velocity toward the *Heart Mender*, the first US registered vessel to enter Cuban waters legally (except for the Mariel boatlift, which doesn't count) since the early years of the revolution. It's almost nine a.m.—starting time—and Doc is in the mood for battle.

On the way out the channel, we split a flotilla of kayakers, the Cuban Olympic team in training. At the marina's headland, the captain opens up the engines, but no sooner does the boat plane, it seems, than he throttles back to trolling speed. The mates ease six lines into the water. We're only a quarter-mile offshore and the depth sounder reads 1,000 feet; another four hundred yards out and the bottom drops to 6,000 feet. And yet we can see people walking onshore. It's like hunting elk in the suburbs.

I retire with our host and the Professor into the boat's swank, air-conditioned salon, and without much prodding Doc launches into a soliloquy on the two subjects he finds most praiseworthy: himself and fishing. It so happens that after he coinvented the intra-aortic balloon pump in 1969, he became a brain in demand, addressing international medical conferences and training surgeons in the Soviet Union and China. In 1989 the Cuban government wanted to enroll his expertise and asked him to be one of the headliners at a national medical conference. Doc said he would if he could bring his boat from Key West and fish. The Cubans thought about it and said, why not? The US State Department said no. But Doc had once operated on Armand Hammer's brother, and . . .

"Doc!" both mates holler simultaneously—the divine interruption. Doc bolts from his seat. It's nine fifteen, and the *Heart Mender* is hooked up, the unlikely champion Dr. Bregman on center stage, a fighting belt strapped around his sizable waist.

The first mate spikes the rod into the holder above Doc's groin, creating a literal connection between the fisherman's masculinity and the furious instinct of the unseen beast. "Tip up," coaches the captain from the bridge. "Let him dive." This is a kill tournament; there'll be no cavalier tag and release. Sweat pours down Doc's torso as he bows forward and reels back, bows and reels. After five or six minutes the beast rises, blasting through the indigo surface, its bill parrying the lethal air. It's a marlin, a stand-up blue big enough to take the trophy, and it dances with magnificent rage for fifty feet or more, the iron-black sword of its bill slashing the Havana skyline.

After twenty minutes, the fish is just off the transom, ready to boat, panting as it lies twisted on its side in the transparent seas, one fierce eye condemning the world above. The mate extends the gaff over the side, maneuvering for the right mark, the perfect moment. Then the marlin spits the hook. With cool contempt he throws the line into Doc's face and is gone, leaving us a silenced, awestruck crew. Doc hands the rod to his mate, accepting the loss with grace.

"A brave fish," he declares in fluent Hemingwayese. He unbuckles the plastic belt, tosses his baseball cap aside, and retreats to the comfort of the chilly salon, dismissing his crew's efforts to console him. He plops down on the couch, the good sport, reflective, storing away the memory.

"Did I have on my red hat or my orange one?" he asks. "I'm a very colorful figure." With a tiny smile of satisfaction, he speculates that a year's maintenance on the *Heart Mender* comes to about twice the Professor's salary.

From the beginning, the Professor offers a dissenting viewpoint to our initial impression of Havana. "No, no, no, senor," he says, which is the extent of his involvement with the Spanish language. What he sees from the balcony is not the city's imminent disassemblage but something on the order of an exotic passion permanently flaunting the edges of self-destruction, semiferal but with a hip intensity, sidling up to disaster and then fluttering away, a city like a Latin woman, beautiful but exhausted, dancing through the perfumed night with a gun in her hand.

We mobilize for an assault on the city's ambiguous appearances, walking first to the Plaza de la Revolución, a vast open space resembling the Mall in D.C. but dropped into the middle of a massive empty parking lot in a tropical Newark. To one side sits a reviewing stand made of white stone, with a marble podium facing out on a macadam lot, its field of telephone poles wired with spotlights and loudspeakers. Here Fidel enacted, in the early days of the revolution, his "democracy of the people," tutoring the masses for hours on end, haranguing them like a fire-and-brimstone preacher, making them laugh like a stand-up comic, building them up to whatever emotional pitch the day's challenges required, until—and this is the vital and democratic part of the ritual—they shouted back to the Maximum Leader in unison: Okay, have it your way, *Jefe*, we want to go home. If you've seen televangelists browbeating an audience, you won't be shocked to learn that this system works, more or less, nor will you be thunderstruck to hear that all domiciles throughout Cuba's cities and countryside, even the humblest shacks—have antennas on their roofs and, down below, old black-and-whites burning blue through the evening hours.

We stroll into Old Havana down narrow cobbled alleys eerily Neapolitan, though Havana's streets are by far the more tranquil and nonthreatening of any I have walked in the Latin diaspora. Urchins flutter around us hoping for Chiclets, but by Monday they'll be uniformed and back in school. In the stone-paved Plaza de la Catedral, a man approaches me, asking for a cigarette. He wants a light, then the lighter, and though I give it to him I take it back, since I have no other and Cuba is out of matches. He gasps when I say we are from the States. North Americans, rare as pots of gold—he loves them, hates Castro.

"Life is very bad in Cuba."

"If you say so," I say, but in truth he looks no worse off than his blue-collar counterpart in Miami. If he had been in Mexico City or Port-au-Prince, or Lima, or Kingston, if he had a context in which to place his misery, perhaps he wouldn't be so quick to claim it. What is absent in his denunciation, what is absent throughout Havana, is the dead tone that marks deep suffering and despair.

Like so many others, my new friend wants to change money, my dollars for his useless pesos. With dollars, a habanero can supplement his government rations—one shirt, one pair of pants, one pair of shoes a year; one pound of meat, five pounds of rice each month—with goods from the astronomically expensive black market. Illegal, of course, but Cubans are being forced by shortages and the government's rigidity to turn themselves into hustlers and sneaks.

Undaunted by my refusal, the fellow offers to sell me cigars—Cohibas, the best—at half the price of the tourist shops. When I don't say no, he suggests we walk down Empedrado, a street as old as the New World, to La Bodeguita del Medio and negotiate over a drink. The Bodeguita is just opening its doors, but already a crowd has assembled outside the establishment, a joint instantly recognizable as one of the solar system's last repositories of cool, a neighborhood hangout with global traffic, a place where dialectics and rum fuse into a collective, joyous, cacophonous blur. Behind the counter two bartenders manufacture endless *mojitos*, twenty at a time, for the relentless tide of thirsty *turistas* who churn through, sweeping in and sweeping out, glancing cross-eyed at the ubiquitous graffiti and taking deep dizzying whiffs of the proletarian smells of bohemian Cuba. Across the street, three plainclothes police officers stand like statuary, arms folded, glowering at the escalating euphoria.

My new friend displays a tremendous appreciation for both rum and drama. "Let's get the cigars," he stage-whispers repeatedly, peering anxiously toward the door. The bartender has adopted Caputo, challenging him with free *mojitos* in exchange for baseball updates. The

Professor sponsors English lessons for two saucy dreamettes who are instructing him in a language of their own: Cognac, they say; champagne. "The cigars, let's go," my friend mumbles. I nod and we're out the door, he walking a half block in front, broadcasting guilt, cringing in posture, the worst black marketeer I've ever encountered. I feel like arresting him myself.

Down Old Havana's strange and marvelous streets I follow him until he ducks into a made-to-order shadowy portal, the arched entrance to a decrepit palace divided long ago into apartments. We ascend a marble staircase, right-angling up through medieval space, musty and decomposing. Sensing our arrival, an old woman, his mother, opens the door. Only a television set places the apartment in any world I know; otherwise, the precise honey-colored shafts of light, the glassless windows, the crumbling textures and bare furniture, the provisional quality of its humanity are, in their extremeness, too unfamiliar for me to recognize except as Hollywood augury.

The deal takes less than a minute. The seller needs dollars; as a skilled tradesman he earns 200 pesos a month—the price of shoes on the black market. The buyer—well, the buyer doesn't need, doesn't even like cigars. The buyer is simply seduced. The buyer finds official Cuba enigmatic, the image formulaic, but how easily and swiftly the rhetorical veneer is scratched and another secret revealed. Bedding Cuba: The historical precedents are countless, large scale and small; it's a North American tradition. Scruples barely make it as a footnote, a tiresome annotation. I zip the wooden box of cigars into my knapsack, and, warned by the dealer's mother to be careful, we return to the Bodeguita, where silence and fear are obsolete.

The question of whether or not we will be able to drive the 780-mile length of this apparently gasless island is resolved the following morning, thanks to Abraham Maciques, the president of Cubanacan, to whom Dr. Bregman had introduced us at the tournament. Cubanacan is the muscle behind Castro's tourist trade, an autonomous government agency not unlike a corporation, free to engage in multinational commerce, free to invest, free to be profitable, free to construct a second society, albeit a ravenously capitalistic and exclusive society—onto but separate from the old system, all in hopes of keeping the revolution solvent. When I inquired if there might be a way to help us secure fuel in the hinterlands, Maciques said not to worry, that he'd have someone take care of us.

By noon we've been provided with a van, a burly middle-aged driver named Eric, and Roberto, a young mustachioed rake of a guide whose services we at first decline, not wanting to be chained to some ideologically rabid government minder.

"Give me a chance," Roberto says with pained sincerity. "You're my first Americans." I ask him if he thinks his country will survive what Castro is calling this "special period."

Who knows? he says with body language, looking untroubled. "The future is the future."

"And right around the corner," I add, "seeing as you're catching on to capitalism so nicely."

"Ah!" says Roberto, touching my elbow lightly, and again with each of his exclamations. "Karl Marx says to take what you can of your enemy's good points and use them for yourself."

"That's not how my mom told me to run a revolution."

"What—your mother?"

"It's a little joke."

"Okay, good, I like the North American sense of humor. But listen," he says, tapping my arm in a brotherly way, "we are very aware of the dangers of tourism and how careful we must be to maintain the principles of the Triumph of the Revolution."

Our van is appointed with a cooler full of juice, cola, and Hatuey beer on ice, with several cases of beverages packed in reserve, including a crate of seven-year-old Havana Club rum. "If we need a little drink," says Eric. With his thick book of gas coupons, we appear adequately outfitted for a Homeric ten-day binge, if nothing else.

As we head east out of Havana I ask Eric to sidetrack off the main highway to the fishing village of Cojimar, home port of Gregorio Fuentes, the now-ancient captain of Hemingway's *Pilar*. As we draw close, the land begins to roll a bit, its soft hills lined with cottages not unlike the conch houses and art-deco bungalows of the Florida Keys. We stop at the turquoise cove where once the *Pilar* was the undisputed queen of the fleet. A small austere park pays tribute to Cojimar's most illustrious friend and patron. After the village heard of Hemingway's death, every fisherman donated a brass fitting off his boat, and the collection was melted down to create the bust of the writer that stands watch over the quay.

We locate Gregorio's modest house, and he invites us to crowd into his living room. Throughout the last thirty years, he has been harassed by curiosity seekers and schemers, but now it seems everyone believes he is dead, and he lives in the isolation he has always sought. Still, he appears pleased for the chance to unscroll the past once more, remarking that it might be his last opportunity, and he talks for hours in firm and measured speech, the incarnation of Hemingway's protagonist in *The Old Man and the Sea*, though the writer couldn't have had any idea back in 1931 that his true subject, twenty years later, would be Gregorio himself, stepping transcendently into the portrait:

> The old man was thin and gaunt with deep wrinkles in the back of his neck. The brown blotches of the benevolent skin cancer the sun brings from its reflection on the tropic sea were on his cheeks. . . . Everything about him was old except his eyes and they were the same color as the sea and were cheerful and undefeated.

From 1935 to 1960 the two men were in many ways inseparable. During World War II they patrolled the coast for German U-boats; during the struggle against Batista, Gregorio tells us, he and Hemingway kept an eye on the local waters to assist Castro and his rebel armies. Hemingway even took Gregorio to Africa to hunt lions.

"Hemingway is the only North American in the world for me," Gregorio says, sitting erect in his chair. He wears a wristwatch with a marlin on its face, though he hasn't fished since saying good-bye to the man he still refers to as Papa.

"Before he died," says Gregorio, "he made his last will and left me a document to hand to Fidel Castro. I was called by Fidel to read the testament, and everything, all Hemingway's property, was for the revolution, but the yacht and the fishing equipment were for me. Fidel said to me, 'When you get tired of the yacht, bring it to me.' And I answered, 'I'll never be tired of it.' After that, many bullshitters came to this house to try to get the *Pilar*, and they left the house in silence. That's why Hemingway chose me to work with him, because I understand things. I want to avoid people who think I should get money from my relationship with Hemingway. I can walk anywhere."

In six weeks, Gregorio will be ninety-three years old, and Hemingway, were he alive, would turn ninety-two eleven days later. They used to celebrate their birthdays together, sharing dinner and a bottle of whiskey on both dates.

"After Hemingway died," Gregorio says, "I maintained the tradition on his birthday. I would go down to his statue by the harbor. I would have one drink of whiskey for myself, and Hemingway's I pour on his head. But I haven't done it for years, because you can't find whiskey anymore in Cuba."

I say I will bring him a bottle—the tourist shops are well stocked. He gives me an *abrazo*, an embrace, and we leave the old captain to puff on his cigar in solitude, bound to the myths he had helped create.

The afternoon wanes; the light on the sea is harsh and tiring as we motor along the pastoral coastal highway toward the resort beaches of the narrow peninsula called Varadero. We pass a coastline too plain for a postcard, strung with clusters of plebian bungalows or dreary cement-block hotels, catering to the domestic trade mostly by means of work bonuses and incentives. Then the shore turns ugly, carpeted with spiky sisal plantations, shelved with razor-sharp ironrock at the water's edge, and punctured by filthy oil wells, Cuba's own Saudi Arabia. Whatever riches lie underground, Cuba seems desperate to suck them forth. Varadero, meanwhile, is presiding over its own oil boom, the kind associated with suntans. On one of the longest (twelve miles), most user-friendly beaches in the Caribbean, every business conglomerate in the industrialized world (except the United States) is vying to see which can build the plushest hotel fastest and cheapest. The French, the Germans, the Spanish, the Italians, even the Jamaicans are building here.

We pull into the drive of a swank, four-star compound, Hotel Tuxpan, a bewildering temple to the gods of generic pleasures. The price is peanuts—half of what it would cost elsewhere for identical accommodations adjoining similar splendors—but it's too expensive in concept, too immoderate in sensibility, for yeoman travelers like us, so tropo-cosmo that it has inflated itself right off the map, out of the Cuban landscape and into an artificial capsule of brochures and charter jet packages, its character now as universally digestible as baby formula.

Over the lobby's pipes, Sinatra sings, "I did it my way," as we check in. I feel hostile, an agent provocateur, more so when Roberto and Eric say that they will be leaving us for the night, since as Cubans they are barred from staying at a Varadero resort. "Tourism apartheid" is what the people call it. Roberto reasons with us to understand, but the fact remains. They are, in theory and in practice, second-class citizens in Cuba's new order.

The Tuxpan is owned fifty-fifty by Cubanacan and a group of Spanish investors, was constructed by Mexicans, and is operated by Germans; Cubanacan retains the supply contract for itself. Five of its staff of 213 are foreigners, and except for a Belgian entertainment director, each foreigner has trained a Cuban understudy who will someday inherit his or her respective position: manager, chef, housekeeper, bookkeeper. The system works: Cuban tourism has one of the best reputations on the European market and the Tuxpan is humming along at 95 percent occupancy in season. "In Varadero," Roberto notes ingeniously, "you see new things every day. You might ask yourself, 'Is it Cuba?'" The answer is unfortunately obvious.

The night sparkles with the gas flares of the oil-drilling platforms across the water. We venture to the disco, where we find the hotel manager, an ebullient, shock-haired Irishman named Eamonn Donnelly, hunkered down in the blast, a giant music disco projected above a dismally empty dance floor. "You can't really get a discotheque off the ground with only twenty-eight German guests," Eamonn shouts through the music. He's pressing to have Cuban locals authorized to come in on weekends, because they're the only ones who could breathe life into the place.

"I can't take any more irony," Caputo screams over the music. "The Cubans are trying to keep the Cubans out. The Irish are trying to get them in."

Cuba has 289 beaches set like diamonds in its twenty-five hundred miles of coastline, and three rugged mountain ranges utterly compelling in their beauty. But unless you're near the shore or around the sierras, Cuba's topography is dominated by its *llanos,* its flatlands, which seem to stretch forever, level as a gridiron and just as parceled out, one agricultural co-op after another. Mile after mile on our way south to Bahía de Cochinos, Bay of Pigs, we watch sugarcane fields and malanga farms pass like continuous yawns, the geography as monotonously fecund as South Florida's, the distant ridges sentineled by royal palms.

From the tourist town of Guamá, where Fidel headquartered himself in an old sugar mill and commanded the counterattack during the Bay of Pigs invasion, the road narrows through mangrove swamp and thick palmetto-scrub forest, the pavement in fluid motion with thousands of insect-size land crabs, their shells black and their legs vermilion, crunching under the tires. As we near Playa Larga, the beach at the top of the bay, solemn concrete monuments rise from the bush, intermittently at first, then with greater density. They honor Castro's troops, 161 killed in action, and they stand where the soldiers fell during the three-day battle in April 1961. Some fifteen hundred Cuban exiles, sponsored by the CIA, were defeated in their attempt to invade the island, and that was the end of diplomatic relations between Cuba and the United States.

"This is a most beautiful place, yes?" Eric observes, with such serene feeling that I turn to look at him. His feeling can only be echoed. The bay, rectangular like an Olympic swimming pool, its waters equally blue, is majestic, and Castro was correct, I think, to turn a place so rich in nature yet so polluted with bitterness into a tourist haven. "Yes, I love the beaches here. I love the water—it's very pretty," Eric continues, something peculiar in his tone.

We drive on toward Playa Girón at the mouth of the bay, where some of the worst fighting took place. We park beneath a billboard PLAYA GIRÓN—THE FIRST ROUT OF IMPERIALISM IN LATIN AMERICA.

"I was with them," Eric reveals matter-of-factly. We stop. "I was a nineteen-year-old student when the invasion happened. I came with the militia brought by Fidel to the final battle. Here, right here." Afterward he had helped guard the captured men. "Yes," he laughs softly, without malice or regret, "I became a major in the air force, but I'm retired now." He fishes out his wallet to show us his identity card—a younger Eric in an officer's uniform, someone who has found thirty years sufficient to quell the hatred, if not the sorrow, no matter what his allegiance.

Eric decides to remain in the van while we tour the museum of the battle with Roberto, whose own father had been tortured by Batista's army before escaping to fight in the Sierra del Escambray. We stroll quietly among the photographs and dioramas, the flags and thirty-year-old weapons, the carefully preserved detritus of the revolutionary process. Eric, meanwhile, has lowered his seat back and is listening to the radio, an old warrior absorbing new music, hearing a new beat.

*　　*　　*

As fast as possible, we speed through the visually tedious province of Ciego de Avila, numbed by its unbroken succession of cane plantations, pineapple farms, banana groves, and citrus orchards, though the air is fresh with Cuba's omnipresent smell of jasmine. We cross into the province of Camagüey, Cuba's largest, where sugar remains king but cows and cowboys register a more poignant effect on lifestyle. Daily flights from Havana bring *turistas* to the city of Camagüey, from there the pale hordes are bused to the encampments at Playa Santa Lucia, and our own destination for the day, three miles of secluded sand and a staging area for access to Cuba's northern archipelago—thousands of keys and sandbars spread over hundreds of miles, most deserted, many unexplored, connected by an underwater system of reefs dwarfing its counterpart to the north and second in size, we are told, only to Australia's Great Barrier Reef. No one has to tell us that those translucent waters provide some of the last unspoiled snorkeling and diving in the hemisphere. At least we could bless the revolution for that, the gift of obscurity to a utopia of coral.

The following day, after a morning dive through coral fields prolific with game fish and lobsters, we leave Santa Lucia pronto to make it to Santiago de Cuba, on the southeast coast, before nightfall. As twilight paints the countryside, we begin to carve our way through the valleys of the Sierra Maestra, the birthplace of Cuban independence and, in the following century, revolution. In 1956, returning from a one-year exile in Mexico, Castro, his brother Raul, and the young asthmatic Argentinean doctor Che Guevara, with seventy-nine other men, were shipwrecked west of Santiago de Cuba and battled their way up into the seemingly impenetrable peaks of the Sierra.

"We identified so completely with the natural surroundings of the mountains," Fidel later recalled to biographer Tad Szulc. "We adapted so well that we felt in our natural habitat. It was not easy, but I think we identified with the forest as much as the wild animals that live there."

Castro's strategy, to nibble away and demoralize his foes, triumphed, but the one enduring mistake he made was to allow himself to become obsessed with the United States. After Batista's aircraft raided a rebel base in the mountains, dropping US-supplied bombs, Castro wrote to a friend:

> I have sworn that the Americans will pay very dearly for what they are doing. When this war has ended, a much bigger and greater war will start for me, a war I shall launch against them. I realize that this will be my true destiny.

It was. Four years later, Kennedy positioned a naval blockade around the island, and Castro brought the world to the brink of nuclear holocaust during the Cuban Missile Crisis, securing his nation's place as one of the pariahs of modern times.

We reach the end of the line, Santiago de Cuba, after nightfall, yet even in darkness it's clear that this is a city surviving on finesse and brinkmanship. The municipality is plagued by a breakdown in its water service; when we check into the Hotel Versailles the taps run, more or less, but stop for good by midnight. The hotel's extensive menu has been reduced to three stewy dishes, and there's no bottled water, though you can drink Miller beer out of the can. There are no cigarettes, no cigars, no medicine, few buses, yet despite the comprehensive crunch, Santiago, Cuba's Hero City, "the cradle of the revolution," is not brittle but resilient. Most of the citizenry appears to be in the streets, celebrating the annual Caribbean music festival.

The day's journey has turned into a grueling marathon, and we have become slap-happy, proposing to our Cuban friends a revolutionary theme park, Fidel Land—in the Sierra Maestra, a roadside attraction for the charter-package hordes that would one day overrun the island. It's a blasphemous tease, and after we stop howling, we apologize, because you don't have to respect a government to respect or fall in love with a country and its people.

Our plan is to spend the night in Santiago de Cuba and then to have the eternally amenable Eric haul our penitent yanqui selves sixty miles toward the western coast and 6,476-foot Pico Turquino, Cuba's highest mountain and a revolutionary shrine. We ask Roberto about the possibility of procuring supplies—food and water—for the climb.

"No problem," he says, which, in a country that has so many problems, is the phrase most spoken. Soon, however, we're ensnared by the hotel's cabaret, the canopy of trees sprinkling us with flowers knocked off their stems by the vibrations of M.C. Hammer on the sound system, and Roberto, a third rum collins in his hand, seems to be smitten by one of the women in the chorus line. I retire around midnight, in the sobering knowledge that we'll be ill prepared to climb anything higher than a porch stoop.

In the morning, as we load the van, squalls bruise the southern horizon. Roberto, bleary-eyed and disheveled, shuffles from his room to the parking lot, an expression of relief brightening his sleepy face.

"Hey, what'd I tell you *locos*, you can't climb El Pico during the rainy season."

We'll do the drive anyway, I tell him, and maybe the weather will clear up by the time we get to the mountain's base. We're Heroes of Tourism, I say, so we have to try, even though Roberto has not kept his promise and we will be hiking all day on empty stomachs.

The coastline is a geologic symphony, the 1812 Overture: the mountains crescendoing with spectacular force into cushiony mulberry clouds; the muscular flanks of the range, thickly wooded and sheer, diving straight into a booming sea; bolts of lightning punctuating the drama off in the direction of Haiti, two hundred miles to the southeast. The road snakes around paradisiacal bays and harbors, each with its rustic fishing village. On occasion the pavement ends where the interface of mountain and sea is too radical to prevent the roadway from washing out during tempests.

We reach the trailhead, finally, after endless delays manufactured by Roberto, who seems to be stalling, unwilling to confront the mountain. Into his water bottle the Professor pours a nauseating mix of Tropi-Cola and energy crystals. I fill mine with all the juice remaining in the cooler and stuff it into my day pack along with my raincoat and a half liter of bottled water. Caputo is married to his sixty pounds of camera gear, but there's nothing else to carry anyway. Behind us, the sea thunders; in front of us, so do the mountains, their tops swaddled in ominous clouds. Suddenly, there's a crack in the overcast and sunlight shoots through. "I'm coming with you," says Roberto. "I'm a Cuban. It's my duty."

We file out of the van and up the first foothill, where we wait for Roberto to catch up. He's sweating and puffing and looks ready to be taken away on a gurney.

"Okay, I'm not Che," he says. "I cannot be a guerrilla. Well, maybe in the city." He walks back down to sleep in the van.

On we push, through the low pastures and scrub. Horses gallop away from us along forest paths; the bells of goats chime in the distance. The sun blazes down on us now, and after an hour we've consumed most of our liquids and the crows have begun to laugh at us.

A few years before the revolution, Celia Sánchez, one of Castro's original confidantes, hiked up Turquino with her liberal-minded father to install a bust of José Martí, the father of Cuban independence. They dreamed that one day his spirit would inspire Cuban patriots to fight the shameful injustices that plagued the nation. If Martí was Cuba's George Washington, few people outside the country were willing to grant that Fidel Castro was its Abraham Lincoln, but there he was anyway, by 1957 in control of an ever-expanding area in the sierra the guerrillas called the "Free Territory." In April of that same year, Celia Sánchez guided a CBS News crew up Pico Turquino to film an interview with Castro in front of the bust. Though he lived in the sierra, Castro had never climbed El Pico, and Che Guevara recalled later that Fidel took a pocket altimeter with him and checked it on the summit to verify that the peak was as high as the maps indicated. The point being, wrote Tad Szulc, that Castro never trusted anybody or anything. I, on the other hand, am willing to believe that the motivation that brought us three Americans to this mountain had something vaguely to do with trust. Then again, maybe this is a misguided and naive notion, maybe this is why we are doomed not to make it to the top, although our parched throats, our hunger, our late start, and the cold rain that has transformed the footpath into a river have contributed to our failure as well. After five hours of rugged climbing, we're above 4,000 feet and tuckered out, sucking raindrops off broad jungle leaves. Ahead of us we can see a faint indentation in the tree line on the mountain's flank, implying a path that cuts a merciless diagonal through woodlands as dense as Borneo's. And beyond, still impacted in clouds and still higher, looms the summit and the bust of José Martí.

It is time to turn back, we all agree, to head down to repose with rebel daiquiris in our hand and make our pal Roberto Cuba's first Martyr of Tourism.

Back in Santiago we walk toward the plaza through a gauntlet of hospitality, deciding to have our dinner on the terrace of the Hotel Casa Grande, an establishment so magnificent in its squalor that it seems born out of an opium smoker's vision, real only by virtue of a technicality. It will soon be closed for renovation.

A guy at the door checks credentials, but the cream of the Cuban crop circulates at will, and we take the last table among a noisy scene of TV crews, politicians, poets, musicians, foreigners, and apparatchiks. Roberto and Eric, delayed by the quest for gasoline, aren't here yet. Again, as before, Cubans initiate the conversations. Here is a trumpet player who has toured the United States but isn't interested in defecting; here is a baseball player who says he snubbed a lucrative invitation to head north to the Show. Here is a twenty-four-year-old black woman who says with passion: "Where is the sugar of Cuba? Where is the rice of Cuba? My feelings are not political, but economic. I ask myself, what is the problem with my country? Why is it so much worse off than other countries? And my answer is, I don't know. I don't know, but things must change before we can go on."

And here is a young black man dressed up in snappy suspenders and wire-rimmed glasses who informs us that the lyric by Grand Funk Railroad—"I don't need a whole lot of money, I just need someone to love"—is an anthem for Cuba's youth. A teenager tells us of a growing split between the people who made the revolution—Eric's generation—and those born into it—Roberto's generation.

Caputo and the Professor, in wonderland, are having an epiphany. The photographer has never before been in a country where it is so easy to take pictures of the people. "It's like they're *pleased*," he marvels.

"That doesn't happen in an unhappy culture," replies the Professor. Which seems true enough. Other than the scarcity of material goods and the thinning effectiveness of services, the everyday culture, away from the resorts, has none of the earmarks of a totalitarian system. No one hesitates to talk with us about any subject. There's an astonishing lack of visible military presence throughout the land. "When the colossus to the north has its heel over your head," the Professor opines, "and the people are this way, you have to say the problems are out of the people's control."

I record the conversation in my notebook, and when Roberto arrives with Eric at the table, I show it to them. "You damn American guys are trying to make me cry," says Roberto, his throat constricting. We all draw deep, sorrow-filled breaths. I excuse myself to the bathroom, where I would have, on principle and out of outrage over the tragedy of US-Cuban relations, kicked everything apart, but everything is already broken.

All that's left is to get the bottle of whiskey back to Gregorio in Cojimar, because he trusted the word of a friend, because some rituals are worth keeping alive, and because, after all, we are neighbors.

(1991)

In Deepest Gringolandia

Gringolandia isn't on a map, but a cultural compass and a little glossy media hype will lead you right to its bamboo or stucco gates. *Gringolandia* is where we North Americans are more and more spending our vacations. What I'm talking about is the network of fun-in-the-sun destinations, the honeyed cash traps, the Otherly fantasylands erected up the mountains and down the coasts of what we call the Third World or the developing world or the postcolonial world—the hot, dark-skinned nations that still bear the shape of Empire's boots across their sweaty backsides. Now, where the Kiplings and Conrads once poked around, hundreds of millions of white people spend billions of dollars each year for the exotic tickle of the five-day, four-night excursion into the mythological but much diluted, faraway but perfectly scrubbed heart of darkness.

There's much about this trend that I find difficult to reconcile with my own point of view as a traveler. When it comes to gallivanting on foreign turf, I crave not the prepackaged but the authentic. I don't care to see familiar faces tainting the view; don't want hideaways intruded upon by "civilization."

But who do I think I'm kidding? Not myself, not much. Bourgeois touring and maverick traveling both spring from the gringo lap of luxury. Even as a Peace Corps volunteer in the mid-'70s, I had the unpleasant feeling that I was little more than the latest style of Roman centurion. And today, as a writer in search of narratives in the islands and hot countries, find me, say, at a military checkpoint along a highway in Haiti and I'm glad to join the hordes and pass myself off as a sun-and-fun-seeking tourist.

Semantics and scale—perhaps these are the only honest differences between the mob that stuffs its madras shorts with credit cards and the bus-riding, backpacking dilettantes, the earnest make-believe anthropologists, and the writers like me. North Americans, boarding their planes, take North America with them—in varying degrees, yes, ugly or beautiful, but North America nevertheless.

Gringolandia. It's global—as far from us as Thailand, as near as our neighbor to the south, Mexico. Mexico, in fact, can be thought of as the model, the original *Gringolandia.* No one in Mexico seems abashed to say it, despite the fact that it summons all the paradoxical truths that define the postrevolutionary state of the Mexican nation. For the Mexicans, *Gringolandia* describes the consolidation of ironies large and small that have transformed the country into something akin to a behemoth theme park.

Two generations ago, the expression merely referred to Acapulco, the first installment in a resort-development epic meant to sustain and nurture the economic optimism of a Mexico invigorated by the business of world war. That was then; this is now: Today, tourism may be Mexico's last best hope. Burdened by a decaying industrial base, an unrelenting population explosion, a catastrophic oil bust, multiple currency devaluations, years of raging inflation, and a $104 billion debt, Mexico now looks to *Gringolandia* for economic salvation. Willfully, carefully, the government has designed and constructed an archipelago of artificial paradises along the country's vast impoverished coastlines. What might rescue Mexico, at least from the stigma of its incessantly predicted collapse? Not crude oil but tanning oil.

The ruling party, the PRI (Institutional Revolutionary Party), now invites an invasion from the north. Mexico's doors have been flung open, the welcome mat's brand-new, its *cerveza es muy fria,* its water has

226

been purified, and the putting greens have a nap as diligently tended as a baron's beard. You get the picture—head south, spend money, relax, party, shake your bottom until the pesos rain out of your pockets.

Late last winter I decided I wanted to visit Mexico's sprawling gringo playland—not to revel in it but to see it all, at one remove, for what it is: a policy, an industry, the new "upriver" world. I booked a flight to Mexico City and there, under Malcolm Lowry's smog-hidden volcano, rented a car and headed for the Pacific coast, for Acapulco, the bright shining hub of *Gringolandia*. I then ventured south hundreds of miles to the newest, most spectacular chamber of the system's heart— Huatulco. Huatulco, as yet unfinished but already fabled. A story.

The clogged boulevards of the capital led me to the toll road that climbed up into blue sky and what little remained of the pine forests, smelling like a Colorado summertime, that once rimmed the central plateau. Past Cuernavaca, I picked up the "superhighway," constructed in the late 1940s during the administration of President Miguel Alemán Valdes. The route, which reduced the previously rugged ten-hour drive to the coast by half, twists out of dense mountains into a pulsing urban jungle, the heights of Acapulco chaotic, the sidewalks made virtually impassable by the city's million citizens, and only a flash of ocean on the horizon to tease me onward. Finally, I found a road that arrowed down to the bay, its shoreline fenced with high-rise hotels. I checked into the Acapulco Ritz, dead center on the crescent of the bay.

Quickly I made my way to the beach beyond the poolside patio and sat among a tribe of white, affluent foreigners under palm-thatch umbrellas in the Ritz's roped-off rectangle of sand—audience to the sun, the glorious sea, and the sales pitch. Here at the Ritz, on the beach in Acapulco, cacophony ruled, the audio assault masquerading as cross-cultural experience. A mariachi band alternately crooned and yapped into microphones. The pulverizing whine of blenders produced an endless freezing river of margaritas. Unbroken clots of traffic gunned from light to light along the four-lane coastal boulevard behind the towering hotels. Boom boxes hollered out Spanish in six-eight time; revving speedboats sliced rooster tails a stone's throw from shore. But none of this din penetrated as deeply as the collective voice of the *vendedores*, the merchant infantry of hucksters straggling past the Ritz's tiny triangle of sandy exclusivity.

Each beachfront hotel has staked an area like this for its guests to lounge, and the hucksters trudge miles over the hot federal sand from one to another. Stations of the Cross for Mexico's underclass practicing the religion of commerce. They line up on the perimeters of an alien yet venerated wealth, whether its incarnations are middle-class *chilangos* from Mexico City, honeymooners from Houston, or undergraduates from UCLA on spring break. (The jet-setters have abdicated the central playas for more secluded villas and five-star pamper factories.)

From a stack he has dropped at his feet, a mestizo unfolds a Oaxacan blanket and spreads it over his chest, his arms raised and his ribs pulled as though he has bravely visualized my particular stable of gringos as a firing squad. For too long he stands just this way, waiting, and when he lowers the blanket to our indifference—how many dozens of blankets have we seen already this afternoon?—there is no mistaking the look of betrayal in his eyes. What I want to know, but can only ask myself, is this: Is the man's expression a professional ploy or a window onto his soul? Such are tourism's questions.

Chiclets, leopard-skin pantsuits, melons, silly hats, garish towels . . . the litany of bargain merchandise is recited in waves, packed cycles, the wares identical although the stream of faces vie for individuality. Some people thrive on the escalated clip of the hustle, but *this many?* an entire city of marching boutiques and ambulating gift shops? The youngest huckster I meet is five, the oldest a stooped great-grandfather hawking sunglasses. The majority are *indios*—the bottom of Mexico's racial and economic barrels, flat-faced and stoic. Except for baseball caps, they dress as if they never left their *ejido*, or communal lands, in the campo.

A sixteen-year-old Nahuatl girl carries a nursling on her hip, selling fruit and peanuts. The mother is happy, humming; the baby chirrups. I ask the girl if she gets tired toting the kid around. She laughs shyly and tells me no, it's nothing she ever thinks about, and on the beach she can stop and play with the baby whenever she wishes. A matron from Dallas leans across the rope to buy a banana from her, and nearby I hear a middle-aged sun worshipper congratulate himself: "Six days, and I don't know who won the mayor's primary in Chicago, and I don't give a shit."

Which problems are my own, which are Mexico's? Who, if anyone, is to blame? Acapulco is seedy, polluted, overpopulated, homogenized, overbuilt, money-crazed, exhausted. Acapulco is one of the world's foremost glamour spots (now overrun by anonymous charters of the you's and me's and our mothers). Acapulco's panorama is breathtaking. Its transactions employ hundreds of thousands; its facilities are modern and comfortable; its opportunities provide a catalyst for democratization. *Choose.*

We know that the decadence of Batista's Havana—its casinos, prostitutes, and narcotics luring a vulgar class of tourists from around the planet—played no small part in the rationale of Castro's mobilization against the status quo. Yet what does it mean, thirty years later, that Castro is reinventing Cuba as a tourist destination? A year before the insurrection the island attracted 350,000 tourists—by 1991 it expects 600,000 visitors annually, who will leave behind an estimated $500 million. What sort of dynamic will develop between faddish, well-heeled guests and their Marxist-Leninist hosts? The advantage to Cuba is a simple one: foreign exchange, *money*. But what are the complex risks to myth and symbology of the revolutionary state? "Exploit the sun," says Fidel. Now, really, if I'm deluded about my self-image as an anti-tourist, what could Castro possibly be thinking in his new job as recreational director?

On the beach at the Ritz in Acapulco, I applied my sun-daunted energies to these questions. But time and again I was distracted by the suffusive presence of the *vendedores*, perpetually tugging my mental sleeve. Of all the hucksters that ever approached me in my travels south, the only ones I remember making a genuine connection with were two preschool boys on the beach at Sosúa, in the Dominican Republic, who sat down cross-legged in front of me and sang a vigorous merengue for a coin, which they accepted with adult dignity. Now the memory is brought back to me, Acapulco-style. Two waifs, neither more than ten years old—a boy with a drum, a girl with a perforated sheet-metal scrapper—make a primitive percussive music, while an even younger girl dances the shimmy, lifting her soiled T-shirt to roll her prepubescent belly. The performance is obscene, and not only for its sexual innuendo; a pallid, sun-blotched man gives the girl money with a frown, paying the troupe not for their performance, which had no worth, no virtue, no conceivable rate of exchange, but paying them to go away.

What's important to keep in mind, I think, is that tourism in the Third World is not some haphazard vestige of colonialism. Acapulco, for instance, was never an unfortunate, accidental yoking of the haves and have-nots, but has always been precisely what it was calculated to be by the Mexican government—an economic detonator at the nucleus of the nonarable, poverty-stricken state of Guerrero, not only a magnet for foreign currency but an alternative destination for landless migrants flooding urban centers, especially Mexico City. Moreover, and no less significantly, Acapulco was envisioned as a proving ground for Mexico's emerging class of managers and entrepreneurs in the late 1940s and '50s, a showcase for their capabilities.

Forgoing the choice between Acapulco's glitzy, overpriced restaurants and the fast-food franchises—Denny's, Pizza Hut, Kentucky Fried—I walked my first night in town to a supermarket. From a row of steaming caldrons, I bought a fat man's portion of chicken mole, had it packed in a take-out container, and went back to my room high up in the Ritz to read the government's own account of the modern history of Acapulco.

This story really begins during World War II, when millions of just plain stay-at-home gringos were funneled into geographies and cultures not their own. Wherever the troops had been stationed, tourists followed, flown by the new commercial airlines. Cuba, Puerto Rico, the Bahamas, and other nearby warm, "exotic" places became tourist meccas.

Mexico took note of the burgeoning wanderlust of the giant to the north. War in Europe had generated a foreign-trade surplus south of the Rio Grande, an advantage it had no chance of holding on to during peacetime. Confronted with a decline in exports and a faltering industrial base, government economists introduced the premise that tourism could take up the slack. By the end of 1945, the PRI had opened tourist offices in four US cities. Public funds were allocated to match private-sector promotional expenses. Almost effortlessly, $35.9 million flowed south and crossed the border—a sum as frustrating as it was encouraging. No infrastructure existed to milk the market for more.

The Alemán government began in the late '40s to build highways and airports and to open new air routes between Mexico and the States. Cash handouts subsidized the construction of restaurants and hotels. Most important, perhaps, Alemán focused on the serene, modest port town of Acapulco, since the 1920s a popular getaway for the better-off of Mexico City. He made the decision to convert the old harbor into a world-class luxury resort (after secretly buying up land for himself). His engineers installed basic city services, laid out streets and housing developments, moved the airport inland. Hotels multiplied along the curving beaches. Bingo! Foreign-exchange earnings from tourism tripled by 1950. Alemán left office having persuaded the PRI that tourism was "the most important economic mechanism for shoring up the areas of national development that were lagging behind the most."

Mexico's next two presidents, however, weren't so convinced. For millions of Americans rotating through Tijuana and other border cities in the 1950s, Mexico was a cheap drunk, a bag of pot, whores having sex with burros. The federal government watched the impending revolution in Cuba and shuddered. Overnight, tourism seemed freighted with political imperatives, forcing President Adolfo Ruiz Cortines in the mid-'50s to preach a more explicit gospel. "While it is my aim to promote this major source of income," he stated, "it is also necessary for tourist activities to respect our customs and ethical principles." He stumped for higher moral standards, natural beauty, wholesome recreation, Mexico's unique history. Simultaneously, he railed against profiteering, "coarse commercialization of activities catering to low human passions and vices." His successor, Adolfo López Mateos, echoed this new creed, emphasizing tourism as a means of "strengthening ties of human understanding and international intelligence." In the minds of Mexico's leaders, tourism seemed to take form as a sort of multinational Chautauqua.

When an imbalance of payments due to insufficient foreign exchange earnings threatened to destabilize the country in the late 1960s, Banco de México began analyzing the sources of foreign exchange—exports, in-bond industries, and tourism—that supplemented the country's oil revenues. Only tourism exhibited a clear potential. For the first time, Banco de México constructed, between 1966 and 1968, a statistical portrait of Mexico's tourist activities. Pondering the reams of data, the bank's theoreticians suggested an idea without precedent—"the building of complete tourist resort cities from the ground up." Consequently, Banco de México funded a meticulous exploration of the country's six thousand miles of coastline. Bank analysts calculated average weekly hours of sunshine. They analyzed soil types and tidal patterns. Research teams evaluated socioeconomic levels and identified routes of supply. Finally, early in 1969, Banco de México recommended to the federal government the creation of "five integral tourist resorts."

An uninhabited barrier island known as Cancún topped the list because of its location on the Caribbean basin. Ixtapa, north of Acapulco, was chosen in the hope that it would alleviate the excessive concentration of tourists in the older resort. In Baja California Sur, an underpopulated region dozing in geographical and political isolation, the bank foresaw a "ladder" of nautical stopovers from the border southward, crowned by the integral resorts of Los Cabos and Loreto. Thus, California's 250,000 boats capable of navigating the Pacific offshore waters would be lured down the Baja Peninsula and into the Sea of Cortés. For the capital of its planned Pacific *Gringolandia*, Banco's team targeted Oaxaca, bastion of the pre-Hispanic past and one of the nation's most destitute states. There, on the belly of the southern Pacific coast, were the Bahías de Huatulco—a cluster of nine paradisiacal bays, an incipient Rio de Janeiro. Here was the last link in the Pacific archipelago: in its dimensions and future potential, Huatulco was to be the grandest resort of them all.

The magnitude of Banco de México's scheme was enormous—a thirty-year comprehensive strategy. The government quickly blessed the creation of an overseer agency, the National Fund for Tourist Infrastructure (Infratur), which just as quickly broke ground for the first two resort cities—Cancún in 1970, Ixtapa in 1971. Three years later, the heretofore irrelevant Department of Tourism was awarded cabinet-level status. Fonatur—the National Trust Fund for Tourism Development, heir to Infratur—was given permission to grant loans for hotels and even build its own, making direct investments in the projects. Although President José López Portillo took office in 1976 in the midst of a deepening financial crisis, he wasted no time in launching the Los Cabos and Loreto projects, certain that tourism had "sufficient economic impact to solve our problems."

By the time of Miguel de la Madrid's inauguration in 1982, tourism had become a lauded national pillar, one that might be counted on to keep the economy from collapsing. All that Fonatur required of the new president was that he promote the industry's benefits not to the treasury but to the public welfare. The president went a step further, asserting that the touristic process strengthened "the cultural identity of our people."

*   *   *

After spending a few days in Acapulco I drove south into the state of Oaxaca. Eight hours on the road brought me to the small coastal town of Puerto Escondido—surf-rat kingdom, haven to retro-hippies, way station for your basic assorted Eurotrash. Not a Fonatur kind of place. Here one could bump into gringos who would cringe at the word *tourist*, though gringo tourists of a sort they were. I found them loitering along the harbor-front street, composing themselves into a bohemian scene—privileged gypsies who more or less wanted the Third World to remain, at least in this place, as loose and carefree as it appeared (to them) to be.

Before driving to the water, I had picked up a pair of hitchhikers who were practicing a slightly more upscale form of drifting—gringos feeding off gringo dreams. Crystal and J.P., down from the States, were time-share sellers, part of a significant entrepreneurial subculture spawned by the burgeoning Third World resorts.

Crystal was thirty-two; J.P., three years older. Married for two years, they'd been knocking around Mexico for one, adroitly harvesting Mexico's money tree despite the fact that neither of them had an FM3, the Mexican work permit for foreigners, which would make their efforts legal. They were following the time-share season south—San Miguel de Allende, Manzanillo, Ixtapa—heading for the heralded Huatulco, two hours south of here. Only, their savings had run out, and now they were stuck in Puerto Escondido. Here there were no condos to hustle. I dropped each of them off on separate money-borrowing missions around town.

We met again in the morning over breakfast. I had requested a mini-seminar on time-sharing. I wanted to hear how *Gringolandia* got sold to gringos. The night before had not been a good one for them. Wounded in Vietnam seventeen years ago, J.P. had been eating painkillers ever since. The rent was due, and he was out of Percodan. Somehow he had lost the key to the padlock on their cabana and shattered the door kicking it in. At breakfast he was woozy and sweating, his face bloodless, but he wanted to talk, get right into it, tighten the focus, redeem himself. I sat back and listened.

"We go into a resort," he said, "and try to talk to the president of a time-share marketing company. They take me as a 'liner,' Crystal as an 'OPC'—an off-property contact. The OPC gets people to come in-house—you're out on the street grabbing them, answering questions, giving them free-drink cards, asking them to go on a tour of the facility. The tour is called lining—the sales effort between bringing the people in and closing them. The liners guide them, take them to breakfast, fill out their forms, warm them up, and become their friends. Then you ask them three simple things. Do you like it? If you get a yes, you write down the word *like* and put a check by it—the visuals are important here. Next, if you had this would you use it? If they say yes, you write down the word *use*. Put a check mark. Next. If this was affordable, if it wouldn't take any bread and butter off your table, da da da, would you buy this today? Most people won't say no at this point, because they've just spent an hour with you and they still haven't heard the price, they're dying to know the price, but you're not going to give it to them until they say yes. So they usually say yes to the third question, and you write down *affordable.*

"At that point," J.P. continued, "you assume the sale. Okay, so now I'll highball 'em. Let's say the product costs $3,995. The going rate in Mexico for a one-bedroom time-share condo—one week a year for life—is about $4,000. I'll tell them $5,500 plus this cost, plus that cost, all adding up to six grand and something. 'Oh no,' they say, 'that's too expensive.' Then we do what's called the drop. Okay, I say, let me give you your free gift then. That's when I call for the back man, the closer. I can do the back hit myself, but the proper way to do it is to bring in another salesman, another gringo—they're almost always gringos. 'Mr. Jones,' I go, 'these people are from Timbuktu, they said they like it, they said they'd use it, but it's just too expensive for them. They like to fish, they like to golf, they love this place because of such and such, but boy, it's just too high.' The backer nods his head for a while and then he goes, 'Well, I've got a special deal today.' Could be a repossession, a divorce, anything. Okay, so the backer drops it from fifty-five to $3,995. Special deal, today only. 'If you walk out the door,' you say to them, 'this nice-looking couple waiting over here is going to get it.' They start thinking—man, $3,995 for thirty years, one week a year, fixed or floating time, 1/52 of a dream come true."

The liner receives four points—4 percent of each sale he is on. As an OPC, Crystal was making more money because of the faster click—anywhere from twenty to forty bucks for getting a client to take a tour whether the client buys or not. And if a client does buy, the OPC also shaves a point. "Not bad for Mexico," she said.

Crystal wanted to know if Fonatur was in Huatulco. I told her yes. "Oh God," she said, erupting with nervous laughter. "It's going to be hard to work as an OPC then. I'll have to be a liner, because where Fonatur is, they'll have Mexicans out front, to show that the Mexicans are capable of getting people in there, but once they're in-house, they need Americans to talk to them. Only Americans. You've got to paint a picture for them of beautiful vacations from now until they drop dead"—her voice turned husky and slow and seductive—"*in places just like this, places just like where you want to go*, and you need to trap them into coming back, into coming back, into coming back."

The road I took south to Huatulco was uncharacteristically straight and conspicuously well attended. I recalled the subtitle from the title page of a four-color, high-sheen coffee-table-style book detailing Fonatur's many accomplishments: "The Imprint of Fonatur on the Geography of Mexico."

Among Fonatur's many achievements have been the following: During the initial stages of each resort project, every hotel room built brought ten new residents to the area, and twice that many by the time the project's goals were completed. While under construction, each hotel room created 2.5 jobs directly and the same number indirectly, and consistently paid these workers above the minimum wage. Similarly, the operation of each hotel room generated four permanent jobs. For every federal peso invested in the projects, ten private-sector pesos chased after it. By last year, Mexico was tenth in the world in tourist revenues. The foreign-exchange surplus represented by the tourist sector during the de la Madrid years of the mid-1980s exceeded $7 billion. Six hundred thousand jobs had been added to the economy during this time, and Mexico's total hotel capacity reached 305,000 rooms—eighth in the world. With customary foresight, Fonatur had built infrastructures for the addition of 50,000 new rooms in the coming years, a capacity equivalent to two more Acapulcos.

About thirty minutes from the heart of the new resort, just past the new international airport, the roadway abruptly convulsed as it wound through the steep mountains that had for so long isolated the coastal plain from any development. My first glimpse of Bahías de Huatulco was not idyllic—I looked down upon the workers' boomtown of La Crucecita.

Situated on the small plain in a valley opening its arms onto Huatulco's premier bays, La Crucecita was, until 1984, nothing at all save a scattering of *palapas*, or shacks. A few miles to the south on the pretty bay of Santa Cruz, forty families grew corn and practiced subsistence fishing, as they had since colonial times. Altogether, fewer than a thousand inhabitants scraped a living out of Huatulco's coast. Local income was below the state average, the lowest in Mexico. There was no electricity. No drinking water. No permanent buildings. No reliable roads, no clear land boundaries. Dengue fever and malaria, though, were there, as they always had been, along with a range of other diseases already eradicated throughout most of Mexico.

Enter Fonatur. Twenty-one miles inland, Santa María Huatulco—a community of two thousand people serving as the municipal seat—was granted legal title to the properties it circumscribed in May 1984. A day later, although individual buildings were unresolved, 52,000 acres of *ejido* lands in the municipality were expropriated by presidential decree. It happened virtually without a whimper yet not without its complications. Santa Cruz, for example, was the proposed site for Huatulco's primary marina and inner-harbor complex of shopping malls, sports clubs, and restaurants. The peasants who resided there were each given a few hundred dollars and a house in outlying La Crucecita. (The relocation was interrupted and stalled when many of them turned around and sold the houses to newcomers, then moved back to their *palapas* on the beach, holding out for more money and houses to budge them a second time.)

The La Crucecita I drove into was home to fifteen thousand people, maybe twenty thousand—it was growing too fast for statistics to be accurate. The master plan's maximum density for the town was forty-five thousand, but that ceiling might prove unrealistic. Now in La Crucecita there were clinics and liquor stores, dentists and a video bar, a travel agency and welding shops. There were factories for ice cubes, floor and roof tiles, adobe bricks. Stores sold restaurant equipment, beds, office supplies, auto parts, hardware, pharmaceuticals. Incredibly, there was a computer store and copy center and an ice-cream shop called Paletas Manhattan.

Everywhere haywire whiskers of rebar (concrete reinforcement rod) rose into the sky, a marsh of iron reeds. Everywhere the gunfire of hammers, the thumping of pickaxes, the thunder and gargle of diesel machinery. Men were erecting utility poles, laying sewer lines. Men were shaping roof beams with machetes, tying the joints with sisal rope. Some thirty thousand rooms are to be built—room enough eventually for two million tourists a year. In front of a nearly finished complex of condominiums, I saw the rarest of signs in Mexico: HELP WANTED.

The demand for workers' housing had been only partly satisfied by temporary construction camps. Men slept in the airy frames of apartments they were building, bathing with hose and bucket. But even after dark La Crucecita worked on, hyperactive, a streetlight casting just enough illumination to saw a board or drive a stake with a sledgehammer. Whoever had knocked off was still in motion, promenading the sidewalks, playing mob basketball under the lights on a gigantic new court.

In weird contrast to these industrious scenes, the *palapa* restaurants on the water in Santa Cruz—a designated tourist area—were empty once the sun went down. One of Huatulco's three hotels in operation, the Sheraton on Tangolunda Bay, was a glittering ghost town. Bats fed happily in its spotlights, and across from the hotel's echoing lobby entrance, unskilled laborers crouched around campfires in the dirt fields, making eerie postapocalyptic tableaux. Only Club Med out on the promontory of Tangolunda Bay jumped to a beat, guarded by soldiers at its gates.

Still, the outlines of the future of Huatulco were boggling. In all directions, the harsh mountainous terrain was being gouged and terraced. Plowed inland from the Sheraton, a golf course had been sculpted, its naked earth awaiting seed. Everywhere I looked there was someone burning scrub, someone being lectured by an architect, someone digging a trench, installing a satellite dish. Huatulco was being prepared for a population of six hundred thousand. It didn't take long for the intricacies of scale to become, for me, conceptually unmanageable, superhuman—it was as if I were bearing witness to a modern-day equivalent of the Zapotecs raising their sacred city atop Monte Albán.

One evening in La Crucecita I met a young journalist named Ismael Sánchez at a meeting of the town's two-year-old Association of Merchants. These fellows were all from Mexico City or some other modern, urban place; they had started a Lions Club and then a Rotary Club. Sánchez, the local correspondent for *El Imparcial Del Istmo*, Oaxaca's only daily, was astonished by the enormous and rapid development. Like me, his sympathies were divided.

"Four years ago," he said, "the people of Santa María Huatulco went to bed at seven. Now they don't even get home from work in Huatulco until then, and stay up until midnight to watch TV. They have money and houses now, concessions for businesses, but they say they were happier being poor than living this new way."

I asked him about the locals who had lived along the beaches.

"They're not happy about the opportunities; they have no interest in them. All the people getting the nice jobs come from outside, and the Huatulcans take the bad jobs. People here are nice, they are special, but not in good ways. They are stupid because they don't want better lives. And still they say, 'Shit on the government.' Everything came so fast, they are in a dream, and they're going to stay there."

Before leaving Huatulco, I got the chance to talk to Dr. Ricardo Ferré, fifty-five, the current regional director for Fonatur for the Huatulco project, appointed by Mexico's new president, Carlos Salinas de Gortari. By this time, my questions had essentially narrowed to one: What, amid all the developing—all the massive hotels and computer stores and video bars—would there be to remind a gringo that he was in Mexico? Ferré was ready for my question.

"I'm a soul engineer," he answered with an ironic gleam, a cocked grin. Huatulco was a shell without soul; he was trying to create a soul, he said, to burn inside this shell. "I'm like God, I'm a demigod. It will be like"—he held his right hand up to his lips, the fingers pinching an imaginary coal upon which he blew until it burst into flame—"*Spirit*! You will come in a year and say, well, Ricardo, you failed, or not."

Ferré is short, stout, white-haired, and has a face like Mickey Rooney's. His job requires him to be part Cecil B. DeMille, part Walt Disney, part Wizard of Oz. But I began to think as we talked that he was mostly the grandchild of Conrad's Kurtz. I heard him called a tyrant more than once, and when I told him this, he seemed pleased.

Ferré is bookish. Within the first minutes of our conversation in his office at Fonatur's local headquarters, he had saluted Marx but disparaged Marxism and paraphrased Santayana as to what directs the path of economics—"We produce things but things also produce us. We live to myths, but myths also create us." He then rose from the conference table where we were sitting and selected two volumes from the bookshelves, handing me one. The book was *Vince Lombardi on Football*.

"This was also one of my teachers," Ferré declared.

"Vince Lombardi?"

"Well, not the person but his ideas. I've been searching for a long time for the material basis of values, ethics. Look, this is another of my bibles, very important to me. Bible in the sense of God, exactly."

The *I Ching*. Vince Lombardi and the *I Ching*.

Ferré has an engineering degree from the Massachusetts Institute of Technology and a doctorate in philosophy, did postgraduate work in Eastern Europe, and has taught at the University of Chicago and the national university in Mexico City. He speaks nine languages, he said. He found a copy of his most recent published article to show me. It was an assault on the scholarship of Octavio Paz.

He then told me of an experience he said he had had on that very day, out on his morning constitutional through the countryside. In the dawn's misty light, he crested a hill and saw, there in the road, horses, "savage horses." They stampeded and, electrified by the sound of their hooves, Ferré had the fantastic feeling he was in prehistoric times, clutching a stone in his hands. I suggested to him that such an event could be placed on the endangered list: five years hence, his revelatory moment couldn't possibly exist in Huatulco. Unless he fabricated it himself, hired a man to import horses from the interior.

"Exactly," he said, and laughed. "But this is a laboratory of what happened many years ago in different parts of the world, a laboratory for what happens when society shifts from a Neolithic peasant pattern into a society that is an urban society. I'm creating it to a certain degree, but the behavior of people is moving us the way people moved into urban settlements many thousands of years ago. It's the new city coming into reality. What I want to prove are the limits of Utopia. If possible."

I inquired about his plans to manufacture cultural ambience in Huatulco. He told me that in two more months Fonatur would be sponsoring movies, music, dances. "Besides that," said Ferré, "I will give some masturbation for the so-called upper middle class so they can see European films, very esoteric films—Bergman, Truffaut."

And traditional culture? I wondered if he'd ship it in from the mountains for the tourists.

"Yes. That's engineering, social engineering. I will take many ideas from Mao's Cultural Revolution." He smiled at his own joke.

Ferré turned to one of his pet projects: to take some of the fishermen on the beach at Santa Cruz and remake them into "businessmen with big, big boats."

Was he committed to making everybody in Huatulco middle-class?

"Well," said Ferré, "not everybody. Some of them. But society is not built according to geometry."

He had an anecdote: "About two weeks ago, one of the very important persons from Mexico City came to see the new buildings we are doing at the beach, a vice director of Fonatur. So this man is a very technocratic person. A typical engineer—very smart, very good, but he has no sense of humor. I refer to him as Don Quixote. He has the shape—very tall, with an eagle nose. So we were strolling to the beach in Santa Cruz. We were chatting with the people, since we are going to build a new restaurant. And there's a man—I'm a small size but this man is smaller than myself and thinner. His name is Don Tesoro. Don Tesoro. So we approach this man's shack. 'Good morning, Don Tesoro, how are you, how do you feel?' 'Ohhh, I'm all right.' And we say, 'Don Tesoro, what about you now agree to move from this area so we can build the new restaurant?' 'You know,' he says, 'I'm an old indio. Please leave me alone. I was born here. I want to be free. I don't want a restaurant. I don't want anything from you. Please leave me alone.' I was so surprised and happy. The vice director was astonished, stunned. 'How is it possible this man is against the progress?' he said. But me—I really love that man."

I wanted to know what Ferré planned to do with him.

"Well, we have to talk with him."

"You're going to change his life, true?"

"No. Don Tesoro's going to move to another area. There are plenty of beaches—he will go there. Well, it is what we have to do."

"You have to get him out of the way."

"No," Ferré said now, reversing himself. "We are not going to move him. WE are going to build around him."

"He can stay?"

"Yes, if he wants."

"Who else on the beach in Santa Cruz can stay? Anybody who wants?"

"Well, Don Tesoro is the only case. He's the only pure man. He's really pure. The others are crooks." Ferré, it turned out, had thrown a beach dweller in jail the week before as a means of getting this message across.

While we talked, a line of petitioners had formed outside the Fontanur offices, waiting for an audience with the boss. Now Ferré had to return to work. But he wished to throw the *I Ching* for me before I left. I asked instead that he throw it for himself and for Huatalco, and he agreed, though he wanted me to toss the coins myself.

While I did this, my thoughts meandered back to another aspect of Ferré's discourse on the philosophical underpinnings of tourism. As he saw it, tourism was a "result of the new loneliness" in industrial societies. "Tourists," he had said, "try to meet people like peasants around here to acquire some of their innocence, their ingenuity."

I threw the coins six times and six times Ferré translated their numerical correlates. With a pencil, he drew the corresponding trigrams until he had sketched a six-bar hexagram, each of its halves, north and south, representing the sun. Double Sun. He flipped through the text of the *I Ching* to the appropriate chapter for an interpretation: *The wanderer has nothing that might receive him.*

"This is Huatulco?" I asked.

243

Dr. Ferré chuckled. "Yes."

Success is through what is small. Ferré giggled. *It furthers one to have somewhere to go.*

There was more, pages of elaboration. Ferré's secretary photocopied the chapter for me, and I was on my way to contemplate its mysteries. What I made out of it was this: The gods want us all to be tourists.

(1989)

The Life I Didn't Get

Kiribati, Christmas Island, erstwhile thermonuclear playground in the South Pacific, two years ago and counting. Neither the beginning nor the end of a journey toward the lightness of being but, for me, more of the same, surfwise, selfwise, further evidence of the truth inherent in the mocking axiom, *You should have been here yesterday.* Yesterday, in fact, is the stale cake of many an aging surfer like myself. Yesterday is what I walked away from, determined to someday again lick the frosting from the sea-blue bowl.

Out there on the Kiribati atoll, we were a small, neoprene-booted family of elite silverbacks—Micky Muñoz, Yvon Chouinard, Chip Post—and brazen cubs—Yvon's son and daughter and her boyfriend; Chip's son. Micky (sixty-one) was the first maniac to surf Waiamea Bay. Yvon (sixty), the founder of Patagonia, legendary rock and ice climber, had surfed just about every break in the world, starting with Malibu in 1954. Chip (sixty), a lawyer in L.A., had seniority in almost every lineup from Baja to San Francisco. The second generation Xers were already dismantling breaks all over the planet. In years (middle), condition (not splendid), experience (moderate), and ability (rusted), I was the odd water monkey in the clan, neither out nor in, and the only one dragging an existential crisis to the beach. The only one who had opted out of The Life, the juice. Maybe I wanted back in, but maybe not. I felt like an amputee contemplating the return of his legs but long accustomed to the stumps.

In the coral rubble of the point at the channel mouth, we stood brooding, muttering, arms crossed on our collective chests, trying to conjure what was not there. The trade winds had developed spinning disease. The glorious, mythical break had been crosswired by La Niña, chilling the equatorial water and deforming the shoulder-high waves, which advanced across the reef erratically, convulsed with spasms, peaking and sputtering inconclusively, closing prematurely, like grand ideas that never quite take shape or cohere to meaning. In years past at this same spot, Yvon and his company of "dirtbaggers" had been graced with an endless supply of standard Christmas Island beauties—precise double-overhead rights, shining high-pocketed barrel tubes that spit you out into the postcoital calm of the main harbor. This time, however, we had traveled far for Oceania's interpretation of Euclidean geometry and we got this, bad poetry, illiterate verse.

Yeah, well . . . this was a hungry crew, and you never know what's inedible until you put it in your mouth. The Xers flung themselves into the channel; the rip ferried them down the pass and out to the reef. Chip goes. Then Yvon, but less enthusiastically. "I'm not going," said Micky, squatting on his heels. I sat too, thunderstruck with relief. Forget that it had been more than seven or eight years since I surfed, or almost fifteen since I surfed steady, daily, with the seriousness and joy of a suntanned dervish. With or without its perfect waves aligned off the point, one thing about this break on Kiribati horrified me. As a swell approached the reef and gathered its peak, the trough began to boil in two sections vital to the fall line of the wave. When the wall steepened to its full height, thinning to emerald translucence, the two boils morphed into thick fenceposts of coral embedded in the wave.

We watched Yvon muscle onto an unreliable peak, gnarled and hurried by the onshore wind. The drop was clean, exhilarating, but without potential. He trimmed and surged past the first spike of coral, the fins of his board visible only a few scant inches above the crown.

Then the wave sectioned and crumbled over the second spike. Without a bigger swell and an offshore wind, it was going to be like that. Yvon exited and paddled in.

"Those coral heads really spook me," I confessed.

Yeah, well. Some risks you fancy, some you don't. When more water piled up, they weren't much of a problem, Yvon assured me. The stay-alive technique was, fall flat on your belly when you left your board. Glide shallow, protect your head, avoid disembowelment or the tearing off of your balls. Solid advice.

"Yeah, I guess," I said.

For a half hour, we watched the rodeo out on the reef, Chip and the Xers rocketing out of the chute, tossed and bucked into the slop. Their rides resembled a five-second saber dance with a turquoise bull, something like that. Micky kept looking up the coast, across the scoop of bay to where the shoreline straightened out in front of a reef I had named, ingloriously, Caca's, because the locals in the nearby village mined the beach with their morning turds. The tide had begun to ebb.

"Caca's going off!" Micky cheered. Yvon and I squinted at the froth zippering in the distance.

"Yeah?" we said, unconvinced, but off we trudged to check it out.

So.

There is a pathology to my romance with surfing that contains a malarial rhythm; its recurrence can catch me unaware, knock the wind out of my metaphysical sails, bring fevers. For a day or two I'll wonder what's wrong with me, and then, of course, I'll know.

I would like to tell you that I remain a surfer but that would mostly be a lie, even though I grew up surfing, changed my life for surfing, lived and breathed and exhaled surfing for many years. Now I can barely address the subject without feeling that I've swallowed bitter medicine, I avoid surf shops with the same furtiveness that I steer clear of underage girls, and I wouldn't dare open up a surf magazine and flip through its exquisite pornography of waves, unless I had it in mind to make myself miserable with desire. In any pure sport, in any art or extreme passion, such disengagement happens sooner or later to all but a blessed few to which the alternatives never quite make sense.

My life only started when I became infected with surfing, moon sick with surfing, a fourteen-year-old East Coast gremmie with his first board, a Greg Noll slab of lumber, begging my older brothers for a ride to Ocean City, two hours away if you drove at ninety miles an hour, which they did. Before that, I was just some kid form of animated protoplasm, my amphibian brain stem unconnected from any encompassing reality, skateboarding around suburbia like an orphan, ready to be adopted and subverted by the Beach Boys, who can still make me swoon when I hear "Surfer Girl" on the radio.

I remember in high school the spraying rapture of the first time I got wrapped—seriously, profoundly, amniotically wrapped—by an overhead tube, an extended moment when all the pistons of the universe seemed to fire for the sole purpose of my introduction to the sublime. This was at Frisco Beach, south of the cape on Hatteras. I remember the hard vertical slash of the drop, the gravitational punch of the bottom turn, and that divine sense of inevitability that comes from trimming up to find yourself in the pocket hammered into a long beautiful cliffside of feathering water. It only got better. There pinned on the wall in front of me, entirely unexpected and smack in my face, was a magnificent wahine ass-valentine, tucked into a papery yellow bikini and, since I didn't know anyone else had made the wave, for a moment I thought I was experiencing a puberty-triggered hallucination, but there she was in the flesh, slick and glistening, whoever she was, wet as my dreams, locked on a line about two feet above me, crouched in what is known in the animal kingdom as the display position. *Surgasm*—can that be a word? You have to understand, I was sixteen and, up to that point, a pioneer of the wonderful world of geeks. The wave vaulted above us and came down as neat and transparent as glass and we were suspended and bottled in brilliant motion, in the racing sea, and friends, that ride never ended, unto this day.

Boy, girl, wave—whew. On earth, I could ask no greater reward from heaven nor define any other cosmology as complete as this. Point, click, put it in your shopping cart. When you're given something good and true you want to stick with it, but it's exactly here, at the impact zone of commitment, that a problem arises. Let the master speak to this.

"I think the biggest lesson I got out of surfing," Yvon told me one night on Kiribati, "is that if you want to take it seriously, you've got to completely restructure your life so that at any moment you can drop anything and go surfing. At Patagonia [headquarters in Ventura], we have a Let My People Go surfing policy written into my employees' contract. You can't underestimate what that means—I don't mean as a business, but as a life. A lot of people end up on the fringes because they're not accommodated by their employers. And it gives you something to look forward to—maybe the surf will be up tomorrow. Tennis is a game, but surfing is a real passion. It's not something you just do when you're young, it's something you do your whole life. I think surfing was the first counterculture, absolutely the first one."

It's a passion, sure, yet like all of the best pursuits and fine indulgences a privilege, requiring generosity from above. Luck. The liberating paradox of obsession. At the very least, a parking place on the overcrowded, overregulated, dog-hating coast.

Most upstanding civilians I know have trouble believing this, but surfing was the energy that formed my identity when I had no other; it was my coming-of-age narrative. Surfing sculpted my ambition, surfing gave me an appetite for the wild world, taught me a value system and the virtues of nature, taught me (through the innovative prose of *Surfer* magazine) to be word-drunk, intoxicated with new language, and prepared me, ultimately, to be free, by making me practice persistence and, as much as I could muster, courage. To set aside fear and paddle out on a day when the beach is lined with fire engines and littered with boards snapped in half by Godzilla waves. To paddle out blind with myopia and alone and lonely into unknown waters. To paddle back out after you've just been seized by an undertow, the strength of which you never imagined.

The first time I declared my irreversible independence and defied my father, it was to go surfing—I was an underage minor boarding an international flight to the West Indies. I joined the Peace Corps to go surfing in the Windward Islands. I moved my household from Iowa, where I was teaching at the university, to the Outer Banks to go surfing. I vividly remember spectacular waves on Long Island, New Jersey, Virginia Beach, North Carolina, Florida, Puerto Rico, Hawaii, the islands of the Caribbean, waves that when I kicked out, through the sizzle of the white water I could hear hoots of astonishment on the beach, which felt like your ecstasy was shouting back at you, and beyond you, to a future where one day you might recollect that once, for a time, you had been a great lover in your affair with the world. You weren't just sniffing around.

But there are many ways to love the world. My sea became literature, my waves rolled into books, my rhythm became the pulse and flow of sentences, not swells. No regrets there, yet I found myself hunkered down on ocean-lonely prairies, striking a Faustian bargain with the gods of success. In my life as a surfer, it wasn't time to move on, it was time to stay, but I couldn't, being deranged by adulthood and its sober illusions. Years later, when the opportunity came up to fly to Kiribati with Muñoz and Chouinard, two of my boyhood idols, though I often daydreamed of riding waves, I just didn't know if I wanted to surf again, to become reinfected with surfing, because I knew there was a chance I would stop living one life and start living another, that I would uproot everything and remake it according to a different sort of yearning, a different set of needs, and I didn't particularly think that was possible. Yes, Bill Finnegan had done it, but no one else, as far as I knew. And as Chip once told me, and not incorrectly, "The greater human enterprise requires more than doing your own thing."

Still, Micky designed me a new board, which Fletcher, Yvon's son, shaped and glassed for me. Still, I flew six thousand miles to Christmas Island, artificially mellowed by some kind of depresso's drug to make me stop smoking. And I gulped back the dread that the point break had induced and walked down the beach with Micky and Yvon and Peter Pan, longing for some of that Old Blue Magic.

What we found there at the break in front of the village was surfing's equivalent of a petting zoo—little giddyap waves, pony waves, knee-high and forgiving—and if these weren't the waves we had come for, they were nevertheless the only waves we were going to get this trip. The silverbacks made every wave they wanted; I made maybe one out of five, my body aching to restore its balance and former grace. Micky and Yvon tutored my rehabilitation, offered comfort: "It's not like getting back on a bicycle," said Micky. "You spend thirty seconds on your feet a day as a beginner or intermediate. Try learning anything else at thirty-second-a-day intervals." "It's the most difficult sport there is," added Yvon, the rock-climbing pioneer. "There's no more difficult sport, absolutely. You have to be young to learn it. You can start snowboarding at fifty years old and get damn good at it. You can't do that with surfing."

Oftentimes when I pivoted my board landward to get in position, the fins would hook up in the reef. I felt clownish, hesitant, my judgment blurred by bad eyesight. But finally none of that mattered, finally I started hopping into the saddle, having fun. That I considered to be a mercy.

I had collided head-on with my youth and what needed resurrection, though not in the boomer sense of never letting go. I had let go. But the dialectic of my transformation had reached a standstill: Surf=No Surf=??? I wanted more waves. I wanted more waves the way a priest wants miracles, the desert more rain. Throughout the middle years of my celibacy, living a counterpoint life, I had prayed hard to be welcomed home again to waves, and these tame ponies on Christmas Island would, I hoped, serve as that invitation. I have since surfed San

Onofre with limited success. Florida too, but only once. I have yet to find the right equation that will spring open my life, rearrange my freedoms, and let me throw my desire back into the sea. My resources are modest, my obligations many; my dreams are still the right dreams but veined with a fatty ambivalence. Maybe the season has passed, but I don't think so. My two lives, and my two selves, have to do the Rodney King trick and learn to get along.

The thing about surfing, Chip told me, is that "you leave no trail." Yes sir, Micky agreed: "It's like music—you play it and it's done."

The strategy, though, that you're looking for is the one that teaches you to hold the note.

(2001)

Mount Ararat

And then I passed on further into great Armenia, to a certain city called Erzurum, which had been rich in old time, but now the Tartars have almost laid it waste. In this country there is the very same mountain whereupon the ark of Noah rested. This I would willingly have ascended, if my company would have waited for me. However, the people of the country report that no man could ever ascend the mountain because they say it pleases not the Most High.

—The Journal of Friar Odoric, AD 1330

Well-trampled Erzurum, one of history's doormats, seemed more than ever resolved to its continued existence, being rather conspicuously fortified. Alongside an airstrip, a village of camouflaged bunkers housed fighter jets. Stuporous conscripts dozed in the sun, manning antiaircraft guns mounded like anthills throughout the arid no-man's-land of the plain. On the outskirts of town, Turkey's entire Third Army was encamped, charged with the security of the eastern provinces. In NATO's dossier of the Apocalypse, here was a vital frontier unit, its troops rotating along a border nervously shared with some major spooks—the Soviet Union, Iran, Iraq, and Syria—each an ancient and sometimes modern enemy, brother, slave, subject, or ruler of the Anatolian peoples of Asia Minor.

The needles visible on the horizon were either minarets or missile sites—easy for a non-Muslim Westerner like myself to confuse, given the times. This part of the world was nobody's idea of a playground, and my journey coincided with another questionable piece of adventurism: Saddam Hussein's surprise trek into Kuwait. Waiting in Erzurum's airport for my luggage, I tallied up the previews to see what I was working with so far: The Middle East. Impending full-scale war. Overwhelming military presence. Alleged Kurdish terrorist activity. A reputedly conservative and xenophobic Islamic city smack in the middle of what is one of the most earthquake-prone venues on earth.

Such facts had been nicely titillating back home in Tallahassee, but the truth was I felt relief to finally be here on Marco Polo's Silk Road, since I was traveling under the strange impression that I had been called to this land. *Called*—not like a god-struck novice or the Son of Sam; more like a delinquent summoned to the tax collector's office. I had the queer feeling that something big was up and that somehow I had a role to play, perhaps as a stable boy to the Four Horsemen. One doesn't argue with intuitions of destiny, one buys a plane ticket and a bottle of Kaopectate. The date was September 7. Two more days and the calendar would provide a most portentous serial: 9/9/90. On that day I would be on Ağri Daği—Mount Ararat—attempting what Friar Odoric had counseled against on the premise of annoying God.

By any account I was a vice-ridden sinner and ill-conditioned to do what I had never done before: climb a dormant volcano-cum-mountain, especially a 16,943-foot one, higher than any peak in Europe or the contiguous United States. I found the friar's words not only provocative but an implicit challenge, meant only for me, because 9/9/90 would also be my thirty-ninth birthday, the starting gate of my fortieth year, crisis time for any nicotine-fouled, under-exercised, previously able-bodied ex-surfer loath to wander far above sea level without a chairlift. Something definitely was up, some lure irresistible to the disposition of my mortal self. I could smell it. Something not too dressy, like Reckoning, or Enlightenment.

I had not come unprepared. In my rucksack I carried an emergency library of the soul, should I have reason to call upon the wisdom of the prophets: a portable World Bible, accommodating all faiths including fire worship; a paperback edition of the Koran; a scholarly survey of biblical sites in Turkey, the "other" Holy Land; the newest translation of the Gilgamesh epic, in case I encountered heavy rains. And since an American could not go anywhere in the eastern Mediterranean Diaspora without that most pertinent of testaments, *The Innocents Abroad*, Mark Twain's travelogue through the Ottoman Empire, Europe, and North Africa, I had that too.

Of personal effects, my toilet kit bulged with Nicorette chewing gum, to prevent me from becoming deranged and inadvertently killing somebody should I elect to stop smoking. I also had with me my new, first-ever pair of hiking boots, broken in by walking the dog to the park. What I lacked, however, were crampons and an ice ax, two items rumored to be convenient atop the glacier-bound summit of Mount Ararat. But I had never seen such equipment in my life, and neither had the Florida outfitters where I had shopped. Come back in January, they had said, amused, and we'll sell you a sweater. In all other aspects of preparation, I was either uninformed or ignorant, and considered both states to be the mother of adventure.

So here I was in Erzurum, where the road to Mount Ararat began. Erzurum had a reputation for being somber and severe, a city "never recovered from winter," and though no one thought to disparage its tenacity by calling it lovely, the negative image seemed unjustified, even if Erzurum did have the only university campus in existence where wolves were a lingering security problem.

I had thrown in my lot with a robust band of mostly German alpinists. Erol, our courier from an Istanbul agency called Trek Travel, ushered all seventeen of us onto a *dolmus*, the Turkish word meaning "stuffed" and referring to grape leaves, aubergines, and minibuses. We were outward bound for Doğubayazit, a four-hour drive east, the staging area for any ascent of Ararat. We slalomed through an army convoy onto the scorched pastures of the valley, the higher landscape a geological punishment—rocky, sunburned, and unyielding. But not infrequently would we top a rise and be treated to a golden vista of bulgur wheat or men harvesting green lakes of hay. The horizon would pour into a gorge, then split open again into a vastness daubed with the parched wheels of sunflowers. Whatever watercourse cut through the distance was described by perfect lines of Lombardy poplars or hairy clumps of willows. The farther we went, the more the land's few resources were given over to nomads, their flocks out beyond, muzzling the scrub.

I had never been among Germans before or traveled anywhere with a single one, so I knew no better than to be glad about it and, for the most part, was. Wolf, a physician from Bavaria, spoke English. White-haired Rudi was an Austrian, splendid to look at, with a profile you could pledge allegiance to and the personality of Kurt Waldheim, circa 1943. There were twelve others, all of them middle-aged, and all had wasted their youths by interminably scaling the Alps and whatever else got in their way. I was, and would remain, the only pilgrim.

Perhaps because of the echoing chill of *Midnight Express*, the gringo hordes continue to bypass Asia Minor, which is a shame, but not for me, since I occasionally see Americans in Florida and get my fill of them there. Besides, there were two others on the bus: Rob of California and Chris of Michigan. Rob, my junior by ten years and a ringer for Superboy, chiseled out a living as a photographer. Chris was an economist for the state government in Lansing. I found his company agreeable, mostly because he was smaller than me and because he was the only other fool on the expedition who had come this far in life without scaling a mountain. Chris and I mulled over the prophecies of Nostradamus, particularly those predicting that, on or near the second millennium, a charismatic

Antichrist (Gorbachev) would reunite the world (Europe), Babylon (Iraq) would be back in business, and mankind could kiss its butt good-bye, as these events would culminate in the Last Judgment, for which we were wondering if we had front-row seats. In the Christian mythology of the Second Coming, Mount Ararat had been approximately targeted as Ground Zero. The Koran located its own End-Days epicenter farther south, a long drive across the border into Syria.

For reasons other than salvation, though, Mount Ararat has been off-limits to foreigners (except NATO snoops) for most of the twentieth century. Only since 1982 had the mountain been officially open; no one can set foot on it without first obtaining written permission, a months-long process requiring a daunting seventy-two signatures. This absolute triumph of red tape explained why Erol was among us and why we clung to him. Trek Travel was one of the very few outfits with a knack for expediting the formalities. Erol's assignment was to escort us all in a piece to Doğubayazit and deliver us to our mountain guides.

Chris and I, brother greenhorns, compared notes we had culled from the available literature. We were most encouraged that the books unanimously emphasized one needn't be an experienced mountaineer to achieve the summit, though they allowed the climb was strenuous and demanded great stamina. We asked Erol to bolster our courage with a little pep talk, and he fortified us with good information. Trek Travel had succeeded in marching 98 percent of its customers to the summit. If our group was representative of the whole, this was heartening news, implying that the majority of Ararat trekkers were well sunk into middle age, and that the mountain was cake.

In Erol's experience, the worst incident to unfold on Ararat had occurred last July, when a trekker—a German trekker, it so happened—somehow concealed a hang glider in his baggage. The packers hauled it unaware to base camp, whereupon the German flew down to Doğubayazit on the day of the World Cup soccer finals, in search of a TV. "If the soldiers had seen him," Erol explained soberly, "they would have shot him out of the air. They wouldn't have known what it was they were seeing."

I asked what the soldiers were doing on Ararat anyway.

"They are guarding the camp against terrorists."

But what was this bull about terrorists—there were none, not this far north, anyway. Yes, Erol conceded, but the soldiers didn't know that. "Whatever you do," he told us solemnly, "don't go outside camp after dark."

"The great provocation," Wolf pronounced, from the veranda of our hotel in Doğubayazit, assessing Ararat in the early morning light. It wasn't just big, you could forget big. The surrounding tableland, flat as a Nebraska cornfield, swept the eye across an uninterrupted horizontal right into a dead stop, whereupon a mountain as perfect and unreal as a child's rendition, a great breast of mountain that had nurtured the very roots of civilization, heaved abruptly more than thirteen thousand feet straight off the plateau. Without outlying foothills to interfere with its immensity, the mountain, skullcapped with dazzling ice, was startlingly exposed, as if it had no other choice than to be naked and divine. I looked at it and felt the awful undertow of attraction.

We were quite a party now—forty-six of us—having rendezvoused with two other groups. One had come, like us, from Erzurum. The other had been hiking a week, gaining unfair advantage, in the Taurus Mountains.

Erol came to notify us of a delay: Our permit awaited its final signature, which it would receive automatically once the commander of the local garrison remembered he had something to do today. As we kicked around, waiting, I noticed that Chris seemed aloof and unwell. As we mustered in the parking lot, our documents secured, our gear collected, he bailed out, citing reasons of health and personal scheduling problems that conflicted with Armageddon. I was sorry to see him go, since I had hoped we might launch our alpine careers together, humiliation being a state best enjoyed with a comrade.

Off I drove with Rob and the Germans and Rudi. We raised a terrible train of dust, bouncing across the plain toward road's end on the hem of the mountain. I was a bit apprehensive about our drop-off point at the tiny Kurdish village of Çevirme, having been forewarned by a guidebook not to violate anyone's *namus* and cause a ruckus. Eyeballing women was strictly out. Pointing cameras at Kurds was also an offense, so I figured that Rob, who couldn't restrain himself, would be beheaded within minutes and that our arrival would result in a flurry of diplomatic gaffes.

I shouldn't have worried. Our appearance on the central pasture of Çevirme was the signal for the population to throw their touchy sense of honor to the wind. They scrambled forward to cull baksheesh and bonbons and to beg for *fotoçek*. Actually, the behavior of the villagers was exemplary, considering they were being invaded from outer space. I retreated to a stone wall fencing a sugarloaf stack of hay and smiled at three prepubescent Cleopatras who judged me satisfactory material to stare at. For reasons of epic length, I was smitten; these were Noah's granddaughters.

It would be unkind of you not to let me say a few words about the ancestor we share. Fundamentalists and frauds, maverick archaeologists, even a former astronaut all have mounted expeditions up Mount Ararat to prowl around its ice cap, hoping to chip out a hatch cover from the old boat. Which would certainly be a miracle.

The story of Noah can rightfully be called the seminal myth of recorded history, the sequel to the Garden of Eden. Something devastating did happen; one winter's snowfall probably was extreme, the spring thaw likely coincided with heavy rains and astronomical tides, the rivers rose, inundating the lowlands. But not to the preposterous level of 16,945 feet, the present height of Ararat, which last erupted in 1840, vaporizing its old cap and, presumably, anything stuck up there.

The Old Testament version is derived from ancient Mesopotamian myths, anyway. The Mesopotamian prototype allegedly landed near the floodplain of the Tigris River, the same region where the Hebrew scribes probably intended to run their Noah aground. But Genesis, which properly set the patriarch down "upon the mountains of Ararat," was misinterpreted immediately. The mountains became one mountain, and Ararat, "a land far away," became Mount Ararat itself. By AD 70, Josephus was swearing the ark was up there in plain view, and Marco Polo reported the same stirring news twelve centuries later, although neither man had seen the ark himself, relying on the accounts of others.

Standing in Noah's front yard, I told myself, all right, it doesn't matter, since I preferred Noah as a metaphor for starting over anyway. Behind the Kurdish girls, atop the stone wall, lay a horse, or rather what was left of one, a long ivory chain of neck vertebrae still posted to their hideous skull, the macabre buck-toothed laugh rudely suggesting the distinction between Noah fact and fiction. The irony moved me along.

Called back to the ranks, we were introduced to our Kurdish guides, Halis, Sandwich (or so the Germans pronounced his name), and Ahmet. We crammed bag lunches into our day packs while the staff loaded the more substantial gear into a Soviet four-wheel-drive Niva. Led by Halis, a rather arrogant sort with the impersonal eyes of a warrior, the Taurus Mountains bunch filed out the back of the village, disappearing into the rising folds of land. I quick-stepped to their rear, anxious to get going, though I properly belonged to Ahmet.

Fortunately, the day's agenda was cushy, a genteel stroll up past the 9,500-foot mark, and the weather was excellent, hosted by a magnanimous sun. Our collective mood was jubilant, even a shade romantic, and already the elevation was handing out rewards. The guides handled us well and were true professionals in their trade, having undergone years of rigorous training and apprenticeship as shepherds. The Europeans attacked the grade in stacked formation, unrepentant tailgaters with the playfulness of mules. This was the poetry of plodding; I found it inspirational, yet every tenth step I seemed to lose the eleventh, slacking off until I had been inducted as an honorary member of the Sandwich contingent. I did what I could to enjoy it until eventually I filtered back through the column, alone for a while before being reunited with my own tribe, who welcomed me with indifference.

Ahmet, however, was pleased to see his lost lamb. He was older than Halis, and clearly wiser, but not a leader. He possessed a sad tenderness, in contrast with the mountain. For ninety seconds we cultivated a warm friendship, until he had exhausted his English vocabulary and I had exhausted myself. "Cigarettes," I confessed, pounding my chest, mock-coughing. Ahmet brightened. He pulled a pack from his shirt pocket and offered me one, which I declined, but he lit one for himself, raising his chin toward the impossible summit and squinting down at me. "Cigarette . . . no problem," he struggled to explain. "Ararat . . . no problem."

This was exactly my attitude, though I could afford it only in spirit. Among my company I was the slowest, the preordained last, eating the troops' dust until I was alone. Every five minutes I stopped to suck air like a vacuum cleaner. I felt fine, but my lungs lacked capacity, and everyone's physical superiority was in dramatic contrast to my own self-inflicted limitations. Repeatedly I lost sight of the procession weaving into gullies, behind crags, but the path was unmistakable and, as I slugged it out in my solitude, it was gratifying to imagine I had embarked on a quest. Noah had been six hundred years old when the Almighty enlisted him in the navy. I had come to Ararat to learn, on the eve of my fortieth year, just how much stuffing I had left in me. The trek was not pure, but then neither was I. I sat down on a basalt throne and, plucking what I thought was wild mint, raised a stinging nettle to my nose.

Base camp was dug in atop a scraped knuckle of ground; above us, Ararat remained the same, monolithic and undiminished. Dinner was set and the field cook stuffed us with a variety of tasteless carbohydrates. I had a beer and was instantly drunk. I lit a cigarette—my sixth of the day, compared with my usual fifty—and was simultaneously stoned.

Ahmet and I sat leg against leg and chatted like two retarded brothers. The sun set and took the world with it. Out in the dusty central plaza of our bivouac, the staff smashed up packing crates and built a modest campfire. The Europeans meditated upon the lambent flames for a minute, then burst into beer hall songs. The clock eased back several aeons, and the darkness muted our many voices, made every gesture meaningful, and offered us the illusion that we were a tried and tested community, which felt nice, as illusions often do.

The next day dawned cold and clear—9/9/90, my birthday, and I fully expected to die, choking either on chemical gas drifting north from the war in Iraq or Nicorette gum or both. As I understood the plan, our objective for the day was to acclimatize to the altitude, promenade up to 13,800 feet, where the high camp was situated, eat lunch, exclaim about how damn high and cold it really was, retreat back down the slope to our feathered nests, and rejoice, each according to his abilities. My plan was more ambitious: I had vowed to forsake smoking the entire day and night, breaking a twenty-year record.

When Ahmet saw me at breakfast, he beamed, all bright and cheering rays. "Bob! We go! No problem!" He shook a cigarette from his pack, tempting me back into the brotherhood. I had no alternative but to flee, slipping in with Halis's veterans. Hands-on, the first and lasting impression of Ararat was of a volcanic dreamscape where a wanderer was forbidden to ask for forgiveness. Massive basalt bombs peppered its flanks in all directions, fanned out like black huts at the lower altitudes but increasing in density the higher we went, until we were picking our way through huge tumbled galleries, the rocks sharply edged like broken lumps of glass. Where there were no rocks, there were baked meadows of field grass, rasping in the wind. The mountain was overgrazed, not by livestock but by the macrocosm. Instead of the expected bears and wolves and wild boars, I could do no better than a ladybug and a half-dozen honeybees. Ararat was theirs.

I began to falter and soon drifted back among Sandwich and his ducklings, all in a row, stabbing one another with their ski poles. I pulled over to let them pass. "Good day." I bowed. "Lovely morning, eh? Auf Wiedersehen." Those who spoke English pecked at me, vicious health harpies, and those who didn't made do with cold neglect. I had not announced my birthday because being celebrated, I feared, would interfere with my growing dignity as a scapegoat. Accordingly, I fell back some more, and there was Ahmet.

"Ahmet, are you following me? I can feel you breathing down my neck."

"Bob! Bob! Bob! We go. No problem. We smoke. It's good."

My conversations with Ahmet were intensely soothing. When I looked up from my feet to speak again, though, there was Rudi glowering at me, and when I looked up the next time, I was alone on Ararat, tracking boot prints through an illicit solitude. I had never *seen* silence of such uncompromised scope, the altitude abstracting the valley and composing the panorama of the horizon into a Euclidean sampler, all swooping, slanting masses, planispheres and primary shapes, glimmering in the thermals. It was as fine a birthday present as I'd ever received.

I stayed with the trail until midafternoon, when I caught sight of high camp, still, at my speed, an hour ahead, and then turned back down. To my surprise, Ahmet was waiting for me, clearly set at ease to see he wouldn't have to go and fetch me. He clapped me on the back and we descended, dropping into another twisty, close-walled gully, so steep our strides grew longer and longer as gravity put the idea into our heads to race. Ahmet whooped and accelerated out of sight. I braked to a stop, red lights blinking. I had thought prudence and good judgment and flexibility would keep me out of hot water, but no one had told me going up was easy, compared with going down. All the unpaid bills started coming due. My return took hours, and it infused weariness right into my marrow. I fell four times, controlled slides through the gravel that sucked out from under me, my legs too weak to fight.

Back in camp, off-duty soldiers were cooling out in the community tent, paying rapt attention to a broadcast from a transistor radio. From our quartermaster, I purchased a bottle of water and joined them at the table. We shook hands, and I asked them to aim high if they saw me sleepwalking. Erol was there, so I had asked him for news from Iraq and Saudi Arabia—were they still on the map? The soldiers said screw the news, screw Iraq; they were listening to a soccer game. I finished the water and begged for hot tea. My flesh throbbed in its cells.

I asked Erol to tell Ahmet I wanted to discuss a few things with him. It was done. Ahmet peered keenly into my face, without expression, then spoke rapidly to Erol, who translated. "He says, 'What do you want to know?'"

"I want to find out the history of the Kurds."

Ahmet studied me and gave me the most piercing look of betrayal I have ever received. And yet I didn't get it. He spoke again to Erol, waited for the translation, and left. Now even Erol seemed oddly without humor.

"Ahmet says he is sorry, but he knows nothing about the history of the Kurds."

What a damn vacant fool I was. The Kurds had been gassed in Iraq, massacred in Iran; Turkey was the one relatively safe haven they occupied in the world, and even here they were under the thumb, however lightly it pressed. The inviolable mountains near the Iraqi border were a Kurdish stronghold and in fact supported an armed (but largely inactive) independence movement. And although the Kurds held elected seats in parliament, the Kurdish language remained banned in all public forms. Essentially, at an expense I had no ability to calculate, I had just asked Ahmet to jeopardize his employment and maybe make a tour of his own in the police stations.

Erol, no dummy, shrugged it off. Nobody wanted the camp contaminated by politics, where it had no place, no use, no point. I felt wretched, then infinitely worse as Erol explained they had summoned another guide up the mountain from Doğubayazit. He spoke English and would be assigned to me alone. Oh, the ignominy, to be coddled with my own guide! And, as my composure failed, he introduced himself—Bulent, a Turk from the Sea of Marmara—and as he talked on, I impolitely cradled my head on the table, with no desire whatever for palaver. He gave up on me and walked away.

I had not smoked yesterday, nor would I today, and I was swaggering a bit after breakfast, because I knew I had high camp nailed. Bulent quickly asserted his own approach to the way things were done. While the Kurdish guides folded their hands over the small of their backs, lending a preoccupied, professorial stoop to their walking posture, Bulent favored ski poles to assist his footing. At the gorge above camp, where Halis veered his squad to the right, Bulent led me to the left, politely suggesting I not step on the fragile grass. For the most part, we spoke little but pegged along, Bulent monitoring my progress and condition. When the party halted for lunch, we were right there.

But then I ruined myself again by clambering into the rocks, my stomach churning. After a particularly long pause to catch my wind, I pivoted summitward to discover Bulent asleep on his feet, bent over his poles. The afternoon turned late. On the perimeter of high camp, I lowered myself down onto the rubble, hypnotized by Ararat. Finally I was here, on the threshold of the summit of the beast. Beneath its white mass, the high camp was like a grotto, cloud-shadowed and mysterious, quarried out from the glacier, its palisades of ice streaked with dirt and volcanic debris. Stones plinked out of the frozen face and rolled musically onto the moraine.

As soon as the tent was pitched, a blizzard raged down on us, stretching prodigiously to the valley two miles below. Rob and I scuttled inside. I could not unzip my sleeping bag. I could not manage the zipper on my day pack or my duffel bag. If anybody had inquired about me, I would have to tell them I had keeled over dead. I lay on my sleeping bag, booted and jacketed. It had grown terrifically cold. Dinner was called, but I could not respond. Bulent brought me a cup of macaroni soup, a thermos of tea. Falling through layer after layer of stupefying aches, I landed on a brittle layer of sleep. Bulent was back at two a.m., rousing us for the summit.

There were stars above the silvered dome, but not many—no omens good or bad. Rob had defected from Halis's group, and together with Bulent we groped our way forward, Bulent's headlamp dabbing into the unknown. On Ararat, I had not made the acquaintance of steep until now. Executing a tight back-and-forth traverse, we made a zigzag stitch right up over the rocks. If you've humped up the Washington Monument with your throat swollen shut and a clothespin on your nose and a chest cold, that's about what it was like on the first section, at least for me.

We constituted a provisional vanguard. Below, the embers of Halis's raiders bobbed out from camp and formed a beautiful jeweled snake, slithering upward. A crag obscured them, and then they came into view again, they were halfway to us, we could hear their dull clank and puff, and Sandwich was coming on. By the time Ahmet waded into the invisible stream of night, Halis had overtaken us, and we halted to let his company pass. The imagery was powerful, militaristic—the solemn clandestine movement under cover of night, the lowered heads and muffled thuds of boot steps, the circumspect cones of dim light preceding each individual, the intense sense of mission that prohibited talk or comment, the implicit glory. The operation was pure war-game and uplifting drama, and since we had no sons to give to it, we gave up Rob, who fastened himself like a burr on the tail of a wolf and was gone.

Sandwich filed by. No one exchanged a word. Ahmet filed by and I thought I recognized a radiance from a visible fragment of Ahmet's smile, wishing me well. Twenty minutes later, when we craned our necks, we could see the almost imperceptible backwash of light from the procession above us; then it flicked its tail for the last time, and vanished.

"Bub?"

"Bulent?" Bulent's English was better than he gave himself credit for, but clogged and submerged in the deep bass vowels and glottal stops, irrefutably male, of Turkish.

"Uh . . . how do you feel? Are you sick? Does your head ache? Do you want to stop?"

This discourse became the refrain of our ascent, an Araratian call-and-response: Are you . . . ? No, boss. Do you . . . ? No, boss. Bulent was my Moses, leading me to an elusive promised land, and I hearkened to his command. In the growing light he seemed more trusting of me, permitting himself to ascend out of view. Ten minutes ahead, I'd find him sagged over his poles, dozing.

To tell the truth, I felt like the most persecuted man on the planet, and I had ceased joking with myself about my prospects or the risks. I traveled only in twelve-foot sections or less, my lungs extended to full volume with each breath, but the wash of oxygen was missing, and I could not be satisfied. Extended beyond my limits, past ordinary reck-lessness, I had put myself in a position where anything could happen. I was aware that altitude sickness buried mountaineers no matter their level of experience, that it was most lethal to climbers with a stubborn streak, and that I was a prime but untested candidate for it. I was suffer-ing as I had never suffered, and yet there was an absorbing momentum, an onward press so inexorable that it never crossed my mind to dig in my foot and make it stop, a perpetual motion aspiring onward, but all the while descending within, unseen, like a deep-sea diver.

I pushed on alone for a few minutes. A storm had enveloped the summit, but the first trekkers would be dancing on it by now. I gazed up from my labor and saw Rudi, picking his way down toward me, on the verge of panic. He shouted in my face, thumping the left side of his chest. I understood the words "heart attack." I nodded with lethargic stupidness and he pushed wildly past, bent forward into an invisible gale.

Bulent and I reunited without mentioning Rudi; he simply asked if I would be happier back in camp.

"Bulent, do *you* want me to go back?"

It wasn't a fair question at all, and I knew he shouldn't answer it. On his deadpan face his own weariness showed from this frustrating

271

trial of his patience. But the question seemed to make him reconsider the unspoken nature of our pact, and he grinned. We rested for a half hour, replenished ourselves with liquids, and pressed on.

After this, everything was different between us. Bulent's brow unfurrowed; a bit of excitement married his eyes. For eight and a half hours we'd been clawing the slope together, and now he suddenly had faith in my perseverance. We had become partners. He looked at his wristwatch. There was still time to reach the summit, he said, if I could increase my pace.

He encouraged one more surge from me, which placed me gasping on a ledge. Before I could catch my wind and move, Halis and his partisans blocked the path in front of me, fattened with self-esteem, and I spent three unnecessary steps climbing off to let them pass. I offered congratulations, but no one looked over at me.

I convinced myself to take the next four steps. I made forty or fifty, at glacial speed, before the next group pushed me aside. Sandwich hailed me on the wing; the others glanced sideways with no fellowship to spare, as though I might jump in their way. This cold shoulder for such hot effort! To hell with false modesty—I'd earned a salute, a nod, *something*. They have slain Mount Ararat, I cried out in righteousness, emulating Noah in that regard. They have bagged their trophy, and must make room on the shelf.

I trudged ahead and came even with Bulent. From here, the seamless bleak roll of the summit was at hand, and we saw Ahmet's company hiking down its curve. Two hundred feet above us the rockscape terminated for good upon a knoll, and nothing beyond but the glacier. Rob appeared on its crest and bounded down to where we stood. He had been among the first on top in order to make *fotoçek*. "You didn't miss anything," he said, downplaying it for my benefit.

This was too much. I narrowed my eyes down the mountain, down toward the valley where all human endeavor had been rendered microscopic—furious, *furious*. "I put a curse on all of them," I snarled.

I condemned them to roam endlessly in search of fatuous triumph, stumbling to keep up with a merciless cigar-smoking guide, spraining their ankles on the bones of sinners that cluttered the trails to Paradise.

"What?" Rob said, his eyes opening wide. "Look, don't worry about them." He told me I was doing great; he was proud of me.

"*Great?*" I snapped. "Phooey. Anyone who wants to climb this mountain can, except for fascist relics in cardiac arrest and diarrhetic junkies." I couldn't help but wonder if tantrums were a little-known symptom of altitude sickness. Noah's sole recorded utterance in the Bible was a curse and a blessing, so there was the mountaineer's precedent.

Bulent and I pressed ahead, atoning for my peccadilloes. I struggled now with a mild headache. Bulent took six more steps and turned to see if I had followed. I hadn't. My pulse roared, I waited for it to calm itself, and we moved on. Ahmet appeared above us on the crest. He threw his arms up when he spotted me and came hopping joyously down the slope as fast as his legs would carry him. From the beginning he had measured me by my own standards. He had studied them as he studied everything, an avid student of all that came his way out here in the remote core of eastern Turkey, and he had not found them wanting—he understood what the mountain was for me. Whatever the price of his tribute and compassion, it was worth it; worth, in fact, more—an Everest or two. He crowed, he embraced me, his face stuck in mine, eyes glistening, nodding emotionally and with exhilaration. "Bob! Bravo! Bravo, Bob!" And then he let me go and was gone to tend his flock.

It was the greatest inducement to endure and do well that a person could expect from heaven or earth, but that was it for me. I had been undermined by Ahmet's goodness. We pressed on, conquering the knoll, and tagged the glacier—16,200 feet. Bulent was very happy. "One hour more. We can do it, we can," he said. "You are so pigheaded. We can."

"Bulent," I said, "I can't." The hour would split slowly and divide into two. There was no chance he could urge me back down before nightfall. I had seen what I could do, and this was it.

An hour above base camp, we threw ourselves down in the dust, propped our backs against a single boulder, slept deeply for a few minutes, and awoke to the light melting across the valley like butter, quieting the emptiness. An alpine coolness circulated on the breeze, refreshing and sweet. Bulent conceded I had used good judgment in deciding to turn back, though he still believed we could have made it. Maybe next year, I idly replied. We had become friends, and we sat together in the stunning peace of the plateau and talked as friends do, about our histories, our politics, our loves; about mountains—he wanted me to see the Kaçkar range, the Little Caucasus, along the Black Sea coast, which he thought the most lovely in all of Turkey. I told him I would—and did, the following week, driving off with Rob to Lake Van, then to Harran, on the border with Syria, where Abraham had once lived; making another predawn climb, this time to the summit of Nemrut Dagi to see the sunrise considered by the ancients to be the most beautiful in the world; then finally to the Black Sea, Bulent's Shangri-la, to marvel at the Kaçkars and wish we were on them . . . but we had run out of time.

As for Bulent and myself, we reached camp at dusk and were enthusiastically received by the whole company. I was of two minds about our welcome, not so anxious to lift my curse, but in the end I relented and replaced it with the other half of Noah's utterance.

(1991)

Dorado

We each have our dreams, and if they are meant to mean anything at all, you hold tight and don't let them go. You can dream of love or money or fame or something much more grand than a fish, but if a fish swims into your imagination and never swims out, that fish will grow into an obsession and the obsession might drag you anywhere, up to the metaphysical heights or down into an ass-busting nightmare, and the quest for my dream fish—South America's dorado—seems to run in both directions.

Of course a fish dream is never just about a fish but about a place as well, an unknown landscape and its habitat of active wonders, populated by creatures looming around the primal edges of our civilized selves. A place like the ancestral homeland of the Guarani Indians at the headwaters of the Paraná River, where Argentina, Brazil, and Paraguay come together. In the Guarani language, *pira* means "fish," and this fish, the legendary dorado, is called *pirayu*, the affix meaning yellow. In my dreams the *pirayu* skyrockets out of its watery underworld, a piece of shrapnel from a submerged sun, like a shank of gold an archaeologist might find in the tomb of an Incan king.

After years of unrequited dorado lust, this year I seized the dream by the gills and finally took off for the Southern Hemisphere. I was hooking up with a guide known worldwide as the king of dorado, Noel Pollak, the best person wired into the fish and its latitudes, the guarantor of the dream and your insertion into its depths. Six months earlier we had schemed to meet in Bolivia at a Pollak-discovered location that had become renowned as dorado nirvana, but we had not been able to manage that trip, for reasons I'll get to in a moment. Instead, we were now connecting at the end of what should have been the fair weather season somewhere in Argentina's vast wetlands, an area two and a half times as large as Florida's Everglades, although the specifics of our rendezvous weren't exactly clear to me. *Get on a plane, find me.* Noel was frequently off in the bush, out on the water, and our communications had been last minute, the logistics addressed in a manner all too breezy and cavalier.

But that's how dreams operate—you fling yourself into their spell and expect it will all work out. What you really must expect, however, is the strong possibility that such immoderate optimism will be sorely tested.

After a daylong flight from Miami, I landed after dark in Buenos Aires, checked into the Hub Porteno past midnight, and was belatedly informed of my itinerary by the staff, a place no one at the hotel had ever heard of—Mercedes Orientes. In the morning, even the placard at the ticket counter in BA's domestic airport didn't identify Mercedes Orientes on my flight's list of destinations. At our first stopover, everybody disembarked but a Chinese businessman and me, and an hour later we put down in Mercedes Orientes, which is probably like flying into Chicken Neck, Louisiana, in 1955. Beneath the low ceiling of clouds as we made our short descent, I could see curls and snakes and catchments of muddy water everywhere, a saturated landscape, a fishery run amok, and I imagined schools of dorado patrolling the pampas like marauding tigers, gobbling up rabbits and lambs.

Someone named Ricardo had come to fetch me in his mud-encrusted pickup truck. Hello, I said, how do you say mud in Spanish? *Barro.* We drive through the somnambulant streets of the provincial town to a two-lane highway and then onto a deeply rutted dirt track, its surface melted to goo. *Mucho barro*, I say to Ricardo, who struggles mightily with the steering wheel. Too much rain, *si*? *Si*. He nodded. The fishing has been affected, *si*? A little, said Ricardo. We pass through endless flat ranch land, small rivers swollen with floodwater, the ditches on the side of the road brimming with water, the pastures lapped with water, sheep and cattle crowded onto the high spots. The clouds roiled overhead, looking ever more threatening, the truck sliding in and out of the ruts until we skate sideways down the track and drop off the roadbed, axle-deep into the slop. It's midafternoon by the time we mud-surf into Pira Lodge. In the middle of the Ibera Marshland, the largest wetlands in the Americas, Pira is the first lodge dedicated exclusively to dorado, built in 2000 by an outfitter called Nervous Waters. The compound is quietly welcoming, an understated outback haven for the One Percenters, although put me to bed in a cardboard box, for all I care, my idea of privilege limited to landing a ferocity with fins.

Of the original team of hotshot guides at Pira, none were Argentinean, the problem eventually solved by hiring a fish-crazed kid from the capital named Noel Pollak, a self-described *born fisherman* who looks like most of the sinewy, bantamweight rock climbers I've known. In 1987, when he was thirteen years old, Noel decided he was a fish geek and taught himself fly-fishing, practicing at a lake in a city park. At age twenty he dropped out of the university to become a professional sports fisherman. For Noel, it wasn't a decision, it was beyond intelligence, it was a calling, like entering the priesthood in waders.

He started giving fly-fishing lessons to friends, one whose father was the editor of a magazine, *Aventura*, which hired him to write articles about fishing. Then Argentina's largest newspaper, *La Nación*, asked him to write a weekly fishing column. But after two years on the beat, Pollack was sick of it all, fed up with writing—actually, fed up with being edited—and he walked away from the job. Instead of buying a car with his savings, he bought a skiff and began guiding in the nearby Paraná Delta, forty-five minutes from downtown Buenos Aires. Then Pira Lodge came into the picture. He guided at Pira for ten seasons; by the third season he was promoted to head guide, eventually managing the lodge. Then in 2006 he took an off-season trip to Bolivia, where he would encounter both glory and betrayal.

Noel takes me directly to the boat dock, where the lodge's pair of Hell's Bay flats skiffs are tied up on a channel of swift, caramel-colored water providing access to the marshes and lagoons and the headwaters of the Rio Corrientes, a tributary of the Paraná. Both the Paraná and the Rio Uruguay farther to the east eventually merge north of Buenos Aires to form both the delta and the Rio de la Plata, the widest river in the world.

Standing on the dock, even a newcomer can see conditions are not normal here. The channel has overflowed its banks, submerging the lower trunks of willow trees, sending water up the lawns of the lodge. Two days earlier a low pressure system over the Amazon basin descended into Argentina and dropped twenty inches of rain in forty-eight hours, resulting in the worst flooding in ten years. Not to be deterred, Noel fished the downpour with his last stubborn client, Jimmy Carter, who had left the lodge that morning to dry out in Buenos Aires.

My moment of truth had now arrived. I'm an agnostic, an unapologetic philistine, one devolution away from fishing with dynamite. Noel puts his gorgeous bamboo fly rod in my hands, wants me to feel its craftsmanship, wants me to love it, wants to see what I can do, but it might as well be a nine-foot piece of rebar in my clumsy grip, and so I show him just how graceless an otherwise competent man can be, stripping out line like an infirm monkey, noodling my cast up and up until it plummeted ineffectually midway into the channel. Because he has teaching ingrained in his personality, Noel seems to think he can help me overcome my deficiencies, and he probably could, but there's too little time, and I had no intention spending it feeling frustrated and dumb. "No one who is learning should ever feel stupid," Noel says, trying to console me, but honestly, screw it. For once, the art is beside the point. I don't want to learn, I want to fish, and I know how to handle my spinning rod.

Noel, unlike the majority of fly fishermen I know, is an easygoing, tolerant guy. He maintains his composure in the face of my blasphemy and we go fishing.

We blast down the esoteric maze of pathways through the marshlands, the channels no wider than a suburban sidewalk. Noel pilots the boat like a motocross driver at full throttle, slaloming through serpentine creeks, making hairpin turns, rocketing ahead across small lagoons into seemingly solid walls of vegetation, the fronds of the reeds whipping my face.

After twenty minutes, the marshes begin to open up into bigger water, providing a clearer picture of why the Argentineans call this region Mesopotamia, the land between the rivers. The horizons are tree-lined, but out here vast clumps of floating islands composed of reeds and their root systems define the ecosystem. As the water gets deeper and as wide as the length of a football field, horses are suddenly everywhere in the stream, washed out of their range. Only their heads are visible, nostrils flared red, chased by swarthy gauchos in pirogues trying to herd them back to terra firma. Farther on, where the marshlands pinch in again at the headwaters of the Corrientes, Noel cuts the motor and climbs atop the poling platform bolted onto the stern and we drift, El Maestro calling out advice and wisdom to me, poised in the bow.

To fish for dorado requires the hyper-accuracy of a marine sniper, every cast by necessity a bull's-eye or you're in the vegetation. Of course as a marksman, Noel uses the equivalent of a bow and arrow, and I'm firing a rifle. His mantra is persistent but gentle—Cast at that riffle, cast at that inlet, cast at that confluence. After dozens of fruitless casts, I'm thinking, fine, let's do dozens more. That old man Jimmy Carter bounced around out here in hard rain for two days and boated eight whoppers. What a dick.

Try over there, says Noel, pointing to an eddy line where a channel runs out of the reeds into the main current. *Kaboom* is the noise you don't hear but feel when a dorado strikes and the next thing you know the beast is in the air, a solid gold furious thrashing bolt of life, and the next thing you know after that is farewell, good-bye, it's gone, and you are inducted into the Hall of Jubilant Pain that is dorado fishing. The fish launches out of the water with a hook in its bony jaws and razor teeth and when it comes back down after a three-second dance it's perfectly free and you're bleeding internally, experiencing some pure form of defeat.

"If you love fishing you're going to fall in love with this fish, but they make you suffer," Noel declares. "They make you suffer, hombre. Like the woman who you really fall in love with, they always keep you at the edge. I will admit it, I like the difficult fish." With the sun about to set, I conjure a second fish into the sky and lose it too.

At breakfast Noel announces he'll wear his lucky hat today, "the one I was wearing when I discovered this place in Bolivia," but then again, Bolivia didn't turn out so well. We took off in the skiff down the channel into the marshlands but the flooding is now unprecedented, its surge has separated vast platforms of the vegetation, breaking apart floating islands, jamming together new ones, and when we finally plow our way out into the Corrientes, what should be crystal clear waters are churned with mud. We pole and drift the edges, both of us fishing for three hours. Nothing. We try every possible combination of structures and depths. *Nada.* Shit. Noel has never seen the Pira's waters like this. The Paraná—a four-hour-drive north—will be better, he promises. The drainage is different, the riparian geology less susceptible to the washout here in the marshes. We headed back to the lodge, packed up, and hit the road.

Fishing guides are in many respects the most innocent people in the world, always believing in the best, believing in the next cast, another chance, embracing a type of aesthetics and idealism found most bracingly in nature. Fly fishermen especially are dismayed by a cretinous mentality, unable to comprehend a certain type of laziness and a certain type of greed.

Noel and I go to the Paraná because we can't go to Bolivia, where he and his investors had built the world-famous Tsimane Lodge up in the jungled foothills of the eastern flank of the Andes. Three years of discovery and development, three years of fabulously successful operations, and then the bottom fell out, all the profits—even the staff's salaries—vanishing into a wormhole, and Noel was left bankrupt. His greatest success was also his greatest ass-kicking, a pattern that seems close to the essence of existence, dorado-style. Back in Buenos Aires, he couldn't even lift himself out of his bed for months. But he had left Nervous Waters, the outfitters of Pira Lodge and in his opinion the number one fly-fishing company in the world, on good terms, and when his depression lifted he approached them with a scheme for a new partnership built around a dorado trifecta—day trips out of Buenos Aires to the delta, a future lodge in Bolivia, and a first-ever dorado operation on the upper reaches of the Paraná, based out of a 100,000-acre estancia named San Gara.

It's a tedious drive north through flat countryside from Pira to the estancia, where we arrived long after dark and met Christian, the son of the owner, and two of Noel's friends—Mariano and Alejandro. Beautiful guys—they have boats, we don't. We're fed beef with side dishes of more beef and shown to austere rooms in what seems to be a converted barracks for the resident gauchos—the estancia runs thirty-five hundred head of cattle and three hundred horses. In the morning I awake to a riot of obnoxious parrots who inhabit, by the hundreds, the crowns of the palm trees clustered at the end of the veranda. The four of us squeeze into Alejandro's pickup truck and tow his boat down to the river, about five miles down flooded gravel roads. Rheas dash across the road, foxes, the huge but rarely seen swampland deer known as *ciero de los pantanos*, flushed out to higher ground. The upper Paraná has been victimized by the same weather system—twenty inches of rain, the river rising three feet out of its normal banks. In fact, as bad as the Pira was, the Paraná is worse.

The river is expansive, miles across, Paraguay out there on the horizon of the eastern bank, separated from us by an archipelago of midstream islands cloaked with impenetrable jungle. The water is the color of *dulce de leche*, whipped by a steady breeze. We roar away to known spots, to unknown spots, scouting and fishing and roaring away again, all of the familiar exposed sandbars and beaches now underwater from the deluge.

Within an hour I have my first dorado but it's minnow-size, four or maybe five pounds, then lose a second bigger one. I'm spin-casting a spoon off the bow and Alejandro's fast-stripping a streamer from the stern, losing fish after fish. When Noel takes his place, the story's much the same, although he boats a half-dozen pirapita, a feisty smaller cousin to dorado, using dry flies. After a couple of hours of happy frustration, we head out to the islands and their solid walls of jungle, the first line of trees and bushes half-submerged, the shorelines sculpted with mini-coves and overgrown inlets and gaps and twisting eddies. It would be impossible to get out of the boat but unfortunately I find a way, kneeling in the bow to retrieve Noel's fly, entangled in a branch just out of my reach, and I fall slow motion into the fucking water. I'm only three feet offshore but there's no bottom to touch and I swim to the stern of the skiff and am pulled back aboard by my wide-eyed friends. As dips go, it was pleasant enough, but with twelve-foot caimans and three-hundred-pound stingrays and truck-size catfish throughout the river, nobody really wants to get in the water around here.

The fishing is grueling. We're casting from about sixty feet offshore into tiny pockets between the foliage, beneath the foliage, alongside downfalls, the trickiest shots imaginable. We're all expert marksmen, but nobody is perfect enough in the wind to stay out of the branches. Farther on into the jungle we can hear the eerie rumbling of colonies of monkeys, their vocalization like pigs, not squealing but a low per-sistent collective grunting. Noel picks up his rod again and now there are three of us fishing, perfectly synchronized, our casts each landing within a yard of each other in separate pockets along the bank at the same moment, and something wonderful happens. "A triple!" shouts Alejandro at the wheel. Three dorado simultaneously erupt into the air, looking like a jackpot lineup of images on a Vegas slot machine, then fall back into the current, gone, all three.

That night two of the Pira Lodge guides, Augustin and Oliver, arrive from the south to join us on the Paraná, a river they don't know but will end up guiding clients on when the Estancia San Gara opens for business in September. In the morning, as a river otter frolics in the shallows, we zoom off in two boats toward the islands. I'm daunted by the wind and the choppy, dirty water and ask Noel how hard he thinks it's blowing—fifteen knots? twenty? That's not the scale I use, says Noel. My scale is Perfect, Nice, Shitty, Awful. This is between Shitty and Awful.

But the day has its rugged magic, at least a window into the magic. Augustin, in Mariano's boat, lands a ten-pound hunk of what's known in these parts as Gaucho Gold, and on an assassin's shot in between two downed trees I'm struck by lightning, so to speak. The strike is immediate, a nanosecond after my diving plug hits the surface, and like a Polaris missile launched from a submarine, up comes the dorado, fifteen pounds, jumping into the air above our heads. Like orcas, a dorado will jump out of the water onto land a full three feet to pursue its prey—in the dorado's case, *sabalos*, panicked bait fish. Somewhere in the sequence I can feel the release of the hook and the fish is free again, but honestly it hardly matters: Noel and Alejandro are hooting and will talk about that fish with a thrill in their voices for the next two days—*Oh man, that fish!*—because it was huge and magnificent and for a moment it was ours. When the two boats reunite, Augustin tells us Oliver has spent the day "harvesting the forest," which means he's been an inch or two too far in all his casts, but at least he hasn't gone swimming. Noel and Alejandro tell him about the monster I hooked and lost. "And then," Oliver, an Englishman, says to me, "you were left with your thoughts." But there wasn't a thought in my head. I was left with only heartbreak. Yet to have owned the fish for a few seconds, to see it in the air, suspended between outcomes, has to be enough.

La vida es sueno, the Latins say—Life is a dream. I think of Noel and his struggle in Bolivia. This time it's not the fish but something much, much bigger, and it stays in the air for what seems like an eternity but in fact is only three years, and when it falls back to the water, it's gone, receded back to the dream—you thought you had it but you never did and its descent is a form of bittersweet devastation. Sometimes you can catch the big one, but the result is pathos and tragedy. And you can lose the big one and yet it persists and remains, a triumphant vision, something to carry forward beyond the dream. There's clarity here— these fishermen, these lovely men, the spread and flow of big water, the dance of the big fish, the ascendant luminosity, a blazing star built of muscle and teeth and fury, the golden arc of sweetness and sorrow, possession and loss. That's what you discover in the marshes, what you bring home from the river. That, finally, is the meaning of the dream.

The next day on the Paraná is a screaming disaster. That evening Noel and I fly back down to Buenos Aires to fish the delta. In the morning we are greeted by squalls but head out anyway into shining moments of solitude and silence, autumn light and autumn colors, and yes, kaboom, up a little creek as I cast a bull's-eye next to a log. Pirayu, the Guarani god of water, strains for the sun. A week later, in the sub- urbs of the capital, scores of people will be swept away by the floods. Any dream has its limits, and this dream had breached its boundaries, waiting to be dreamed again, and better.

(2013)

Gorongosa

On a sun-broiled morning in central Mozambique, we headed eighteen miles into the bush, our destination a shrinking stretch of soupy pool, one of the last remaining catchments in the drought-withered river, where the hippos had hunkered down during the wasting days of a dry season that refused to end. Afterward we would be choppering to other sites—remote wonders, unique to the area—although my attention had drifted when the itinerary was explained. The limestone gorge, perhaps, where the East African Rift Valley arrived at its southern terminus? The lacy cascade of waterfalls off the westward escarpment? The cathedral-size grottoes housing countless hordes of whispering bats? Not that it mattered—bad luck, you could say, since we would never get farther than the hippos.

Because of the heat, and I guess for the breezy fun of it, Segren, the young pilot up from South Africa, unhinged the front doors off the R44, a Bell-manufactured helicopter aviators call a "little bird," and we strapped in, the four of us, and ascended skyward from the small grass airstrip at Chitengo, the headquarters of Gorongosa National Park, once considered among Africa's premier game preserves until it was destroyed by decades of unimaginably brutal war and savage lawlessness, its infrastructure blasted to rubble, its bountiful population of animals slaughtered, eaten, reduced to gnawed bones and wistful memory.

In the copilot seat, with the panoramic sweep of the continent expanding out my open door—loaves of mountains on several horizons rising like a time-lapse video of Creation day, the veldt ironed out into a haze of coastal plains spread east toward the Indian Ocean—I adjusted the mic on my headset and joined the conversational squawk behind me, Greg Carr and Vasco Galante stuffed into the rear seats, already sweaty between doors that could not be removed, although they were dressed much more sensibly than I was for the tropics, or what would have been sensible if the word *malarial* were not so lethally affixed to Mozambique's ecology.

Greg and Vasco, it was becoming clear to me, were fearless, a matching set of *muzungus*, white guys, with a true affinity for the bush. Like Greg Carr, the American philanthropist who had committed his time, wealth, and considerable energy to the restoration of Gorongosa, Galante too was a successful business entrepreneur who slammed the brakes on the life he was living, threw away his map of old assumptions and foregone conclusions, made a U-turn, and went to Africa.

Many of their sentences began, *During the rainy season*, and I would be directed toward something in the landscape that was not as it should be this deep into December—the evaporated Lake Urema, shrunk from seventy-seven square miles to four; a wilting Gorongosa massif and its deplenished watershed; the raku-cracked and burning floodplains of the savanna. What now expressed itself as terra firma would require boating skills during the Southern Hemisphere's approaching summer when the park's bottomlands swelled with watery overabundance. Awed and exhilarated, I leaned out into the rush of air watching the scatter of antelope below.

At Greg's instruction, Segren eyed a safari track to navigate out toward where the platinum thread of the Urema River emptied from the traumatized lake into the dusty jungle. The pilot dipped the helicopter down into the river's high-banked channel and we roared along its downstream course at treetop level, my companions remarking upon the bed's sorry condition—black patches of dampness embroidered with a fringe of hoofprints, scum puddles churned by expiring catfish, and, increasingly, weed-clogged runs where the absent flow had encouraged a vibrant bloom of flora, the greenest thing in sight.

Last year, when CBS's *60 Minutes* came to Mozambique to produce a feature on Carr and Gorongosa, the hottest conservation story in Africa, they had filmed the river from the air as scores of Nile crocodiles flipped one after another off the banks into its robust current. Maybe there were some crocs down there now, nestled in the mucky overgrowth, but we couldn't see them. Reedbucks and occasional impala bolted across the bed's golden sand into the cover of the jungle, but it was Africa's flamboyant birds who owned the desiccated river. Egyptian geese, grotesque marabou storks showcasing the ass-bald head and plucked neck of carrion eaters, graceful herons and lanky crowned cranes, majestic fish eagles. Then we were hovering over the upstream edge of the pool, the squiggle of crocodiles visible in the khaki-colored water, and Greg pointed to a grassy bar about three hundred yards back where he wanted to put down.

On the ground, Segren announced he would stay with the aircraft and keep the engine running and we climbed out with the rotors thumping over our heads and began walking through the high grass at the base of the steep bank towering above us.

This was my first time in Africa, but even before Vasco's warning, I realized we were in elephant country, their rampant footprints postholed shin deep in the hardening cake of fertile soil, an ankle-twisting hazard. I had also registered Vasco's sudden intensity of manner, the heightened alertness, his head rotating as he scrutinized our surroundings. "Okay," he said, trying to sound lighthearted, "this is a place where elephants come. If you see an elephant coming from the north, you go south. Turn and *go*."

Although more people are killed by hippos than any other wild animal in Africa, the elephants—the remaining elephants—of Gorongosa were unforgiving. For generations now they had been engaged in a kill-or-be-killed war with humans, the once prolific herd decimated by rebel soldiers harvesting ivory to finance their insurgency or gathering a windfall of meat for their starving cadres or just gunning down the giants for the wicked hell of it. By the end of Mozambique's civil war in 1992, only three hundred of an elephant population ten times larger were left alive, and those three hundred, according to *National Geographic* cameraman Bob Poole, who had been filming in the park for a year, were "skittish and aggressive." If you were on foot, as we were, walking into an elephant's range of smell or sight could be justifiably categorized as suicidal.

But as we approached the pool, crocodiles underfoot in the soggy weeds, or a land-foraging hippo spooked by the sudden appearance of humans between it and the water, were a more immediate and tangible concern. Greg and Vasco traversed the bankside, climbing higher for a better vantage point to scout downriver and, I suspected, to be better positioned in case of a charge.

In the wild, the pittance of what's left of it, the ancient primal verities still apply. (Extreme) caution and (mild) anxiety translate as ingrained virtues, rational responses toward the perilous unknown, yet once Greg and Vasco trained their binoculars on the water, I could feel the tension in the air undergo a euphoric meltdown. Hippos! Exactly where they should be, according to their birthright, at peace in their own habitat . . . after being wiped out completely, thirty-five hundred of them, during the endless war.

As my companions dialed the aquatic spectacle into focus, I began to share the joy, unpuzzling the strange visual logic of what I could see, a rippling logjam of glistening tubs of chocolate flesh, googly-eyed and agitated, clustering down below in the muddy water, choreographed by paranoid shifts and rearrangements that never really changed the tight composition of the jam until a bull slide-paddled forward to calculate the threat of our presence. Saucer-size nostrils flared and exhaled spray, a wet snort like the release of hydraulic brakes in the fragrant stillness, now absent the distant background thrum of rotor blades.

The pilot, for a reason known only to him, had shut down the engine. Occupied by the marvel of the half-submerged pod, we simply noticed an improvement in the depth of the silence around us and made no mention of it. There we stood, spellbound and revering, allowed by the moment to believe in an Edenic world so harmoniously, benevolently perfect, one forgets to remember that the most readily available dish on the menu might very well be you.

The glory of the hippopotamus seems shaped by bizarre hallucinogenic juxtapositions—the utility of its rounded amphibious design packaged in the exaggerated ugliness only seen elsewhere in cartoons; its blob-like massiveness adorned with undersized squirrel ears and stubby legs akin to a wiener dog's, bullfrog eyes that are nevertheless beady, pinkish peg-toothed jaws like a steam shovel's attached to the compressed porcine features of its face. We were enthralled, flies on the wall of hippo heaven. Then we withdrew as gently as shadows, back to the helicopter, which maybe had a problem. But dreamy and high with hippo love, we didn't much care.

We climbed in, Segren muttered something about weak batteries, we climbed out. "I don't think I'd let my mom ride in this helicopter," said Greg. He and I walked upriver and sat cross-legged across from baboons collecting on the far bank, remarking on what we could figure out about the tribe's hierarchy and habits, occasionally extrapolating our insights into opinions about the monkeyshines of the primates half a world away on Wall Street, the two of us content and carefree. Then Vasco walked down the bank to tell us what we had already suspected—the helicopter, with a dead starter, wasn't going to get us out of here—and even then we greeted our predicament as a frivolous interruption to an otherwise magnificent day.

But we were in no-man's-land, the great bloodthirsty Darwinian free-for-all, probably twenty klicks beyond the Chitengo compound's cell phone range, the VHF radio on the little bird was of no use, and we had to guess our chances of being rescued before tomorrow were zero, since no one knew of the fix we were in, let alone where, exactly, to come looking.

There was a boyish brightness in Greg's eyes when he suggested we go for the full unadulterated experience, seize the rare opportunity to traipse (illicitly) in the park, cross the river and hump all day through the forge-like heat of the primordial jungle into the happy zone of cell phone reception, and text message the cavalry.

"So what do you guys think?" Greg said as we stood on the wrong bank of the croc-infested river. "Wanna walk?" Vasco and I looked at each other and shrugged. We were not bound to see much indecisiveness from Carr, a man whose permanent optimism was exceeded only by his irrepressible, well-aimed, and sometimes kooky enthusiasm (like plopping down on a restaurant floor to do push-ups). Anything could happen tramping around in the jungle, but we faced one certainty: It was not yet noon and we had to be safely back to civilization by sundown, the predatory commencement of people-eating time.

"I was hoping to show you a lion tonight," Greg Carr told me the night before, the first thing he ever said to me, yet I had arrived too late at Gorongosa to enter the locked preserve. The lion Greg had in mind, however, had roared throughout the evening, and early this morning, before commandeering the helicopter, we had driven out into the bush looking for it but found only vultures convened at the skeleton of its kill. Now, less than twenty-four hours later, Greg's desire to hook me up with a lion was quickly losing all of its appeal.

I asked if either one of them had the foresight to bring along a side-arm . . . *you know, just in case.* Greg said no, and Vasco said, Yes, this is my pistol, showing me the miniature penknife he carried in his pocket. I was the only one with gear, a shoulder bag crammed with nothing useful except our water bottles, and to lighten the load I removed a book, William Finnegan's chronicle of Mozambique's civil war, and tried to give it to Segren, who had chosen to remain behind, but the pilot did not want it. What else have you got to do? I said, frowning. Regardless of his schoolboy's distaste for reading, the book was staying.

For several miles we hiked upstream along a game trail flattened through the grass, the riverbed still glazed with stagnant water beneath a lush carpet of weeds, an ideal habitat for lurking crocodiles as advertised by the warthog carcass we hurried past, its hindquarters shorn off as it had tried to flee. Farther on the channel's vegetation began to get mangy, exposing islands of muddy skin, their crusty appearance more to our liking as we walked ahead, the bed drying out until Greg had convinced himself conditions were favorable for a clean and effortless crossing. Let's try it, said Greg, and I watched in horror as he and Vasco took six steps out into what I assumed was quicksand, their legs disappearing in a steady downward suck. I responded in the manner most typical of twenty-first-century Americans, grabbing my camera to record the flailing of their last astonished moments.

It seems implausible that some lives might ever intersect, separated by every divide destiny can thrust between two people, yet should their story lines somehow twist together, they form a single braid of near-mystical affirmation for unlimited possibility. Say, for example, an African warrior—Beca Jofrisse—and an American tycoon—Greg Carr: the unlikely pair of administrators who occupy the summit of Gorongosa's organizational chart. One a former Marxist-Leninist freedom fighter, the other a capitalist swashbuckler who made his fortune developing information technology.

A genuine introduction to Lieutenant Colonel Beca Jofrisse's country begins with the unsettling sight of an AK-47 assault rifle emblazoned on its national flag, and the story of modern Mozambique—its tyrannies and bloody struggles and ideological promiscuities, its surprising transformation from the planet's biggest nightmare (in the early '90s Mozambique was the poorest country on earth) into one of sub-Saharan Africa's very few nations where hope, peace, and stability are not delusions—can be found contained in the proud generation of woefully scarred and stoically victorious people like Jofrisse, a gentle statuesque man whose frozen stare into the whirlwind of the past is regularly broken by embracing smiles.

In 1968 at the age of nineteen, Beca Jofrisse began his long walk north across the length of Mozambique to the border with Tanzania to join the *luta armada*—the armed struggle for independence from Portugal, which had inflicted a five-hundred-year-long battering of the mainland's indigenous populations since 1498, the year Vasco da Gama rounded Cape Horn and landed at Ilha de Mozambique, claiming the shoreline he sailed past for the Portuguese crown. The white man's ravenous enterprise had many appetites—in the seventeenth century gold, in the eighteenth century ivory, in the nineteenth century slaves—and in 1891, during the European powers's "Scramble for Africa," Portugal established formal control over three colonies—Mozambique, Angola, Guinea-Bissau—which seventy years later would erupt in open rebellion.

The battle for Beca Jofrisse's country was waged by Frelimo—the Mozambique Liberation Front—from its headquarters in Dar es Salaam. When Beca finally crossed into Tanzania to enlist in Frelimo's revolutionary army, he could scarcely have imagined that more than twenty years later he would be fighting on, his country still a raging war zone, his enemies his own misguided people.

In Tanzania, the literate Beca excelled as a student of military basics, which earned him a trip to the Soviet Union for more advanced training and an indoctrination into the tenets of communism. Returning to Tanzania, he was deployed back across the border into the fray and in 1972, ordered to cross the Zambezi River, his unit battled their way south to spread the war into the province of Sofala, the home of Gorongosa National Park, forced to close in 1973, engulfed in combat and the scorched earth campaign of the colonial military.

By 1974, Portugal's trifecta of wars in Africa had proved to be a losing ticket, and in July of that year a new government quickly agreed to hand over Mozambique to Frelimo. The independent Republic of Mozambique was proclaimed the following year. Overnight the Portuguese, 250,000 of them, pulled out of the demolished country in an orgy of sabotage and vandalism, leaving behind an infant nation with too little infrastructure and too many guns.

Out of this maelstrom of "peace" and economic chaos another monster was born, the Mozambique National Resistance (Renamo), a disorganized but homicidal insurgency assembled by its sponsors— first white-ruled Rhodesia and then apartheid South Africa—to ensure that black majority rule in Africa became synonymous with disaster. Renamo's objective was to sow havoc, wreck everything, and paralyze the country, and it would bathe Mozambique in blood for the next sixteen years.

Central Mozambique absorbed the brunt of these atrocities, and Gorongosa itself became a shooting gallery, a shifting headquarters for both armies, the area swarmed by destitute refugees, the footpaths throughout the countryside rigged with land mines, its animals serving as a type of ATM machine to fund and supply the combatants. Protected as a private hunting reserve since 1921 and designated as a national park in 1960, known romantically by tourists as the place where Noah left his ark, Gorongosa's 1,455 square miles once hosted more predators than South Africa's Kruger, denser herds of elephants and buffalo than the Serengeti, and thousands upon thousands of plains animals. By the end of the civil war, the body count was numbing—the elephants decimated; hippos exterminated; the largest lion population in all of Africa reduced from five hundred to a few dozen; thirty-five hundred zebras gone; two thousand impala gone; rhinos, gone; forty buffalo left from a herd of fourteen thousand; a herd of seven hundred sable antelope reduced to zero; three remaining wildebeests from a herd of fifty-five hundred; 129 waterbuck from a herd of 3,500; the ubiquitous warthogs nowhere in sight. Cheetahs, wild dogs, hyenas, and jackals apparently exterminated. Leopards, no one could say.

When the civil war blazed into existence in 1976, Beca Jofrisse underwent a metamorphosis from jungle guerrilla fighter to an elite member of the newborn nation's high command, stationed in Maputo, the cosmopolitan capital. By the early 1990s, Frelimo, disavowing its Marxist ideology, signed a peace agreement with Renamo. The catastrophic decades of hostility and ruination were over. Beca, like the soldiers on both sides, had lost scores of friends in a conflict that had left more than a million Mozambicans dead and millions more wounded or maimed. He retired from the army, pursued an engineering degree, and dedicated himself to the reconstruction of what had been lost.

As the new century rolled out, the nation's hatred and mistrust slowly exhausted itself and Mozambique was alive again, though not by any measure discharged from the intensive care ward of the underdeveloped world. But for the first time in memory, the country seemed to be sitting up and smiling. Its near-death experience imbued Mozambicans with a laid-back joie de vivre balanced by a sustaining sense of civility, the correct antidote to fratricidal madness. About the same time that Greg Carr parachuted onto the scene in 2004, Beca realized the war had left behind in him an unrequited love—a passion for nature and the forests of central Mozambique, the beauty of the thousand-year-old baobabs, the surreal haunted groves of yellow fever trees in the provinces where he had fought as a young warrior to liberate his country.

Lieutenant Colonel Jofrisse's friends in the Frelimo government encouraged him to consummate this old but dormant romance and sent him to study natural resource protection at the Southern African Wildlife College. Then in April 2008, at a signing ceremony between the president of Mozambique and Greg Carr, formalizing the nonprofit Carr Foundation's forty million dollar, twenty-year agreement to resurrect the national park, Jofrisse, representing the government of Mozambique, and Carr together became Gorongosa's pair of overseers, partners in a pas de deux quite unlike any heretofore performed in the continent's jungles.

*   *   *

High in a tree in Africa a desperate woman clutches a baby, her feet submerged in floodwaters of biblical proportion. For Greg Carr, like most people watching CNN's footage of the devastation caused by Cyclone Eline when it slammed into Mozambique in 2000, this wretched image blipped the obscure southern African nation onto the screen of their awareness, however momentarily, and even then, like Carr, many of those viewers would be hard-pressed to articulate a single fact about the country beyond a general pronouncement on its condition: hell on earth.

Later that same year in New York City, a mutual friend introduced Carr to Mozambique's ambassador to the United Nations, a congenial diplomat who asked, Why don't you think about helping us out? It was a question Carr had come to expect from well-intended strangers. What else really would you ask a philanthropist sitting atop a stack of money, in this case 200 million dollars, an amount that for Carr served as the answer to a question few masters of the universe ever bothered to ask: How much wealth is finally enough? Carr deferred, telling the ambassador he would think about Mozambique, but his hands were tied with other projects.

In the mid-'80s, by the age of twenty-seven, Carr had already morphed into an über-capitalist, turning away from a path into academia. A history major at Utah State, he left his hometown in Idaho Falls, Idaho, exchanging the mountains of the west for the ivory towers of Cambridge, enrolling in Harvard's Kennedy School of Government, which he saw as a springboard for earning a PhD in linguistics. While finishing up his master's degree at the Kennedy School, he began an intensive study of the breakup of AT&T's monopoly on telecommunications, smelling opportunity in its divestitures.

He convinced a friend, Scott Jones, a twenty-five-year-old scientist at an MIT lab, to go into business with him, maxing out their credit cards for start-up funds. In 1986, their new company, Boston Technology, democratized voice mail services, marketing the system to the emerging Baby Bells. Four years later, Boston Technology was the top voice mail provider in the nation. By the mid-'90s, Carr was CEO of both Boston Technology and a second technology venture, Prodigy, an Internet service pioneer. Then in 1998, a very rich man with, he says, "a pretty bad case of attention deficit disorder," he walked away from it all to create the Carr Foundation, its charter targeted on three areas of philanthropic pursuits: human rights, the arts, and conservation.

Visionaries resist typecasting, though with a pince-nez and roughrider garb Greg Carr could pass, in stoutness of physique as well as spirit, for a younger Teddy Roosevelt. To explain how he thinks or to illuminate his moral universe, he quotes Buddhist philosophers, Nelson Mandela, and David Foster Wallace, and he cites the authors—Darwin, Harvard biologist E. O. Wilson—he considers seminal to his swooning love of nature. Were Carr a more conventional businessman, when he took a powder from his fortune-making enterprises at the age of thirty-eight, the temptation to describe his action as a midlife crisis would have been irresistible, yet for Carr it was a long-awaited chance to shift gears.

Behind the change was a lifelong conviction that the span of a career should contain separate but interlocking halves, a yin/yang of profit and nonprofit, an exuberance for making money married to a passion for giving it away to support causes dearest to one's heart. Passively giving *back*, just checkmarking the do-gooder box, wasn't the point. The point was unleashing happiness, animating your value system with injections of old-fashioned fun, which is precisely what he thinks rich guys without a sense of largesse are missing out on. Darting an elephant to replace the batteries in its radio collar ranks high on Carr's list of Fun Things to Do After Breakfast.

On a deeper level, though, he saw capitalism without a conscience as a socioeconomic steroid, proving itself no more useful to humanity and its huddled masses than other abused ideologies. Rise alone, fall together. The selfish detachment of cowboy capitalism from the welfare of a community created mayhem, a danger not only to itself but to the planet, plundering the resources of an ecology with the same rapacity of soldiers pillaging a national park.

Ideally, making a busload of money allowed you to cut to the front of the line as an agent of meaningful change, and by 2000, Carr was inundated with projects: turning the former headquarters of the Aryan Nations into a peace park in Sandpoint, Idaho, constructing cultural monuments in Boise. He built the Market Theater in Harvard Square, then donated eighteen million dollars to establish Harvard's Carr Center for Human Rights Policy. He produced a movie, then started a radio station in Afghanistan. He was conducting a marching band of altruism, on fire with intellectual stimulation yet yearning for something more visceral, adventurous. The recipe had to include "a little vision to it, some mystery, some romance, some difficult problems to solve," and satisfy his lust for immersion—"Do theater to understand theater and do conservation to understand conservation. Don't just read a book. Combine ideas and action. Exist in physical reality."

Intrigued by the ambassador's invitation, he began to systematically research conservation projects in the southern African nation and traveled to Mozambique for the first time in 2002. Two years later he returned to climb aboard a helicopter with government officials to tour six potential sites Carr had identified that fit both his personal goals and the political mandate—to weld environmental restoration with human development into a sustainable business model based on tourism and agri-industry, thereby enabling absolutely marginalized communities to have a future. The second stop was Gorongosa, the park in shambles, long forgotten as a destination, a lost cause. Nothing there anymore worth bothering with, Carr heard often, a sentiment that collided with his intolerance for cynicism. But when he first set foot on Gorongosa, "it was, boom, *Let's go!*" Returning home to pace around the house and think about it would have been antithetical to the tally-ho style of his decision making.

What Carr saw at Gorongosa, with a historian's perspective, was Yellowstone, the park he had grown up with as his neighbor in eastern

Idaho. Yellowstone made it easy for Carr to conceptualize the Gorongosa project. "When Yellowstone was made a national park in 1872," says Carr, "the animals had been extirpated. It wasn't this pristine thing and the government said, 'Oh, we better protect it.' No, no, no. It had been hunted out. The bison, the elk, the bears were gone or mostly gone. The point of Yellowstone Park was to recover it, and a hundred years later it's back. I look at Gorongosa that way. This was the first national park in the Portuguese-speaking world. Both parks are the flagships of their respective nations. Both of them have big charismatic fauna, including carnivores. Both are dangerous places." The parallels struck him as personal and beckoning.

For the next two years, he consulted with aid professionals, searched for suitable experts to bring into the project (more difficult than he imagined), and negotiated with the Mozambican government (in Portuguese, a language he did not speak), "just trying to sign a piece of paper and get started." That contract, a Memorandum of Understanding signed in 2004, essentially stated, said Carr, "Look, this is one day at a time, toss me out whenever you want, and let's just get to know each other." He wasn't buying the park, or leasing it, or taking it over as a concession, but instead agreeing to manage Gorongosa on a provisional basis. It was by any account an unusual arrangement, an auspicious foreigner assuming control over an iconic sovereign asset, and Carr hoped it would provide a template for saving stressed-out national parks throughout the developing world.

Gorongosa's business manager, Joao Viseu, calls Carr's approach "the new philanthropy—not just giving but doing," a paradigm splitting the difference between two more recognizable patterns—the Paul Farmers of the world, who start with nothing but a calling and gradually accumulate resources because people believe in them, and "the rich guy who has his billion dollars and then says, *There you go.*"

At age forty, with piles of money on hand, Carr rode the elevator to the ground floor, the place where everything looked and felt different—where Carr looked and felt different. "I didn't sit in Washington, D.C., and mail checks. I came here and said I'm going to be here for twenty years, and I'm going to wear these silly cutoff shorts. To make things work in rural Africa you've got to be hands-on, and you run a real risk of making things worse if you intervene from a distance."

One night at dinner—grilled prawns, gin and tonics—I listened as Greg and Beca, Gorongosa's two lordly patriarchs, got to know each other better, discussing an issue of vital importance: the forthcoming annual soccer game between management and staff. Carr suggested that, as co-administrators of the park, he and Beca should be the goal-keepers. Or, given their age, the two of them together would make one goalkeeper.

"Maybe," said Beca doubtfully. "I'm not good."

"Or maybe we should be somewhere else," said Carr, who had never played soccer, and the two of them leaned into each other like broth-ers, laughing.

"But we can," insisted Beca.

"*Sim, podemos,*" Carr agreed. Yes, we can. The game, with Carr and Beca on the field against the youthful staff, would end in a crowd-cheering tie.

From where we sat in Chitengo's soaring new open-air rondavel-style restaurant, gazing out into the beast-filled wilds just a minute's walk away, I found it difficult to imagine the devastation Carr had encountered here three and a half years earlier. When he first drove in with his new multidisciplinary team (scientists, engineers, business managers, economic advisers, tourism developers), there was no water, no electricity, the few walls left standing in the rubble were riddled with bullet holes, bomb casings were lying around. They were embedded within the miserable heat of a hazardous jungle sur-rounded by crippling poverty and the vestigial tensions of civil war. He hired a labor force from the local communities, former Frelimo soldiers and Renamo rebels who required occasional stern lectures on the rewards of playing nice. Slowly Chitengo's infrastructure—tourist chalets, reception center, meeting hall, staff housing, mechanic's shop—began to rise from the ashes, its reincarnation adorned with Internet satellite dishes. Until he moved into a spacious campaign tent, Carr slept outside in the back of a pickup truck, high enough off the ground to keep safe from snakes and (he hoped) lions, a star gazer's preference that landed him in the hospital, semi-comatose with the first of three bouts of malaria.

An intrepid hiker back home in Idaho, Carr, with an entourage of biologists and local guides, quickly became an obsessive explorer of the park and its environs, gleefully "discovering" thermal springs, waterfalls, caves, unknown species. The animals were not entirely gone, as he had been led to believe, but hiding, what was left of them, still harried by rampant poaching. A revitalized team of rangers, many of them former poachers themselves, began to patrol throughout Gorongosa, its dry season plagued by wildfires set by illegal hunters to drive game into snares or harvest the large rodents that burrowed on the savanna. By 2006, with the completion of a fenced sanctuary, the park had begun to reintroduce large numbers of grazers—wildebeest and buffalo—back into the overgrown grasslands, and supplement the antelope populations with breeds that hadn't been seen in years. Last year more hippos and elephants were trucked in, but the zebras Carr hoped to import remained unavailable behind Zimbabwe's nearby border, trapped by political turmoil.

Tourists trickled back to the park, thirty or so camping out the first year, fewer than a thousand in 2005, eight thousand (a mix of tourists and other visitors) in 2008, compared to twenty thousand in Gorongosa's golden years in the sixties, when the park's original restaurant, now rebuilt in soaring rondavel style, often served four hundred meals a day. From day one, Carr understood that the long-term fate of Gorongosa depended on ecotourism, a tricky proposition for an unfamiliar destination so distant from the world's centers of dwindling affluence. In ten years, the project believes it will be able to easily accommodate one hundred thousand tourists a year, an egalitarian mix of self-drive campers and luxury-addicted adventuristas, and even at four times that capacity Gorongosa would still maintain the same "tourism density level" as Kruger National Park in South Africa without damaging the character of its wilderness. Right now, the top-quality safaris Gorongosa offers use only 75 miles (of a potential 620 miles) of game-drive roads.

Yet before tourists could be seduced back to Gorongosa, the project's near- and long-term success depended on its ability to cultivate the support of the 250,000 villagers living in the park's buffer zone and surrounding district, the overwhelming majority of them subsistence farmers living in a sprawl of mud-and-thatch villages and scattered homesteads, vulnerable to disease and famine, too poor even to generate garbage, which explains the remarkable litter-free cleanliness of the countryside's roads and footpaths.

Humans and the environment invariably compete with each other, yet without synchronicity between the two, Carr believed, both were doomed. The Gorongosa project, dedicated to floating both boats simultaneously, put itself at the center of a controversy in conservation science, positioned between a movement called "back to the barriers," basically turning the natural resource into an off-limits fortress, and a more decentralized and porous community-based management approach toward environmental stewardship.

Across the planet loss of habitat, an apocalyptic problem approaching critical mass, requires increasingly radical change in human behavior, yet barricading Gorongosa from its swaddle of communities, Carr told me, was both infeasible and perhaps morally arrogant, an artificial separation between integrated ecosystems (an astonishing fifty-four distinct ecosystems) and social patterns that would have minimal effect on the three practices that most endanger the park's well-being—slash-and-burn agriculture on the watershed, charcoal production in the buffer zone, and hunting—and offered no incentive to lure people away from these traditional activities. And Carr believed fervently that a dense, rich, and age-old culture, better attuned to contemporary realities, was no more or less worthy of preservation than a rain forest or wildlife population. The key to all of this, of course, was to enable self-sufficiency by galvanizing everyone with a financial stake in conservation.

The first priority was an educated, healthy workforce. The day after our jungle march, we waded hip-deep across the Pungue River to visit Vinho, the community closest to the park's headquarters. As we scrambled out of the flow, I mentioned that Gorongosa's head safari guide, Adolfo Macadono, had told me that a week earlier, a villager had been eaten by a crocodile while fishing at the same spot where we were standing on the bank. "I think about it as getting hit by a car in Harvard Square," Greg said. "It happens." Need I say I found no comfort in this analogy. Drying off as we toured Carr's work in Vinho—a brick-and-mortar school with a Wi-Fi computer lab, a clinic and nurses' residence, a bore well drawing potable water—Greg told me he had promised to construct a hundred additional schools and twenty-five more clinics throughout the district. By 2009, Gorongosa employed six hundred newly trained locals, an additional five thousand people benefiting from their paychecks.

When Carr reached out to the villages dotted across the buffer zone and the Gorongosa massif, many peasants had rarely, if ever, seen a *muzungu*, and certainly not one bearing swag— cloth, wine, tobacco—to appease the resident spirits. Near Nhatsoco, a settlement on the mountain, Carr was rebuffed by the area's *curandeiro* (spiritual leader, witch doctor—take your choice) when he sought the priest's alliance in his effort to stop people from clear-cutting in the rain forest. His team had arrived in a flurry of bad juju—their helicopter was a sinister red color, a village chief wore inappropriate clothes, an unhappy ancestor—a snake—chose to make an appearance. Sent away as a rude meddler, Carr, an innately humble man, apologized but persisted, eventually gaining the priest's blessing. By 2006, locals were being paid to guide tourists up the sacred peak, build tree nurseries, and begin replanting hardwoods across the slopes.

Everywhere Carr goes in the district these days, he is treated inevitably like a rock star distributing goodwill and golden eggs. In return Carr asks the villagers to stop setting fires in the park, give up poaching, forgo hacking down trees. Not surprisingly, perhaps, the bad habits carry on, at least for the time being, though a shift in attitudes is palpable. Carr, with no illusions, says, "It starts somewhere"—a more felicitous life, a less destructive way of doing things—but by the time he hands back Gorongosa to the Mozambican government twenty years from now, no one doubts that its human and ecological landscapes will have undergone a mind-boggling transformation. The project's staff, 98.5 percent Mozambican, already light up with the feeling that that future, with its attendant sense of triumph in their remaking of a war-torn country, has pulled into the station.

For the record, the only foreigner on Gorongosa's team of managers is Carr's wry-humored communications director, my slimed and footsore companion Vasco Galante, a tall, balding, solid-bodied former basketball player for Portugal's national team.

It wasn't quicksand after all but a bog of liquefied silt. Greg and Vasco bottomed out crotch-deep and eventually extracted themselves from the goop and we continued our march upriver, though in a matter of minutes, Greg, undaunted, had plunged into another bog. This time as he struggled free he began to notice that wherever a plant with tiny yellow flowers grew, the bed would support his weight, and farther on we came to a place where the flowering zigzagged across the channel. Heedless to my admonitions, Greg racewalked toward the far shore as if he were trying to beat oncoming traffic. Perhaps he worried about crocodiles hidden in the weeds, although I had begun to learn that Greg's momentum was an indomitable force, at times imprudent, and uninhibited by ambivalence. Certain now that what we were doing was a variation of crazy, I looked across the river at the opposite bank, the feral tangle of thicket, vine, and scrub palmetto roasting in the feeble shade of blanched trees and spiked ilala palms, and resigned myself to the crossing.

We scrambled up a natural drainage chute carved into the bank, found the seldom-used safari track we had hoped was there, and followed it back downstream for two miles, a stretch where several days later Vasco and I would find elephants coming up off the river, and a hippo cow and calf napping in the bush not thirty feet from where we now walked. Then the track turned away from the river into the windless, stifling heart of the jungle, and we were soon inhaling intense fumes of the unforgettable leathery piss odor of wild Africa.

For the first half mile the trees were stripped, smashed, toppled over, leaf-eating pachyderms passing through like a tornado, and we became instant students of their mounded dung, studying the color and relative dryness to determine the herd's proximity. "Just keep talking," Greg said hopefully, and whenever our conversation flagged, I would loudly announce to the jungle that we were, in fact, still talking.

We walked with relentless determination, which is how one walks when Greg Carr sets the pace and you intend to keep up with him. With the sun overhead there was little shade on the track, the sauna-like ferocity of the heat as threatening as the thought of lunging carnivores or slithering black mambas, and after an hour it was evident that we lacked sufficient water to stay hydrated. Magically my shoulder bag filled with rocks and we began to share the punishment of lugging it. Sweating profusely in jeans and leather boots, I envied my companions' bwana shorts and minimalist footwear—Jesus sandals for Vasco, preppy sockless boat shoes for Greg—the current *muzungu* styles for a jaunt through the goddamn jungle.

The second hour, Vasco and I began to drag our feet ever so slightly, the monotonous slog of the trek contradicting its urgency. Greg, on the other hand, was having a terrific time, supernaturally energized to be shipwrecked in the middle of nowhere, an opportunity flush with the thrill of rule breaking, and by the third hour, as my need for two-minute breaks became more frequent, he would shuffle restlessly, unable to stand still as Vasco and I squatted in the shade, parched and mindless. Our slowdown finally summoned Greg's inner (antsy) child and he suggested we stay put while he went on alone searching for the elusive cell phone signal. No way, Vasco and I protested. Our pride would not allow it, and we stuck together for another mile until, on the verge of heatstroke, it became painfully obvious that our pride wasn't quite the virtue we had imagined.

We shook hands, wished Greg Godspeed, and watched his blithe disappearance around a bend in the track, wondering what body parts he might be missing if we ever saw him again. The late afternoon sun had begun to splinter into golden beams, planting shadows in the jungle, and, unable to depend on the success of Greg's solo mission, we began walking again, our pace marginally faster than zombies. After a ways Vasco snatched up a long stick. What's that for? I asked a bit dubiously. Just in case, he said. For animals. Minutes passed in silence and I kept thinking I should pocket one of the occasional rocks I saw in the track. Vasco, I said, what kind of animals are you going to hit with that stick? You never know, he said, and we both laughed at this absurdity. He told a safari joke that ends with a hapless fellow preventing an attack by throwing shit at a lion, which he scoops out of the deposit in his own pants.

By four o'clock we arrived at a landmark that Vasco, for the past hour, had expected to see any minute now—an old concrete bridge spanning a dry wash. This is it, said Vasco, removing his shirt and collapsing flat on his back. I pulled off my boots and socks, rolled up my pants, unbuttoned my shirt, and laid down as well, dazed and blistered and generally indifferent to what might happen next. We had walked ten miles from the near side of the river, plus another three or four trying to find a crossing. It was unlikely yet that Greg would be in cell phone range, four and a half miles farther on, and so we were puzzled when we heard a search plane overhead, flying out toward the hippo pool, unaware that our failure to return in the early afternoon had set off an alarm with Beca that had now reached the highest levels of the federal government, or that a large herd of elephants was nosing around the disabled helicopter while Segren, engrossed in Finnegan's book, read the first eight chapters.

Barking signaled the approach of baboons, challenging our right to recline on their bridge. The jungle dimmed toward twilight, its harshness replaced by a counterintuitive sense of abiding peace. I closed my eyes, remembering the quizzical eyes of the antelope—oribi, waterbuck, nyala—we had seen throughout the day, poised to flee but not in any rush as we passed by in quiet admiration of their elegance and beauty. What a shame, I dared to think, that we had not seen a pride of lions or trumpeting elephants. A sun-stricken fantasy, akin to a death wish. When Vasco asked what time it was, I told him four thirty. They'll come for us by five, he predicted, and, as night fell upon Gorongosa, they did.

We found Greg blissed out, up to his sunburned neck in the cool blue water of Chitengo's new swimming pool, eating a bowl of fresh fruit cocktail, a full moon rising behind the happiest philanthropist on the face of the earth. The safari guides would call us *damn fools* for our reckless misadventure. Fair enough, and we would have to live with the mischievous glow of that assessment, persuaded that our bad luck—an outlandish privilege, a backhanded gift—might never again play out with such serendipity, marching across Africa in league with just the sort of heaven-sent fool a better world could thrive on. A world, I would expect, where standing around waiting to be rescued is not an option.

(2010)

What I Did with the Gold

Although the island has taken on great significance for me, it's no more inherently beautiful or meaningful than any other place on earth. What makes a place special is the way it buries itself inside the heart.

— *Richard Nelson, from* The Island Within

Someone—a literary critic—has written that twenty years of distance gives us not just an event or place to return to but also our former self. Or, I might add, *somebody's* former self, not especially recognizable as your own.

Van Britton's younger brother was certain he remembered me, offering as proof the details of my residence on Old Providence Island when I lived there in the early seventies.

"Mistah Bob, you used to live in Freshwater Bay."

"I lived in Old Town," I gently corrected him, "near Raimundo Lung."

"You used to ride a white horse," he continued, undaunted.

"No, my horse was red."

"Your wife's name was Sherrie, no?"

"I wasn't married," I felt obliged to tell him. "My girlfriend was Marta, the *panya* girl who lived with her mother and sister and brothers in Old Town."

Van's younger brother paused, momentarily subdued, trying to untwist this piece of information. After a minute his head slowly bobbed, his face brightening into a shy expression of the pleasure that comes from remembrance. "Mistah Bob," he insisted. "Back then, you didn't have a beard."

Back then, he was only thirteen or so, what the *isleños* call a sprat, a sardine. I had never fished with him, as I had with his older brother, up on the Serrana Bank, and I didn't know whether I knew him or not since his affliction—a right eye that rolled back into his skull when he shifted his line of vision—was peculiar, I seemed to recall, to more than one of the Brittons.

"No," I had to tell him. "I had the beard."

"But it was black, eh? Now it is white."

"That's true."

"Yes," he concluded triumphantly, his right eye rolling blank. "I remember you, Mistah Bob. It is very nice to see you again, mahn."

"It's very nice to be back," I said, acquiescing.

Throughout the exchange, Van had been giving me knowing looks, studying me with a wry half-smile. I had come upon the two brothers at their compound—sort of like a rasta camp for nonexistent tourists—in the middle of a jungle clearing, the two of them enjoying a quiet late summer day, sitting across from each other on log benches muscled into position on both sides of a long, handmade wooden table. I sat down next to Van, who automatically reached behind him for a calabash gourd filled with pungent weed.

"Do you remember me?" I had asked Van. We had not seen or spoken to each other in almost twenty years. He peered into my eyes for a second before he answered, resolutely, *Yes*, and then remained silent while his kid brother, exercising his right as an islander, constructed a past for me that wasn't even remotely true, yet nevertheless plausible. Now I suspected that Van himself was bluffing, that he didn't know who I was either—until he suddenly spoke up.

"Mistah Bob," Van began, squinting through the smoke of the stick of ganja he brought to his lips, finalizing his appraisal. Behind us, his girlfriend stirred a Dutch oven set over a wood fire, boiling rice. "Mistah Bob," Van began again. Apparently he had scoured his memory to his satisfaction and I was there, loud and clear, yet once again transformed, another island variation on the theme of my identity. "Mistah Bob," he said a third time, exhaling a river of blue smoke. "What did you do with the gold?"

I suppose there was bound to be some misunderstanding about that, but whatever I said would only complicate matters. Providence is a small place—*small*—and the smaller the place, I've learned, the more it thrives on mystery, intrigue, conspiracy, shadow play, and the intimate connectivity of myth. Nobody is quite anonymous, but no one's story is ever quite reconcilable with the facts. There's no contest—the fecundity of an island grapevine would put many a novelist's imaginations to shame.

Gold, the breakfast of empires.

There was once a golden highway in this part of the western Caribbean Sea—these days resurrected but snow-blown with narco traffickers—running from Cartagena to Campeche, whereupon it dog-legged eastward with the Gulf Stream toward Havana, turned north up the coast of Florida and east again below Cape Hatteras to direct its trade across the Atlantic. This route was the legendary Spanish Main and throughout the sixteenth and seventeenth centuries, on its prevailing winds and favorable currents sailed the fabulous wealth of Mexico and the Americas, transported to the royal court of Madrid aboard the plate fleet, the treasure-laden galleons of the Spanish Crown, and forever at the mercy of God and hurricanes, uncharted shoals, and, of the utmost relevance to my tale, those rogue seamen and cutthroat adventurers known as the buccaneers. Multicultural long before such ethnic stews were fashionable, the pirates of England, France, and Holland bivouacked primarily on three strategic islands scattered along the Main: Jamaica and its blasphemous Port Royal; Tortuga, off the coast of Haiti (where barbecuing sank its New World roots); and, approximately 500 miles north of Cartagena and 150 miles off the eastern coast of Nicaragua, the island then named Santa Catalina—St. Catherine's—known today as Isla Providencia or, as its Afro-Anglo inhabitants have always called it, Old Providence (its colonial designation, Catalina, passed on to its tiny sister island, now connected to Providence by a footbridge). Regardless of its far-flung obscurity, Providence was considered prime real estate by the privateers, for virtually all homebound ships sailing north to the Atlantic from South America passed within sight of her timbered peaks, like fattened geese adrift on a pond, and more than one was raided and sunk, or plowed into the island's thirty-six square miles of barrier reefs to end up permanently established on the bottom, its ghosts counting the centuries until the invention of the aqualung.

By 1600, Dutch pirates were holding cookouts and cocktail parties on Providence, a style of social life you might expect to have altered radically when, in 1629, the Company of Adventurers of the City of Westminster sent aboard the *Seaflower*, of all people, a stiff-spined batch of Puritans to scrape out a few plantations. The gin, however, proved mightier than the Lord, once the Puritans realized they had been situated in a most divine position for plundering Spanish treasure ships. It was a Welshman named Henry Morgan, though, who would soon place Providence on the bloody map of history.

The future Sir Henry greatly desired, wrote his Dutch surgeon John Esquemeling in *The Buccaneers of America*, "to consecrate it as a refuge . . . unto the Pirates of those parts, putting it in a sufficient condition of being a . . . storehouse of their preys and robberies." Which is precisely what Morgan did—or so say the islanders today—when he arrived in Providence in 1670 with two thousand fighting men aboard thirty-seven picaroons to stage his most infamous, daring, and brutal exploit, the sacking of Panama City. The fleet proceeded from

Providence to the Caribbean coast and off-loaded twelve hundred banditti, who marched across the isthmus to the city and marched back three weeks later, leaving Panama's seven thousand houses, two hundred warehouses, eight monasteries, two cathedrals, and hospital burned to the ground. Of rape, torture, and cold-blooded murder, there was plenty. "Of the spoils thereof," said Esquemeling, "he [Morgan] carried with him one hundred and seventy-five beasts of carriage, laden with silver, gold and other precious things."

The contemporaneous value of the loot, it has been estimated, was between three and six million dollars. Back on the Caribbean coast, Morgan went secretly aboard his flagship and put out to sea, followed by three or perhaps four vessels containing the greatest part of the treasure. Contrary to the historical record, Providence islanders argue passionately that Morgan stopped there on his return from Panama, sailing into local waters with three ships, though only two proceeded on to Jamaica, because, the folklore has it, either one of the treasure ships hit the reef on its approach or, most insist, because Morgan scuttled a ship after unloading its golden cargo and burying it with several slaves to guard and enchant the trove. Then the pirate hoisted sails for Port Royal and, caught up in the volatile politics of the day, never returned.

After Morgan, Old Providence experienced, like Gabriel García Márquez's fabled Macondo, one hundred years of solitude. A sanctuary for outcasts, fugitives, and escaped slaves, it was resettled in 1788 by Francis Archbold, the Scottish captain of a slaving ship, who established a cotton and tobacco plantation on Catalina (where the Archbolds—or Archibols—reside to this day). This explains why the people of Old Providence speak a vaguely Elizabethan patois—*You vex me, mahn. Tis as I say, Alphonse.*—with a Scottish accent—*Gid mairnin, sah*—but it doesn't explain why the islanders claim, rather emphatically, that they are descendants of Henry Morgan, his beautiful red-haired mistress, his captains Robinson and Hawkins, and his crew.

Of course, I didn't know any of this stuff when, in December 1973, fresh from a university miseducation, I decided to step back from the forthcoming betrayals of the nascent Me Generation. I didn't know, for instance, that Providence islanders, in the words of one anthropologist, were keen on generating hypotheses concerning the whereabouts of the treasure, or that over the years they had dynamited and dug up the length and breadth of Catalina, and a good many sites on Providence, or that the Colombian government itself had sent soldiers to excavate the old ruin believed to be Morgan's fort—everybody down here running, in effect, a high fever searching in vain for pirate's gold.

Actually, I had never even heard of an island named Old Providence when I boarded the cheapest flight in Miami that would deposit me, at least technically, on Latin American soil. The flight's destination was San Andrés, the main island in an off-the-map archipelago and a budding Colombian resort. From there I planned to boat-hop to the continent in pursuit of a romantic's itinerary, the adventurous dreams of youth: I wanted to sweat in the oceanic jungles of the Amazon, scale the Andes, surf in Peru and Brazil, smell the fires of revolution igniting. Free and restless, I had just turned twenty-two and wanted out—*out* being not only a destination but a hazily imagined lifestyle.

I never made it, though, to the South American mainland. On the flight down, fate's ever-playful travel agent booked me a seat next to a fellow I had observed in Miami checking in an egregious amount of excess baggage: footlockers, duffel bags, scuba tanks, an air compressor no one could lift. He had gleaming eyes, a brush mustache, and hair like a clown's wig, and from the start he impressed me as a genius of self-importance. As we entered Cuban airspace, he began to fiddle with a long cardboard tube, removing nautical charts that he rudely unscrolled in my face.

"Here," he said without even looking at me, "hold the end of this."

With the index finger of his free hand, he tapped three or four meaningless spots clustered in the archipelago we jetted toward, mumbling to himself and behaving like an ass. Impatience, not curiosity, got the best of me.

"All right already," I said. "What's your story?"

Howard was a dive instructor from Chicago who had once worked in Isla Mujeres, where he had befriended an American couple—Tay and Linda Maltsberger—who now lived in Providence, and somehow were in possession of an exclusive license from the Colombian government permitting them to salvage old shipwrecks in the clump of islands. Since we were both cheapskates, that night Howard and I shared the expense of a hotel room in San Andrés. In the morning before he left on the weekly flight to Providence, Howard made a most casual, semi-serious invitation: Should I happen to be in the neighborhood, he'd teach me how to scuba dive. The impulse to take that forty-eight-mile detour, I have since thought, was tantamount to trading a massive illusion for a small unknown. In my imagination the continent struck an obscene pose, pursed her lips, and beckoned me with a gesture of unlimited possibilities, yet here I was contemplating a blind date with an unheralded island I felt no special interest in. I'll go for a week, I told myself, but the week ballooned into a year as Providence began, however clumsily, to shape me into a writer.

An old raconteur once suggested that one-third of all criminals are nothing but failed adventurers and that the vocation of adventurer is ultimately as tragic as that of youth. Even in the best of circumstances, treasure hunting is a slippery business, 98 percent bluster, bravado, and self-delusion, and when the bullshit stops, treachery has been known to rewrite the script. Typically, a salty impresario will con a group of investors into financing what amounts to a wild-goose chase. On Providence's reefs, however, centuries-old wrecks weren't difficult to find— the locations of at least a dozen were common knowledge among the local fishermen—but without the equipment or resources to salvage them, such information fell into the category of useless.

When I landed in Providence, two weeks after Howard, and tracked him down, I was grateful for his effusive welcome, only partially tempered by his announcement that, if I went halves, he could now afford to rent a launch.

"Let me get this straight," I said, amazed. "You're going to salvage a galleon, *but you don't have a boat*?!"

It could have been worse, I suppose. He did, after all, have the air compressor and scuba gear—the first on the island. My career as a treasure salvor began and ended with our third dive, which also was my last with crazy Howard. My journal entry, dated January 24, 1974, begins: *Our object was a Spanish galleon sunk 300 years ago ¾ of a mile off Morgan's Head on the island of Santa Catalina.* Reading this today, twenty years after it was penned by my adolescent hand, I wonder, however briefly, if I made it up. Is it early evidence that I was already being influenced by the islanders' habit of thought that aggressively blurred the lines between fact and fiction? For instance, what about those details? How did I know the wreck was three hundred years old, a galleon, or even Spanish? Did Linda or Captain Tay tell me, or are these morsels of verisimilitude my own invention?

Whatever the case, we did indeed dive that day on the visible remains of a ship lost during the colonial epoch—a scenario that would have produced yawns in Hollywood. After snorkeling all morning across a grid of reef off Catalina, we spotted what we were hunting— a prosaic mound of ballast rock, round as the cobblestones that paved the alleys and esplanades of the New World. We skin-dived down four fathoms—as generations of former wreckers might well have done—to inspect a brass cannon nestled in the sand, and an enormous fluked anchor nearly twice my length, cantered against the rock pile. I recovered a page-size sheet of whitened lead, an oxidized iron or silver rod with four symmetrical nodes on its crown, coral-encrusted shards of amphora. Fixing the general location in our memories, we moved up the reef to spearfish and then returned to Providencia for lunch. A small crowd had gathered on the dock, anxious to learn if we had found Morgan's treasure. No matter what we said, it was assumed we were hauling up gold by the bucketful. My journal advises me that I was too excited to speak, and that someone commented on the wild, lusty look in our eyes. After lunch, Howard and I returned to the site with tanks and crowbars. The journal entry ends anticlimactically, but with a trite and grandiose flourish: *We found nothing of great significance, except to me, but we know of two more galleons, and these have never been dived on—so there is this possibility called tomorrow.*

Christ.

We were the most hapless bunch of treasure hunters the world has seen, our naïveté only exceeded by our incompetence. I'm not entirely sure why, but I never dove on a wreck again. Anytime we took a boat out to the reef, however, it seems, now, the entire island grumbled: *Dem fellas takin' we gold.* We had the license, the scuba gear; we were gringos. We were chronically half-assed, but that trait seemed to elude the *isleños.* In their minds, two plus two equaled millions, equaled Morgan's treasure.

Meanwhile, a better story unfolded, far richer in potential: the island itself, its astounding beauty, and the fascinating singularity of its people. I rented a house on the beach in Old Town, on the other side of the harbor from Town (which no one called by its actual name, Santa Isabel). The house had no furniture and, like everyone else's, no running water (we bucketed water out of a cistern squirming with mosquito larvae), and though it was one of the rare houses in Old Town with electricity, the power plant only managed to function three hours in the morning and two more in the late afternoon, keeping the fishmongers' freezers in a state of perpetual thaw.

I purchased a kerosene stove and lamp, removed the kitchen door from its hinges for a table, with seats made from driftwood, ordered a hammock from Moraduck the hammock-maker in Lazy Hill, and began to feel, with an overwhelming inner sense of arrival, at home—a feeling that my new neighbors, welcoming me with fresh-baked johnnycakes and plates of food, did not discourage.

For twelve dollars I became the owner of Reeva, a spirited Paso Fino, and we began to explore the island, galloping bareback on the palm-lined beach at Southwest Bay, reining the horse into the turquoise ocean until the bottom fell away and we swam together in liquid air, my hand wrapped in Reeva's black mane. In rum shops I sipped the local moonshine—called Jump Steady or Jom's Toddy—and heard the braggadocio of the fishermen. Ingesting the mushrooms called duppy caps—*duppy* meant "ghost"—I climbed into the mountains whacked out of my mind to stand on the peaks in the raging wind, the sea an expanse of fox fire and tumbled jewels below me.

Howard moved in and set up his compressor on the veranda; so did a woman named Beth, from Friday Harbor in Puget Sound, whose brother had once worked for the Maltsbergers in Honduras. I began courting the only available Latina on the island—twenty-year-old Marta, uprooted from an upper-class life in Bogotá with her younger sister, Clara, and two little brothers and transplanted unhappily in this most remote of places by her beautiful but slightly demented and unforgiving mother, a relative of the Archbishop of Colombia, who exiled herself and children to an alien paradise upon learning of her husband's infidelity. Marta's overprotective mother despised me, naturally—I was the first boyfriend of her oldest and favorite child. She'd come hammering on my front door to rescue Marta from my caresses; her shrieks would send Marta dashing out the back door, scurrying across the mudflats to be home waiting not so innocently for *madre*'s tempestuous return.

Life for all of us grew more immediate, less gold struck, more devoted to the quotidian pleasures of survival, island dramas, the textures and subtleties of a community where poverty intensified, rather than corroded, the honest joys of existence. Assimilating into their rhythms, we flared with modern schemes for short periods, then relapsed into timeless slothful bliss, taking to our hammocks with a book, savoring our Cuba libres. The Maltsbergers' efforts to lure investors into the wonderful world of treasure hunting never got far off the ground. Linda and I came up with an idea to write a cookbook, but the project lost momentum and nothing ever came of it. I pitched articles to magazines, collaborated with a photographer, worked tenaciously, ran out of money . . . and nothing ever came of that either.

Before long I went native, joining up with a pair of Old Town spearfishermen—Raimundo Lung and Gabriel Hawkins—leaving before dawn each morning to sail out of sight of land in Mundo's lanteen-rigged catboat, learning the labor, fear, and glory of their profession and bringing home dinner to a house now crammed with a revolving-door ensemble of wanderers, outcasts, and expatriates. Then the collective magnificent weave of the year unraveled and overnight, it seemed, we were all gone, riding away on the currents to our separate futures, leaving behind in our wake a minor but nagging contribution to the island's mythology, another screwy installment in Providencia's leitmotif of gold.

To tell the truth, I did not want to go back. For a long time, that's how I felt.

Coming back, though, was also part of the ethos of Old Providence, as was the act of leaving. "What defines islanders," says the writer P. F. Kluge, "is not the way they live on islands but the way they move between them." The islands—all islands—depended on the human flow. On the profound restlessness that leads to self-exile; on remittance; on the magnanimous return of the prodigal son. Travel as a rite of passage into manhood or some variety of marriage.

This is what happened when you lived on a remote island, an unimaginable distance from the push and shove of things, the commerce and convenience of the temperate latitudes and the developed world, the dubious but seductive advance of the nuclear age and its postmodern spawn. An island where men, under their own power, went to the sea each day for their living, challenging its caprice in the smallest of boats. Where families took to the sea on holidays, to visit and to celebrate. Where obtaining a government permit, or buying a bag of cement, or keeping a doctor's appointment meant risking the hazards of the sea. One day you were talking with someone, playing cards with him, dancing with her. The next day they were never to be seen again, and you were dreaming of them falling, slowly, with macabre beauty and grace, through the blue, ever-darkening thickness of space, and the dream never stopped but at its bottom lay all your missing friends, looking up through the water at the moon.

Here is what I remember:

Shortly before dawn each morning, Mundo would send his little girls down the beach to wake me, like songbirds. *Mistah Bob*, they'd whisper cautiously. *Mistah Bob*, they'd whisper through the open slats of my window, their melodic voices barely audible over the lap and hiss of the lagoon. *Me faddah say you sleepin' long enough, mahn.* I would growl theatrically, they would giggle. *Mundo say git up, Mistah Bob. Is time to go fishenin.* They were beautiful cherub-faced girls with gap-toothed sunny smiles. I could see their silhouettes in the lavender light of the window, their long wavy tresses braided and beribboned, the pleasing line of their plaid school dresses. *Mistah Bob*, they'd persist, *Mistah Bob*, until I threw open the door and stooped for their quick kisses, and that would be the end of our lovely game.

The year 1976 was the last time Mundo and I exchanged letters. His read: *Bob, I have a sad story to tell you. My two daughters went to San Andres for Christmas and on their way back the Betty B* [an old inter-island cargo and passenger boat] *burst open and more than half the people drown. You must just know how I feel. Margarita and Virginia died.*

With great reluctance I had sailed on the *Betty B* myself, and I had sailed on the *Acabra* too, which was even less seaworthy than the *Betty B*, and proved it by sinking first, only a few months after I had sailed away from Providence, overcrowded with passengers but close enough to shore for all hands to be saved. And a month or so later, my friend Captain Ibsen Howard would disappear one night in the passage between San Andrés and Providencia, washed overboard his own boat in heavy seas.

However you got yourself to Providence, your faith in everything—God, man, technology, yourself—was sorely tested by the voyage, and never so wantonly as when you flew Cessnyca and its nine-passenger twin-engine Beechcraft, apparently maintained by obeah priests. My final letter to Mundo, hastily scrawled from the Windward Islands in the summer of 1976, where I was a Peace Corps volunteer, was to report that I had been assaulted and stabbed; stay tuned, I wrote, because further conflict seemed to be brewing. Except for that one night in my life when someone woke me in my bed and tried to kill me, I had never experienced moments of sheer terror except courtesy of Cessnyca.

On my inaugural flight during December's stormy weather, the fucking *pilot* knelt on the tarmac, crossed himself, and prayed before boarding the plane in front of me. Airborne, we roller-coastered through tremendous thunderheads, my surfboard levitating in the aisle. On my second flight to Providence, the pilot lost control of the steering as we touched down, the dirt runway turned to muddy soup from a recent downpour, and we crashed sideways through a stone wall, coming to rest in a mangrove swamp. Another day, my photographer friend arrived at the airstrip to find the flight crew wrapping a rope around one propeller and yanking it, the way you would a lawn mower, to start the engine.

Twenty years later, getting on and off Providence still seemed like risky business, at least psychologically if not statistically. By the time I arrived in San Andrés from Bogotá I was understandably wired and struggling against a creeping sense of depression. No surprise to see that San Andrés hadn't changed much—its fate was to be a teeming, overbuilt tropical shithole, eternally engaged in the process of making itself uglier, a low-lying featureless free port roamed by sunburned hordes of Colombia's equivalent of Kmart shoppers, loading up on faulty appliances. The only difference seemed to be that now the mafia—meaning, the cocaine cartels—was doing its laundry here, building tacky mansions and chintzy resorts, apparently designed by architects using the Jersey shore for their aesthetic model.

On the other hand, San Andrés's frenetic shabbiness had always been the perfect foil for the purity of Providence's unassailable beauty, multiplying a traveler's sense of thanksgiving and wonder, seeing for the first time its exotic peaks, its stunning cobalt reefs, its raw charms, experiencing the midwestern hospitality of its people. Island-style here was an irresistible production, sort of a blend between *Sinbad the Sailor* and *Little House on the Prairie*, performed by a very mellow all-black cast directed by uptight, but absentee, South Americans. The kind of destination you truly only connected with in your imagination, because its existence was oftentimes too good to be true. A place endangered, ultimately, by your desires.

If leaving was a mistake, I figured coming back had the potential to shake out as an even bigger one. Why break my heart reconfirming the trend, proving to myself that Providence was, after all, neither a quirky utopia nor an idyllic glitch, but a doomed fragment of a fragile, shrinking world? When the developers and speculators deployed—as surely a battalion had by now—who was going to be the fool who played Diogenes, rejecting their temptations, scoffing at their inevitability? Twenty years ago, I listened to the alcalde of Providencia tell me that he hoped the personality of the island never budged, never came to resemble San Andrés. "I watch my children riding horses bareback into the sea," he said wistfully. "I leave my doors open at night knowing no one will enter and put a knife in my back. We live in peace and to destroy this would be a serious crime. If we can reject the influences of big capital, if we only allow the building of cabanas and reject any project bigger than this, then we can preserve our home in all its natural beauty."

Twenty years ago I believed this guy but now, as I sat eating my lunch at a little makeshift restaurant near the airport, waiting for the SAM flight to Providence, I entertained grave doubts that his vision, however sincere, could have withstood the onslaught of the forces playing late-century hardball capitalism in this part of the world. Reject the influences of Big Money? Yeah, right, I thought sarcastically. I fretted that I was coming back too late yet I didn't know, I had lost touch absolutely, and since Providence was so vital a part of my past, had performed in fact a catalytic role in my self-definition, it was time I found out. As if, in judging Providence after twenty years of distance, I would also be measuring the life I had led against the life I might have lived, had I remained behind or had dismissed the impact Providence had delivered to my heart and soul. And what of Marta, whose mother had denied her the twentieth century by flinging her backward into the primitive world of a colonial pioneer? What of the two fishermen who had allowed me to share their lives as well as their boat—Gabriel, who had made me his brother, and Mundo, in so many ways my father?

Long ago I had heard that Gabriel went to Jamaica looking for work, then shipped out on a freighter headed north. Had the northern ports bedeviled him, turned him into something as rare as murder on Providence—a racist? Had he ever raced home to marry his sweetheart? And what of Mundo? The Canadian novelist Robertson Davies once wrote that a man, in his youth, has several fathers, and his biological one isn't necessarily the most significant. I had three: the one who fathered my physical self; a professor in Missouri who fathered my passion to be a writer; and Mundo, the third and most adroit, a poor black fisherman, the father of my spiritual point of view, who taught me how to persevere past hardship and never to be afraid of life. Mundo, I was convinced, was dead.

It didn't really eat at me, the life I never chose, and to say I missed Providence would not be entirely true, though Providence is the only place I've ever lived where I envisioned myself not leaving. But years ago my island fever metamorphosed directly into an obsession for writing and swept me off into another life. I had never been homesick for Providence, though I often felt as if I had been born there, but I was aware of it always, embedded there in my existence, like a phantom limb. I was never homesick for Providence but, more to the point, I was utterly bewitched by it. I was haunted, though in a kindly way.

My past on Providence wasn't ice but fire, burning with indelible images that kept reappearing in my fiction writing; the last thing I wanted to do was mess with the mojo, or spoil a dream year's delicate aftertaste by indulging in the overrich confections of nostalgia or, likewise, the thin broth of pity and regret and disillusionment.

I finished my lunch but not my despondent mood. I ambled back across the road to the airport and asked a taxi driver whatever happened to Cessnyca.

"It dropped," he said, an answer that required no further elaboration.

As I sat in the departure lounge watching the weather deteriorate, I kidded myself into believing I'd been through too much over the years to feel trepidation about the flight. Even buckled in, finally, on the sweltering, claustrophobic nineteen-seater I was more or less fine, a little jittery maybe, but the jolt of takeoff reawakened the religious conviction of the woman across from me and, damn it, it makes my skin crawl when people stutter their prayers out loud on small airplanes. With horrific noise, rain blasted against the cockpit windows; a downdraft slapped us into a steep bank. I closed my eyes—here was the old dread, an overwhelming sense of déjà vu—and when I opened them again we had busted through the squall; below us spread the inside reef like a celestial swimming pool, and in front of us humped the musky, verdant mountains of the island that had gotten deep inside me, so deep it seemed to have rearranged my DNA. I had flown back not into time but into some other stage of my imagination, my serendipitous literary collaboration with place, back into the genesis of my own symbols, themes, and fictions.

I jumped into a taxi; the road—the only road—had, like the landing strip, been paved some time ago, and already it begged repair. Larry, the amiable driver, smiled when I told him I wanted to get a room in Town. Alvaro's residencia had a new life as a general store; the Hotel Aury now housed the bank and some municipality offices. Now the hotels were all in Freshwater Bay (*Aguadulce* in Spanish) and having to rely on them underscored my unfamiliar status as a tourist.

*   *   *

Driving through Rocky Point, through Mountain, and down into Town, I was cheered to find that, at least on the surface, Old Providence had not been inspired or coerced to re-create itself for a profit. We gossiped, Larry and I.

"There was a fisherman in Old Town, Raimundo Lung . . . " I said, tentative, providing a lead.

"Yes, yes, Raimundo. He was our most famous diver on Providence. Guys would come from all around—Cartagena, the Caymans, the States—to dive against him. But they never beat him, you know. He was our best man with a speargun. Now nobody dive in Providence these days except with tank."

Finally I had to ask: Was he still alive?

"Livin' right there in Old Town still," Larry told me. Suddenly I was euphoric with relief, and coming back made sense. But then, just as suddenly, our conversation had a trapdoor in it, which sprang open underneath me. I asked about Marta and her sister, Clara. What had become of them?

"Them still here," Larry said. This was unexpected—wonderful—good news.

"No," a passenger we had picked up along the road corrected him. "One of them is dead."

On December 1, 1979, Marta and eight other passengers boarded the flight to San Andrés and took off into what turned out to be catastrophic weather. That was the last anybody saw of them and no trace of the wreckage had ever been found.

I was numb with sorrow when Larry pulled over in front of Mundo's house. What I had attained, exactly, by my return to Providence was an invitation to an emotional slam dance. Through the greenery, I could see down the path where Mundo stood, leaning over a worktable. Age had sucked at his muscles and carved into his face; his hair was graying, but then so was mine. When he realized it was me we embraced, tears in our eyes and now I was back among the living.

"Mistah Bob," said Mundo tenderly, "I thought you were dead. I am a grown man, but when I received your last letter, and then no more came, I lay in bed at night and cried, telling myself them rough fellas in St. Vincent killed you, and you was dead."

We held each other's hand like lovers, reluctant to let go.

"But Bob," Mundo continued, "just last week I was fishenin' with Armando, and I tell him, *Somehow I feel Mistah Bob is alive.*"

Anyplace else, coming from anybody else, Mundo's declaration would have struck me as mannerism, the exaggerated rhetoric of a good friend, but Providence had a way of forcing the supernatural down your cognitive throat, and twenty years ago, Mundo had startled me with his clairvoyance, again and again, until years later, a student at the Iowa Writers' Workshop, I was compelled to write about his eerie talents, fictionalizing the truth of events I was unable to comprehend, and although I had crafted an alter ego for myself, it seemed unnecessary and even somehow wrong to give Mundo any other name—or reality—but his own. In life, he had always been larger than life.

The same goes for duppy-haunted Providence, rubbing itself so intimately against the cosmic shanks of nature. The island had always played *Twilight Zone* tricks on me, suggesting, among other mysteries, that there were moments of inexplicable mysticism in the human act of expression, especially the act of writing, moments that would reach out to tear a souvenir off the coattails of the future. Where does an imagination come from, I found myself asking on Providence, but the island always answered back with a riddle—Where does reality come from?—and a biblical reproach—In the beginning was the word. It's the language, dummy. There was no other link between real events and the imagination but language and nature and the imagery that hovered between the two.

Our reunion drained me. I was both exhausted and exhilarated, heartbroken remembering Marta and, remembering her, chilled by the fact that an image of her death—a woman sinking to the bottom of the ocean—had been with me—I could date it in my notebooks, since 1979, the year she vanished into the deep.

I needed a room, a shower, stiff drinks, food, and a bed. I promised Mundo I would return tomorrow and we'd go fishing Monday. Not Monday, he said. We'd be hungover Monday. For a few minutes more, we said what needed to be said between us. Then, as I was poised to reenter life under the microscope in the nineteenth-century village that was still Old Providence, Mundo paved the way for me.

"Mistah Bob," he said, his tone a mild warning. "When you left everybody said you took the gold. But I told them no, I knew you well, you were not that type of man, that was not you."

The Monday after Sunday's fete at Mundo's, I couldn't determine if I was actually hungover from aguardiente or if my beaten-up feeling could be written off as emotional decompression. My former self chastised me for renting a *moto* in Freshwater Bay to tour the island, opting for convenience and speed over the old-fashioned rewards of putting one foot in front of the other, because even though the number of cars and pickup trucks had doubled to about sixty since I was last there, as had the population—about 4,500—the underlying pace of the island was still dictated by the start-and-stop stroll of pedestrians.

Whom I didn't overly blame for not stepping out of my way as I puttered past like a mechanical mosquito. Before I could click into third gear, I had left behind Aguadulce, Providence's only bona fide tourist zone. In my day I would ride my horse, Reeva, here from Old Town, or walk the distance with Marta—an hour-and-a-half Spanish lesson, one way—to sit on an empty beach in a prolifically empty landscape. Marta and I loved our sense of sole ownership, making out in the sand. By the end of my year on Providence, a mainland *panya* visionary had constructed three rustic cabanas under the shade trees behind the beach, easy to scoff at since the one-room clapboard shacks sat unrented, unwanted. Providencia wasn't for tourists, it was for travelers, traffickers, drifters, exiles, runaways. Sail in, sail out.

Now the paradisiacal beach had eroded to a narrow crescent, and Freshwater Bay supported a thriving but inoffensive village of restaurants, open-air bars, and lodging. No grand projects, cash only—even your traveler's checks were no good. Providence simply lacked the infrastructure and accessibility for corporate greed to take root. In this insular nook of the world, greed was still the prerogative of individuals mostly lacking deep pockets, the damage they caused less visible: a few kids knocked into outer space by drugs, several luxurious hideaways for nameless kingpins, ruinous land speculation.

"It [the island] will be totally private ten years from now," one of Providence's new entrepreneurs told me. "A few of the large landholders will get rich, but everybody else will be fucked. They'll have to move up into the mountains, or to San Andrés. Their children's children will never be able to afford to live here." What he described I accepted with fatalism for I had witnessed it happen again and again, a centuries-long heritage and way of life suffocated overnight, assigned to the archives. Make way for the twenty-first century, where the gold is electronic and all acts of piracy in the global village are cultural.

Over a hill that plunged precipitously into blue-green waters, I motored onward to Southwest Bay, once the island's most magnificent beach, yet despite considerable erosion it remained wide enough to accommodate Providence's most colorful spectacle—the Saturday morning horse races. I'd come to find the Brittons—Van, his father Burgo, his sister Indiana. Mutual friends in Miami had asked that I take them a gift, a modest amount of money, a fresh reminder of caring, old bonds renewed. But Burgo, I soon learned, had fallen out of a sea grape tree and broken his back; Indiana, two years younger than I was, had a heart attack—they were both dead. I followed directions to a trailhead into the bush, parked, and hiked through the scrub to scout Van's weird, serene—as if it were intentionally vacant—tourist compound and give him the money.

Hey, remember me? Yeah, you took the gold.

Back on the motorbike, I traversed the hilly southern tip of the island, dismayed by the sight of well-armed marine guards posted at all four compass points on the sun-scorched mountainside. The Colombian Navy found itself high and dry here in a garrison ostensibly built to show the flag to those bellicose Nicaraguans, who for some unfathomable reason were nursing a Falkland Islands territorial fantasy about Old Providence. That would be an interesting turn of events for a population who has no communal memory of institutionalized colonialism or slavery, only of being ignored and forgotten, thanks very much. Most islanders wouldn't readily admit even to being Colombian. What are you then, I'd ask. *We is gyad-dyamn Englishmen, Mistah Bob.*

Down where the eastward slope flattened on the outskirts of Bottom House, I stopped to ponder an unpaved turnoff I'd never seen before. Had someone bulldozed a road up over the densely jungled hill to Manchineel Bay, once only reachable by boat or by a perilous horseback ride along the cliffs? The Manchineel Bays of paradise were reserved for lovemaking, one of those spots you would never bother to go to without a date, one of those places where you unabashedly worshipped sensuality, enslaved yourself to it, where you ended up contemplating, if you were male and so inclined, the metaphor that if islands were women, tropical islands were women who riveted you with lust, and how many islands would it take to soothe the itch, you licentious dog? How many islands before you came to your senses, settled down, and married Ohio?

I couldn't imagine that a road, however rocky and washed-out, would enhance Manchineel Bay's reputation for intimate liaisons. Better go see, I thought, and what I thought was true—cookshacks, snack bars, thatched ramadas shading picnic tables, a covey of sunbathing tourists, some Bottom House locals playing dominoes. I bought a bottle of beer and sat down, feeling irrational, feeling jilted. Things weren't so bad at all. The beach was still spectacular, peaceful, its atmosphere like an erotic daze. So what if Manchineel had lost her virginity? That didn't make her a whore, at least not yet and maybe never, even if the municipality went ahead, as promised, and paved the road.

Still in love with her, I began to brood, took a walk and a swim to sort out my thoughts, ease the ever-increasing pressure on my heart. Rather than disoriented, I felt surreally connected, more, perhaps, than I wanted or deserved. Come back to Providence and all of a sudden you're loaded up with dead people. My own personal ghost fleet of souls, and the manifest was growing daily. The worst of it was, and not without its tragic beauty, I had become a medium between the two worlds, the one here and the one not-here, not just an emissary from the past but from the afterlife, toting around the images that survived beyond death. There they were, the bulge in my day pack. My books, of course, and two carousels of slides, previously thumbed by a curious *National Geographic* editor twenty years ago and then returned with apologies.

In this poor place condemned to poverty and isolation, no one had pictures of their dead, no one could recall the faces of their lost children, fathers, sisters. Last night at Mundo's we had tacked a bed-sheet to the wall, turned off the lights, and I began the show. Neighbors crowded in the doorway. I was prepared for the bittersweet taste of peeling back time, but I hadn't counted on opening so many graves.

Now everywhere I went, sad-eyed but hopeful islanders were flagging me down on the road. Like Miss Daci in Old Town, who waved me over because she had lost three of her four young sons with Mundo's daughters on the *Betty B*. Someone at Mundo's had recognized the eldest, an iconic shot of a fourteen-year-old boy standing up to his chest in slate-green water, fishing with a hand line. Her surviving son, Roy, now the cashier at the bank, had only been a few years old when his brothers drowned. He had no memory of them, and Miss Daci herself couldn't quite reassemble their faces in her mind, it had all happened so long ago. So it was I began making house calls, delivering back the disappeared to their families and loved ones, and two nights later I set up shop in the town square, running an extension cord out of the bank, which had agreed to remain open for this purpose and, as twilight fell, I projected my mixed bag of phantoms and former selves across the wall of the erstwhile Hotel Aury. *Duppyshow*, I would overhear someone in the enthralled crowd say, matter-of-factly.

There's Oscar Bryan, my uncle, said the bank manager.

Three schoolgirls sitting splay-legged on the ground: *My God, mahn, the one in the middle is my wife!*

Ah, look, poor Winston. He get crushed by a truck.

Lookout House—it burn down, you know. Yes, I know, and Linda's dead now seven years, her ashes scattered off the Turks and Caicos.

Margarita and Virginia, angels, no? Raimundo and Miss Pearlie's girls. Marta. Hello, Marta. Good-bye.

I turned around to see who had identified her so quickly. It was the island's agent for SAM airlines. "Bob," he said, extending his hand, "you don't know but I am Roberto, Marta's youngest brother." He was four years old when I left, had inherited my surfboard, which still hung on his bedroom wall. His older brother and sister had moved to Miami; Roberto had stayed behind to look after his mother, who had not come out of the house since the day Marta had died. No, Roberto told me in answer to my questions, Marta had never married; according to Clara, after me she never had another boyfriend either and, as for Clara herself, she hadn't become the aviator she had once dreamed of being, a sixteen-year-old girl sitting in the moonlight on my veranda, staring at the sea, but she had read about my books in the *Miami Herald* and knew about my life. It meant a lot to Clara, Roberto said, that things had worked out for me.

There was just so much of this I could take. My stoicism collapsed into melancholy and I began giving away the slides, shedding my collection of spirits like a retiring schoolmistress dismissing class, sending everybody home for the last time. I escaped to the boat bar tied up to the wharf—Glasford's boat, Ibsen's brother—where I could sink into a pair of island traditions equally eternal as its ghosts: listening to country and western music, the more sentimental the better, and firing back a bottle of Medellin rum. Bullshit optional, but just as time-honored.

Mistah Bob, mahn, listen, Mundo's new wife, Concha, is going to say to me, the day before I leave again. *When we are bairn we are each given a destiny, not so?*

I want to answer petulantly, wearily, cynically, *I know, I know.* But I don't know, really.

Or I want to say, *Deaths, yes. Destinies, no. Destinies you wrestle with, until they shake you off.*

I don't have a new revelation about Providence, but instead a revitalization of my original one: Time and chronology are two different animals; the latter tame, a beast of burden, always hungry; the former wild, unruly, popping in and out of existential holes, coming at you from all directions, everywhere at once.

Sunday, we sat at a table moved out to the yard to eat the stewed conch, beans, and rice Concha had cooked for lunch. Chickens and cats scavenged at our feet, Jim Reeves crooned on the cassette player. Gabriel was there, returned from the world to marry his gal, Vivian, and take a government job, night watchman at the new hospital. His domesticated paunch and burgher's affability made a poignant contrast to Mundo's wizened poise. In went the food, out came the memories.

I had first met them as a customer, wading out on the flats in front of Old Town to join the queue surrounding Mundo's catboat, attempting to buy a fish. Mundo gave me a five-pound slab of red snapper but would not accept my money, which made me uncomfortable. Next day, same thing. Who did he think he was, Santa Claus? Take my pesos, I urged, but on the baffling basis that we were neighbors, he kept refusing. Neighbors, according to my upbringing, were nothing more than the people next door, a fuzzy part of the scenery. You didn't need them, they didn't need you.

Where did a white kid from the D.C. suburbs go in 1973 to develop an abiding sense of community, family, tolerance, and generosity? *How would I know?* I would have replied at the time. *Seek virtue* was not ranked on my list of Things to Do in South America. I would have regarded any suggestion to go live among poor black people in the Third World as dubious indeed. Maybe even more so today, having done quite enough of it for the time being. All I know is that it *was* my destiny to alight in Providencia for a year, to rent a house in Old Town, to have Mundo as my neighbor and friend, then as my teacher. His pedagogy was rudimentary: Watch and learn. He rarely gave instructions or advice or reproach, except where danger and harm were imminent. He allowed me my mistakes, and I accepted his affectionate bemusement with my awkwardness.

Occasionally he would say, about something good or bad, wrong or right, *That is the black man's way.* Occasionally I would say the same thing about whites, but generally the issue of race was so mundane and pointless we never discussed it, except as a joke. I could never get him or anybody else on Providence to stop calling me *Mistah*—I even retaliated for a time with *Mistah* Mundo, with no success. It became my name, yet when Mundo requested my most earnest attention, he'd drop the formal, slightly teasing designation in a second. *Bob,* he'd say in his soft-spoken voice, *I am a grown man and my father is dead but still I hate him for taking my future away from me to give me this life of hard work and suffering.* In his youth, famous as a baseball player in Cartagena, Mundo was scouted by the gringos and offered a crack at the minors, and an education, in the States. A good son, he returned to his father's house in San Andrés to ask permission, but his father said no and in those days, Mundo emphasized, you obeyed your father.

Or, we'd be out on the reef, I'd be rowing, Mundo diving, when suddenly he'd spring up to rest his elbows on the gunnel, his face a bowl of euphoria. *Bob,* he'd say, *put on your mask and come look. This is a beautiful spot, bwoy. Beautiful.* He didn't place a lot of faith in my nautical abilities, though he held to his conviction that, since I had voluntarily crossed the threshold into his world, on land or at sea, under his protection and guidance, I would endure, and that single belief became my own, became deeply self-defining. In return, I trusted him, probably far too much, not to kill me when he went a-cowboying beyond the limits of sane seamanship in his livelihood, half profession and half blood sport. It was a most unusual alliance.

In went the food and beer, out poured the memories. Mundo and Gabriel exhaled laughter, reminiscing about the first time they carried me fishing. We went outside the reef into big swells; for eight hours I lay tucked into a fetal curl, awash in pink slimy bilge, puking, dry heaving, getting scorched with second-degree burns. That was the end of my life as a fisherman, they assumed, but at dawn the next morning I was on the beach with my gear, ready to go, and was never seasick again. My skin turned brown—*When you come to Providence, bwoy, you cyan't stay white for long.*

Now we had to talk about the first day they trusted me to row the catboat while they both dived. *Mistah Bob come back sayin', "My hands! My hands! They all bloody! What did you do with my hands!"* The first time they let me share the diving: *You swam ugly, Mistah Bob. Ugly. Like duck.* My first encounter with a shark, which had just bumped me and wheeled around for a second pass—*I never see a fella fly into a boat so fast as Mistah Bob. And him shoutin', "Fuck this, fuck this, I ain't punchin' no more shark. Fuck this you motherfuckers."*

More beer, more memories and hoots of laughter. Our two-week excursion up to the Serrana Bank aboard a mother ship, the time the *panya* cook pulled a knife on me and Gabriel stepped between us. Serrana, where some of the men in the catboat fleet went ashore on one of the atolls and robbed the eggs from the nests of boobies, terns, man-of-war birds. The eggs were overdeveloped and mostly rotten; they ate them anyway that night. Serrana, where you didn't have to dive, just wade, to fill up a boat with conch, where the sea turtles were as plentiful as hummingbirds in a garden of bougainvillea. Where Mundo announced one morning he had a "sign," had dreamed that night that he had sex with a man, and that meant this day he was going to shoot a big male hawksbill. And did.

338

Mundo's dream interpretations of the future, their accuracy—I'm at a loss for what to say about them. Or what to say about the psychic coincidence of a moment like this: In "Hunger," a short story I had written about Serrana, there was a line I penned about Mundo's mother, the only line I ever wrote about her, something about how she looked at the white man "as if he had come to steal the toes from her feet." Naturally, I wanted to know what had become of her, since she had lived with her son but obviously wasn't around anymore. With great pain, Mundo told me she had died only last year after long suffering. She had scratched her ankle, contracted blood poisoning. Mundo took her to the hospital in San Andrés, where they amputated her foot. Just coincidence, I know, but one of an abundance, offered to existence as a novelty. Like certain poems, the incident seems to beg meaning but eludes understanding, perhaps because I've lived so many years with these people in my imagination.

After lunch I unzipped my day pack and brought out my books, flipped through *Easy in the Islands*, showed Mundo and Gabriel their stories, later read aloud from "Mundo's Sign." A tribute. If, as Debussy said, "music is the space between the notes," then stories are the space between the islands, between lives. Mundo's reaction was, well, demure; he regarded the books with a thin, aloof smile and, disappointed, I returned them to my bag. There were other people I wanted to show them to anyway.

Fishing again with Mundo brought another twinge of heartache, like watching a former winner of the Kentucky Derby being roped up to a plow. Forget sailing, forget catboats—everyone used a motor launch now. The whine of the two-cycle engines replaced the hum and slice of the wind. Free diving was out, scuba tanks in. Plastic Clorox bottles instead of calabash gourds for bailers. The reef itself was in robust good health but you had to go farther and deeper to find the fish.

The result of our hard day's labor: not even enough of a catch to pay for our gas. On the way back in Mundo began telling me a story of another day he had spent in rough seas. A year after I had left, he built his first launch, took it eighteen miles up north to the top of the reef, and went outside into the indigo water. Then his engine conked out and the bad seas stove in one of the planks along the keel. He wedged his shirt into the hole and, with a piece of iron, banged the board back into place. Now they wouldn't sink but they had to bail constantly. As night fell, he threw out the anchor to slow their drift through the open ocean. When the sun came up, he waited for Cessnyca to come searching for them and send a rescue boat, but there was no plane, and no rescue boat, and when the sun went down again he told himself, *Fuck it, they think we're dead,* nailed a sheet of plywood to the bow to catch the wind, pulled the anchor and told his mate they were going to Nicaragua on the current. And for three days and nights, without food or water, that's what they did.

Mundo, I wanted to say but didn't, you're planting another story in me.

This is what I remember.

These are the lives I imagine.

These are the recurring images that inhabit me, outside place and time:

The ballet of a man and turtle, their pirouettes through the sorrow-filled loneliness of a blue universe. A black man gorging himself from a bucket of rotten eggs. Sharks like a whirl of gnats around the head of a diver. Boys racing horses on an endless golden beach. The spiral arm of a hurricane, like a serpent's tail, lashing against the coast. The sleepless eyes of killers and the grin of the barracuda. A quiet day, fishermen asleep in their boats. A naked woman eating a mango, juice dripping off her chin. Rain like a swarm of crystal bees. A catboat heeling into a squall and going under. A machete slashing the arched throat of a hawksbill turtle. A man playing the jawbone, the bounce of the quadrille. An old black woman's frown of suspicion. An old black woman's prayers for my safe passage. The phantasmagoric light of the flambeaus, the slap of dominoes against wood, and children drowning. And this, first written in 1979 on the beach in Cape Hatteras, revised in 1980, coming to final rest in '81, at home and at rest finally, in a short story called "Easy in the Islands." A woman crawling along the ocean's floor, weightless as a feather, her hair in flames of phosphorescence. Unbidden, after her death, without my knowledge of her death, Marta came to me, and comes to me, to construct another type of romance altogether.

On my last day with Mundo I gave him, as I had always intended, the book containing his story. I wasn't certain he wanted it, or what it meant to him, or if he thought of me, ultimately, as nothing more than a voyeur and a thief. "Ah," he said softly, "I finally have it. Here it is in my hand," and, to my astonishment, he raised it to his lips to kiss its cover and complete a twenty-year circle, spinning out into that place where everything exists but our flesh.

Now it is time to confess. This is what I did with the gold.

(1994)

Wartime Interlude

America's Marriage to the Far Away

1. The Bittersweet Lightness of Superbeing

The numbers stagger and overwhelm, and thrust us far beyond weeping over the endless constellation of lives, so many many lives, brutally discontinued. Twenty-five million men and women in uniform slaughtered in two world wars; 60 million? 70 million? dead civilians. Nobody really knows the count; they are uncountable. Millions more in all the other wars of our time, our century, the American century, history's bloodiest century. Surely the last to die will fall into a ditch or alley in some forsaken place, a bullet in his chest, shrapnel through her skull, on the very eve of the millennium as the dazzling ball of the future descends in Times Square.

For the living, the endless expanse of blood is indivisible from the blessing, *Pax Americana*, or so I thought, watching the Sea Harrier jets come home last May to the USS *Kearsarge*, on whose hot deck I stood with the flight crew of the 26th Marine Expeditionary Unit, peering out over the calm blue Adriatic, here at the end of this century held too long in what Rudyard Kipling called "the whirlpools of war."

Two fighter jets appeared out of the haze, their silhouettes no bigger to the eye than a pair of migratory geese. Where they had come from, what they had done, that they had found their way back to us—these gave weight to the moment. So it was sobering to see the Harriers circle and break their coupling, the first jet banking for its cautious approach, its landing gear extended like stubby feet, a terrible bird of prey hovering above the stern. The second Harrier blasted in a few minutes behind it, turbines winding down like sirens. Beneath the dull gray wings, the undercarriages were empty; the planes had dropped their bombs on Serbia.

Released from the colorless anonymity of his warplane, the first aviator, all business in his olive-green flight suit and helmet, shook hands with the flight crew, his manner laconic, uncomplicated, elite. The second pilot, the squadron leader, was different, though: what was apparent to me, from the moment I approached him, was that he had a soul, pure and transparent, there for all to see, should they choose to look. Not all men make such an impression, and when I say *soul* here, it is to remember the words of Vietnam veteran William Broyles, talking about combat survivors: "If you come back whole, you bring with you the knowledge that you have explored regions of your soul that in most men will always remain uncharted."

The emblem screened onto the fuselage of the pilots' jets—a knight's armored helmet over a crossed battle-ax and sword—resonated with the second pilot's features—long face, long Norman nose—tightly framed by his own flight helmet, which made him seem so much like the reincarnation of a medieval crusader. His fingers, too, were long and unexpectedly elegant, and on the back of one hand were inscribed target grid coordinates he had written with a ballpoint pen. His mouth was wide and elastic; smiles contorted into grimaces, toothy laughs into the pained resignation of his jaw. He was, for the few minutes he stood by his warplane, separated from its awesome glory and yet still bathed in the light and darkness of the run, a mythic figure, exalted and tortured by grave responsibility.

Today, the pilot allowed, was a good day, splendid weather, and they were able to get their ordnance off. That combination always made him feel better, less frustrated, but his eyes held the contradictions of his mission in the Balkans, or, for that matter, the role of the American military here at the end of the twentieth century. He had flown Harriers during Desert Storm too, but there was a not insignificant difference—the feeling, he said, that this was less than a conflict and more like a training mission in the States. Later, belowdecks in the officers' mess, we would talk about the Orwellian corruption of language—NATO labeling the bombing a "humanitarian intervention"—which the pilot found distasteful, as if the bombing were the equivalent of philanthropy, one of the many illusions that contributed to the current notion that people don't, or shouldn't, get killed in a war or that fed the more airy delusion among politicians and the public that somehow America, here at the end of a war-saturated epoch, had achieved the immutable end of war itself.

"Is it a fair fight? No, it's not a fair fight," he said, asking that he not be identified by name. "I don't bother to comfort myself with the humanitarian cloak. My job is to just attack." But later, with his dark eyes weathered and sad, he said, "I pray that it works," meaning the air campaign, bowing his head. "I pray that it works. We've got to end it soon, end the suffering."

Maybe such humanity in one of our own warriors shouldn't have surprised me, given the acute sensitivities of contemporary American society, but it did. Then again, humanity is a luxurious byproduct of waging yet another "war" so abstract, distant, and sanitized.

After almost a decade of America's secular jihad against ruthless disorder, it is the sacred and profane pairing of the humane warrior—forged by the military, the Clinton administration, and the counter-culture-turned-popular-culture—with the volume of inherited history that much of the nation and much of the world finds curious, puzzling, suspect in its claim to virtue. Repeatedly throughout the bloodshed in Kosovo, the punditry referred to the "new military humanism," the defense of human rights, as a righteous, or self-righteous, form of armed conflict.

In the mostly illusionary void created by the end of the Cold War, America, too, like nature, reflexively abhors the relative emptiness of a vacuum, filling it with bursts of policy, another type of gas, and not necessarily inert, but more often than not perfumed with what the nation chooses to believe are good intentions: free markets, democracy, international order, the shining light of moral crusades. Applied to the United States, however, the phrase "military humanism" seems oxymoronic and dangerously unrealistic. Better to sort out the confusion generated by the de facto intertwining of military operations and humanitarian operations. How to distinguish between each entity? Where does the persona of soldier as samaritan end and his identity as killer begin? Can the so-called end of ideology really be extrapolated to mean the end of war, or has it merely afflicted the military and its operational doctrine with paradox, ambiguity, and ad hoc missions? Have we turned our military into a force of steroid-bloated cops stationed at the door of a reform school for regional delinquents, or has America truly evolved into the supreme do-gooder, "the ultimate benign superpower," in the words of *New York Times* columnist Thomas Friedman, "and reluctant enforcer" of an imperial but enlightened globalism? In other words, here at the triumphant end of the Cold War, if we have regained the military and economic superiority that characterized America at the end of World War II, have we also regained the moral stature that accrued to us after the defeat of fascism, or has the subsequent defeat of Communism somehow muddled our collective value system, leaving us inspired but directionless in the absence of an apocalyptic pairing of good and evil?

Oh, the bittersweet lightness of superbeing, alone in the world in our greatness, alone with the imperfect mirror of our ideals. Our power both ends grief and begins it. Against great harm we enact greater harm, preventative or corrective or sometimes even punitive, in the name of hope and abiding decency and the beckoning future. While history will perhaps measure our good intentions with approbation, our conspicuous goodness, as writer and World War II combat infantryman Paul Fussell has suggested, might be part of the trouble, allowing us to mislead ourselves and others into believing an ancient, terrible lie:

that somehow war can be something less than "the very quintessence of immoral activity." Immodesty of purpose and certainty of belief— two aspects of America's vaunted optimism but otherwise known as sanctimony—never have been a particularly wise or holy mix.

But if, as Fussell insists, all war is a crime, what then are OTW— military operations Other Than War? Can war itself be decriminalized by separating it from ideology and vital interests and instead hitching it to moral imperatives and parceling it out as humanitarian actions? Or, as one of the Marine captains guarding a refugee camp in Albania put it to me, "If we go to war for economic reasons, why not for moral reasons? I don't want to get emotional about it, but for Christ's sake, man, is NEVER AGAIN just a bumper sticker?"

Both answers, the affirmative and the negative, seem applicable to the historical moment.

2. Slouching Toward Clintonism

In a Kosovo Liberation Army training camp in the foothills of northern Albania's mountains, I ask Ilir, a young officer back from the front, the question du jour: Had he lost any family members in the ethnic cleansing? *"Everybody* who's a victim in Kosovo is my relative," he said emphatically, providing perhaps the only answer that could justify the existence of an insurgent army and its steady resolve against charges of terrorism.

One might be forgiven for thinking that Bill Clinton and the NATO leaders had reached the same impassioned conclusion about their own relationship with the Kosovars. Select crops of the administration's "relatives" have sprung up near and far across the planet, while other tribes of victims have been, either ruefully or cynically, shamelessly or pragmatically, disowned. The selective motto I FEEL YOUR PAIN, embroidered over a scarlet background of apologies, is one of the more fickle pennants overflying America's currently chivalrous foreign policy.

But however freshly restyled its overt sentimentality, the philosophy of virtuous compassion urging us as a nation toward a higher calling has been seeded into the American experience since Day One.

Great powers always cast their actions as demonstrations of moral superiority. Our sense of exceptionalism arrives in nascent, quasi-mystical form with the New England Puritans, who believed they would supply a "moral example to all the world," and flows, contracting and expanding but mostly unbroken, to the Vietnam War. Thomas Paine wanted America to begin the world over again. John Adams brazenly declared that the United States "will last forever, govern the globe and introduce the perfection of man."

At the dawn of the American century, following the United States' brief but ugly flirtation with colonial acquisition during the Spanish-American War (Mark Twain did not hesitate to call American soldiers terrorists for the atrocities they committed in the Philippines), it was Woodrow Wilson who imagined that America would provide "a positive moral example to all the world" by refusing to join Europe's continental war and the insupportable callousness of its ruling classes. But Wilson failed even to persuade his own countrymen that his crusade was worth it. The naïveté and hubris of his sense of American moral superiority, compounded by the venal self-interests and ethnic hatreds of European politics, resulted in a peace badly made. Thus the first world war begat the second—the clear-eyed commitment to destroy Hitler and the Japanese, the Jehovah-like wrath of Dresden and Hiroshima—and the second, its intemperate sequel—the rise of the Soviet Empire and Maoist China, and postcolonial mayhem on three continents. After the tens of millions slaughtered, saving the world now meant saving it for *democracy*, which really meant defeating, or at the very least, stalemating, Marxism-Leninism in any of its various incarnations.

For this we were presented with a one-size-fits-all strategic tool, the Truman Doctrine. "It must be the policy of the United States to support free peoples who are resisting attempted subjugation by armed minorities or by outside pressures. . . . ," the president informed Congress in 1947, creating a foreign-policy environment of endless interests (containment of the Reds, which often meant active support for such thugocracies as Duvalier's Haiti or Mobutu's Zaire, Somoza's Nicaragua or Suharto's Indonesia), endless entanglements (Korea, the Persian Gulf, Cambodia, Cuba, Taiwan), and dishonorable intrigues (Guatemala in 1954, Iran in 1953, Chile in 1973). The Truman Doctrine committed the United States to the defense of legitimate governments against insurgencies. Legitimate simply described the immediate postwar status quo and its effete colonial handovers, before the Soviet Union launched its international juggernaut in its ascent as a superpower and a supercolonizer. America the missionary battled or subverted or boxed in the godless menace around the world, sometimes directly but more often clandestinely, through proxy wars of increasing intensity.

But just as Wilson's crusade for globalism had recoiled back into isolationism, the Truman Doctrine's global embrace vanished in the jungles of Indochina. Vietnam imploded not just our sense of exceptionalism; the damage went beyond that. Americans started to believe there was something essentially wrong with our vision of the world. If there was such a thing as a national destiny vis-a-vis the world, we were fairly sick of it.

In 1975, after the humiliation in Southeast Asia and the angst of Watergate, sociologist Daniel Bell, one of the many voices announcing the nation's descent into self-doubt, proclaimed the End of American Exceptionalism. Americans could no longer believe that their country had a uniquely moral role in world affairs, he wrote. We were, Bell concluded, "a nation like all other nations." The idea sprang open a trapdoor in the American psyche, leading to the upwelling of malaise that Jimmy Carter dared to acknowledge. But a scant twelve years after Bell's eulogy, Ronald Reagan had resold America to Americans, repaired the national spirit, rediscovered the nation's place in the world, and set the stage for a new era of "crusading interventionism" despite the public's indifference to or shallow understanding of America's international role. The Iran hostage crisis not only demanded that Reagan seduce us back from self-induced impotence into proactive foreign affairs but spurred the extraordinary technological advance, professional competence, and increasingly unconventional shape of today's military.

"In dealing with such Third World issues," wrote Simon Serfaty, the director of the Johns Hopkins Foreign Policy Institute, in 1987, "the Nixon-Kissinger-Ford foreign-policy administration had attempted to introduce the country to the imperatives of history—a predilection for might over right. . . . Next, the Carter administration sought to return the country to its historical right of birth—a predilection . . . for right over might. . . . Thus the Reagan administration's opportunity was to attempt to develop a blend of right and might."

Late in Reagan's second term, political scientists noticed that he combined Carter's vision of a virtuous American foreign policy with an image of strength and confidence, resurrecting the messianic idealism of Wilson. Whereas his predecessor had declared "our policy is designed to serve mankind," Reagan upped the ante, echoing America is "the last best hope of man on earth," and his ensuing call for a "crusade for Freedom" became known as the Reagan Doctrine, in which the president declared the legitimacy of active American military support for guerrilla insurgencies on three continents.

America then anointed teams of rebel surrogates in Nicaragua, Angola, and Afghanistan, avoiding the direct use of our own military forces except in Beirut and Grenada in 1983—the first a "peacekeeping" catastrophe, the second akin to a local 911 call. America was kept free from war until history could play Santa Claus for Reagan—the collapse of the Soviet Union, peace in Central America—and Reagan's Cold War rebel surrogates would morph into Bush's blue-helmeted UN surrogates in Bosnia.

It is more than a little ironic that whereas Reagan saw the globe through the eyes of a crusading liberal, drawing comparisons to himself with his Democratic predecessors in the White House and their robust rhetoric directed toward "saving" the world, Clinton sees it like the moderate, cautiously realistic Republican he appears to actually be. Still, the advocacy of human rights is a fundamentally interventionist posture. Human rights, the liberal *cri de coeur* during the Cold War's final decades of realpolitik, have become a geopolitical beachhead for the rapidly evolving activism of international law and the apparently noble motivation for a steady deployment of battle-ready American troops—peacekeepers, we are told to call them.

Enter, then, William Jefferson Clinton onto the chaotic streets of world affairs, lungs full with the legacy of precedent, his eyes illumined by the exceptionalist light of hope, pockets heavy with the fervent globalism of the corporate class, all the while enjoying the most powerful military ever offered by history to back him up. The Clinton Doctrine, such as it is, is not quite a "new Wilsonianism." These days America is not trying to save the world. Rather, we operate a sloppy triage, trying to keep the neighborhood from hemorrhaging in too many places at once; or we administrate a postnatal ward, indifferently or arrogantly baby-sitting the planet's infant democracies. In zones of conflict, Clinton feels the compulsion neither to support existing governments (Truman) nor to undermine them (Reagan) but to *Americanize* them. The old "moral equivalency" of the American and European radical left (the United States and the Soviet Union said to represent two sides of the same evil coin) has been replaced by the new moral equivalency of the Anthony Lakes and Sandy Bergers and Madeleine Albrights (sans Slobodan Milošević): treat the terrorists and the pro-democracy coalitionists as equally legitimate forces in Haitian society; ditto Croats and Muslims in Bosnia, Serbs and Albanians in Kosovo, Palestinians and Jews in Israel—thereby avoiding the Somalia syndrome, where taking sides proved politically disastrous and cost the lives of American soldiers. What the president most seems to desire is the removal of images of atrocity (at the top of that list, scenes of lifeless American GIs dragged through the streets of some Third World dump like Mogadishu) and their substitution with images of virtue (soldiers helping hurricane victims in Honduras)—to replace war with operations other than war, an empty space in an army's traditional reality, where there are no friends and no enemies, no front or rear, no victories and, likewise, no defeats, and no true endings. At the beginning of 1999 the United States had seven engaged deployments of its army somewhere around the world. Last year the Army's Special Operations Forces alone deployed 35,500 personnel on 2,500 missions into 112 countries. Altogether there have been twenty-seven large military deployments to date, costing at least $20 billion, during Clinton's deceptively maximalist administration. On average, he has ordered one cruise missile fired every three days of his administration. As the century ends, and the millennium with it, so ends a distinct epoch in the role of the American military—its identity, its use, its own worldview, the public's perception of it.

And yet, until some unforseen day, the military's culture *is* war, will always and must be war, not peace. Kill, win. Upon these roots only can be grafted the fruit of humanitarianism. Society's responsibility here is to ask the questions: Kill whom? Win what?

3. War, the Rock Concert

Man-made humanitarian disasters—famines caused by civil wars as much as by ethnic cleansings or religious persecution—are directly wired to political meltdowns and spiritual bankruptcy. Outlaw states, failed states, lost states, self-murdering states, leaderless states; name the collective psychosis, and somewhere on the globe it is raging through a formerly stable society. Humanity has come this far only to look back into the future at its oldest archetype, its savage, predatory face. Heart-wrenching imagery, the pornography of violence, flashes into our living rooms from cameramen in the field but, as U.S. Army Captain Dave Johnson asked me during the annual Special Forces Conference and Exposition at Ft. Bragg last April, "A picture's worth a thousand words, but what if every one of those words is irrational?"

The captain had a point. The Powell Doctrine required that the deployment of troops be contingent upon the support of the American people, but irrationality—impulse buying, obsession with lotteries, addiction to sensational entertainments—often describes the unreliable emotions within the consumerist soul. The increasingly preferred answer, I suppose, to the captain's question is this: Pack your ruck, show up at the airstrip in the morning, get the bloodbath off the networks and cable by tomorrow afternoon.

The conference's theme, Regional Engagement and the Future, had the high command wrangling over what the Army was going to look like in the year 2020—the Army After Next, as it had been formally titled and gamed. "There are still men in uniform wed to the past," groused the towering chairman of the Joint Chiefs of Staff, General Henry Shelton, who flew in from Washington after a night spent reviewing the Belgrade bombing target list with the Pentagon's lawyers. At least the conference nailed the basics, unveiling quality-of-life improvements for soldiers in the field, including the next generation of gourmet MREs (meals ready to eat): seafood tortellini, black-bean burritos, and Hooah! energy bars. But the bigger issues—Who are we? Where are we headed? What are we supposed to do when we get there?—were still unresolved.

The conference's most repeated slogans—EQUIP THE MAN, NOT MAN THE EQUIPMENT, and HUMANS ARE MORE IMPORTANT THAN HARDWARE—signaled the cause of the confusion. In the next fifteen or twenty years, the development of on-the-ground technology, the battlefield immersion into virtual reality, and the real-time communications network, both visual and auditory via personal satellite hookups wired into helmets and headsets, means soldiering will finally be transformed into the much prophesized ultimate video game, with targets—people, machines, buildings—zapped off microscreens like so many bloodless clumps of electrons. *Way cool*, the next iteration of extreme sport, and only the bad guys eat it.

In the language of pop culture, it's no-pain, high-gain Baby Boomer warfare, executed by Generation X technokillers who, because of the increased lethality and precision of evolving weapons systems, can close down the rock and roll in a time frame more associated with dance marathons and spring break—weeks, days, hours—unless the politicians screw things up. This is not the vernacular the military thinks in, however. Pointing with laser pens to high-tech graphics projected ubiquitously throughout the conference hall, the brass spoke of politicians or chiefs of state as "clients"; they talked about "what sells"; about "how to guarantee the product"; about "zero defects" (translation: everyone on our side comes back alive); and made knowledgeable references—"the holistic approach," "our core ideology"—to a professional-development book entitled *Built to Last: Successful Habits of Visionary Companies.* They talked, as you might expect from the largest politically correct institution in the galaxy, about "enabling" and "empowering" their men and women to explore their own capabilities to be all that any locked and loaded human being could possibly be.

It did indeed sound brilliant and farseeing. But there was a sense at the conference–as the cruise missiles slammed into Belgrade from Navy ships and Air Force bombers, as the Marines lashed out at Serbia from their floating platforms in the Adriatic, as Special Forces forward observers ripped off their American flag shoulder patches and slipped into Kosovo (a KLA colonel told me), and as the 1st Infantry hunkered red-faced in Macedonia minus three POWs—that maybe the conventional army itself was lagging toward a form of obsolescence, a big, brawny scarecrow, overmuscled, risk-averse, and not so productive, the last ones interpreting the Powell Doctrine's criterion of marshaling overwhelming force against an enemy to mean *a whole bunch of people with a lot of heavy equipment but nothing much to do.* There wasn't even a demand for 155mm howitzer rounds anymore. In the new tactical environment, in which the Gulf War was more of an aberration than a foreshadowing, one last spectacular hurrah for conventional infantry and artillery, the Army could at least take comfort in the fact that it was no longer being fielded as cannon fodder. "No casualties" by definition meant, first and foremost, no ground wars. The Air Force didn't shape the battlefield in Iraq, it destroyed it, and all the Army had to do was sweep up. In the absence of monolithic threats, the soldiers were going to be *occupiers*, the folks who drag ass into town after the pilots and Marines and Special Operations snake-eaters had taken care of dirty business. Well, it's a job.

Any understanding of the Army's fin de siècle thought process begins with its perception of the changing nature of the enemies on the horizon, described in military-speak as asymmetric threats: terrorism, guerrilla warfare, information warfare, enemies taking sanctuary in inaccessible and urban terrains, theater missile defenses, the byzantine relationships forming between terrorists, criminals, failed states and non-states, and of course the spread of weapons of mass destruction, biological, chemical, nuclear. The Pentagon, closely examining the decade's operations other than war to determine what the dimensions might be for real warfare, noticed a trend: the bad guys were paying attention, learning from our mistakes as well as our successes. Compounding the problem was the accelerated exportation of state-of-the-art technology that the military would rather keep for itself. "The operational edge—owning the night [with night-vision equipment]—is not as decisive as it once was because of the international market," lamented General John Abrams, who runs the US Army Training and Doctrine Command, a lesson the Russians barely lived to regret in Chechnya. In Albania, at Task Force Hawk, I'd hear another Army officer shrug and say, on background, "There's very little we can hold on to. All technology gains are temporary." For the past fifty years, the central tenet of the United States military strategy has been to make war far too expensive a proposition for anyone who might dare to challenge us, which has worked on the macro level, superpower to superpower. But history's Goliaths have trouble remembering that stones are free and slingshots easily stolen.

The Cold War monolithic threats spawned fixed patterns of response based on military doctrine, but now the decision-making process had to be rethought for asymmetric threats—adaptability

takes precedence over traditional models. Abrams, whose presenta-
tion was academic and abstract, high on reasoned solutions, loved to
talk about "transcending the dogma," refining the uncertainty factor
"so the enemy can never predict our actions," and more than once he
genuflected before the blinking altar of information technology. The
general was, as were so many of the officers in the room, a warrior-
scholar, ornamented with postgraduate degrees alongside combat
medals. Cerebral and flinty, eggheads with guns, as overeducated in
theoretics, I sometimes felt, listening to their esoteric badinage, as the
Modern Language Association. Not that they didn't exist, but you had
to go out of your way to find a certified idiot in this crowd.

The idea was to balance the dynamic of war—coercion—with the
dynamic of peace—influence. Simple enough, but it meant a radical
shift in the military's approach to non-war-fighting tasks. In order to
avoid war, the Army's Special Operations wanted to build professional
regional engagement forces (REFs) for dealing with operations other
than war—counterproliferation, combating terrorism, foreign internal
defense, pyschological operations, civil affairs, direct action, unconventional warfare, combat search and rescue, counterdrug activities,
humanitarian assistance—in recognition "that the military was continuously on an operational footing." But the regional engagement concept was not without its troubling aspects. For one thing, it reflected,
as the head of the US Army Special Operations Command, Lieutenant
General William Tangney, explained, *constant presence*; that is, military
globalization by any other name, but with a lighter footprint than the
massive worldwide encampments of the recent past.

But as I listened to the conference's three days of symposia, it was
apparent to me that the REF concept wasn't going to propel the Army
into the twenty-first century anytime soon. As General Shelton warned,
the hierarchy of the conventional Army still didn't quite grasp what
its own Special Operations Forces did, though many of the officers in
attendance believed the entire force was going to become more SOF-
like in the future. "Only a small group in SOF are trying to make the

concept of regional engagement happen," said another general, Sidney Shachnow. "The majority couldn't care less." Another panelist worried that REF, because of its focus on global scouts and information, would precipitate significant changes in the law that, without proper vigilance, would "break the firewall between intelligence gathering and operations that has been there for thirty-five years." Another speaker was even more pessimistic: "With every passing decade, the media and the international community's sensitivities are more attuned to what you're doing. We didn't invent Special Forces to do peacetime engagement. SF is not going to be used as Mother Teresa. The SF pulls off the humanitarian mask and is suddenly doing covert operations."

The discussion turned frequently toward the role of the individual soldier. Major General William Boykin, head of the Army Special Forces Command (Airborne), was not happy with the SF recruiting ads, which focused on humanitarian assistance rather than warrior skills. "Train warriors," he said, "and everything else will fall into place. This nation needs warriors."

Major General Shachnow: "There are two extremes of soldiers—the warrior door-kickers and the great humanitarians. The SF doesn't emphasize one or the other but operates across the full spectrum . . . whether they're dealing with a waitress or a guerrilla leader."

General Peter Schoomaker, commander of US Special Operations: "We have a fundamental problem in the well-resourced Western world dealing with warrior-class cultures. Sometimes I wonder if anybody's been in a fistfight, deep down within that logic."

From a military point of view, Schoomaker was right: the bombing campaign was a coercive political tool, really designed to affect the morale of civilians and soldiers, a textbook Clausewitzian extension of policy meant to persuade Milošević that he couldn't afford the political cost of keeping his forces in Kosovo. From the perspective of a senior Army officer deeply involved in combat operations at Task Force Hawk on the ground in Albania, this political reliance on the Air Force, which the Air Force eagerly embraced, in effect deep-sixed the Powell

Doctrine, allowing politicians to underresource the military without accountability, and that path was booby-trapped with familiar hazards.

"The Air Force preaches you don't need all the tools," said the officer, but then you regressed back to a Lyndon Johnson scenario, signaling the key to your enemy's eventual success. The polar extremes of the US military, labor (the Army) and technology (the Air Force), were tumbling out of their correct proportions. The thinking, called Halt Phase Strategy, was that you didn't need a big army, or even an active army; you just needed reserves, because the Air Force was so good. "But if you run across a completely committed foe"—say, for instance, the Somalians, rather than the Serbians—"if you use technology, all you do is drive the conflict down the scale to guerrilla warfare. If the question is, How do you want your armed forces structured in twenty-five years? your determination to advance technology and forget labor will always be for naught."

Well, maybe. This is an ongoing argument in which the Air Force will likely persevere, but the ironies generated by the clash of operational doctrines are profound riddles. Unlike Kosovo, the Battle of the Black Sea in Mogadishu was a military victory for the United States, but it was a political disaster exploding through American society, and so no victory at all. The political victory in the Balkans, though it took ten years and cost hundreds of thousands of civilian lives, was, as an example of American military power, something along the order of a grand nonevent—a steely gesture of morality. It's not unfair to say that the military wasn't even looking for a "victory" in Kosovo.

The ambiguity of the relationship between the Kosovo Liberation Army and the United States and NATO underscores the paradox at the core of the post-Cold War doctrine of humanitarian intervention: we do not deploy our military with belligerence in our hearts. Instead, we merely choose to believe we have no enemy, just countries we deal with when their behavior crosses the line of what we find acceptable. With such an absence of long-term strategy or a consistent foreign policy, tactical operations applied to the moment—bombing Serb positions in

Bosnia, protecting Kurdish refugees in northern Iraq, removing a tyrant in Haiti—create the illusion of a genuine, coherent, and extended political commitment to justice, democracy, and nation building. In fact, the post–Cold War interventions have been mostly marked by futility, a lack of resolution, and a lingering sense of betrayal, because what we ultimately seem most willing to invest in is the status quo—Iraq out of Kuwait, a weak Aristide returned to his palace, the refugees back in Kosovo. Beyond that threshold, the costs mount, the risks escalate, the political will falters, and our good intentions are met with skepticism. In such an environment, the Army's concepts of constant presence and perpetual operations dwindle toward hollow self-justification.

4. Singing Songs with the Refugee Girls

The smallest female officer in Marine history, four-foot-ten-inch Captain Gabrielle Chapin, insisted on lending me her sleeping bag. "It's clean," she wanted me to know, though I would have been equally grateful if it were not. I was being choppered ashore from the USS *Kearsarge* with a platoon of reinforcements to Camp Hope, a refugee camp in central Albania, where the 3rd Battalion, 8th Marine Regiment, provided external security.

Daily life was almost too welcoming, wholesome, and affluent aboard the *Kearsarge*, which at times seemed nothing so much as the military's version of Lake Wobegon—the women strong, the men good-looking. "Our Marines are motivated, and the food is good," Captain Chapin would say in a self-mocking tone, parodying her assignment as the 26th Marine Expeditionary Unit's public affairs officer, responsible for coddling the visiting press, invariably bored with the *Kearsarge*'s insularity and unnewsworthy narratives until they discovered the ship's ATM machines.

And the food, as she wryly advertised, was good. In the four mess halls, the ship's nutritionists had carefully labeled each slice of cake or serving of fried shrimp with its caloric count. The cappuccino machine was appreciated, the salad bar outstanding—unless you knew about the 1st Infantry's salad bar in Macedonia, extravagantly supplemented by an individual pizza bar, a burger bar, a taco and burrito bar, a fruit bar, and a tantalizing dessert bar stacked with locally made pies and tortes, all this bounty in addition to a full-service cafeteria line, the feast wolfed down beneath the flickering images of the mess hall's big-screen TV and then worked off in Task Force Sabre's warehouse-size gym.

Here on the ship life was mellow, almost festive at times. Occasionally there'd be a barbeque on deck, or tuna fishing off the belowdecks stern with the crew in charge of the air defense guns, or even romance. Of the approximately 850 personnel on the ship, about a third of them were women. (At Task Force Hawk's vast compound ashore, plenty of the troop tents were coed.) Belowdecks, when the ship went to red lights in the early evening, there was easy laughter, archipelagos of music, brash flirting, only infrequently punctuated by the far-above whoosh of Harriers taking off, the noise punching down through the decks like a massive airlock being secured. College instructors traveled with the MEU, so you could work on your degree. The ship had centralized television, its own channel stocked with a thousand movie titles. And for anybody who still felt, as at times everyone did, that he or she was in a faraway place, engaged in a faraway war, and that this wasn't real life, or a real family, homesickness had been diluted by e-mail.

"It's very deceiving," said a female sailor, an African American from Philadelphia, as we stood in the forecastle the morning I left the ship, looking at the sun rise over the mountainous Albanian coastline. "It's all so beautiful out here, and there's so much horror on shore."

She wished she could go in and do something to help, cook for the Marines, hand out blankets to the refugees, anything to feel she was more a part of it. "It's surreal to be out here, everything so calm, on such a beautiful day." Above our heads, there was a sudden crack of M-16s—live fire practice up on the flight deck, the bullets slapping into the water about a quarter-mile off the port side. The Marines practiced every day:

marksmanship on the deck, or, down below in the ground transport cargo hold filled with hovercrafts and armored Humvees, they learned a few phrases in Serbian and Albanian—*Drop your weapon! Lie down now!*—and rehearsed detention and arrest techniques, or practiced how fast they could drop to one knee and jam a fresh clip into their rifles. Unlike the conventional Army, they actively trained for humanitarian ops too, to prepare for what the Marine Commandant General Charles Krulak called the corps' three-block model—feeding people in the morning, house-to-house fighting in the afternoon, low-intensity conflict in the evening.

The beauty of the day remained by the time I walked off the Sea Knight helicopter into the blazing heat of the Albanian plain; what had changed was the feeling that you were getting closer to war, somebody's war. Every night, in the hayfields surrounding the refugee camp, you heard AK47 fire and unnerving bursts from machine guns, standard nighttime fare, the entire population toting assault rifles after the nation disassembled in 1997. Several nights before I moved in, the company of Marines guarding Camp Hope had come under direct fire, bullets impacting in the dirt throughout their wide-open compound, whizzing over their new Eureka! tents. The gunnery sergeant had brought forward a Humvee-mounted TOW antitank missile launcher and used its thermal sights to locate the gunmen out in the pastures, then sent a stream of illumination rounds streaking past their heads.

Nights grew considerably quieter after that, but force protection, so abused by the conventional Army in Haiti, had become a legitimate obsession. Backhoes had clawed out firing positions, berms of sandbags were stacked waist-high, battle-ready Marines in full body armor manned checkpoints and snipe positions throughout the area twenty-four hours a day. In the irrigation canals that bordered the camp, frog gigging was locally popular after dark, and the Marines had given villagers chemical lightsticks to keep them from getting shot.

"There ain't no business as usual around here. Period," drawled Major Bill Jurney, an amiable, squint-eyed, fearless gentleman from

North Carolina. He had been to Liberia, the Gulf, Cuba, Haiti, Panama, and now this, commanding the first Marines ashore in Albania, tacked on to the first Joint Task Force Shining Hope mission. The 160 men, the major explained as he showed me to my quarters—a piece of cardboard covering the bare ground in an open-walled supply tent—had come up against "a good dozen shoot/don't shoot situations" since they arrived on Easter Sunday. Jurney was continuously, persistently, reevaluating his security measures, in dogged adherence to Patton's growling axiom: *Plans should be made by the people who are going to execute them.* "You create your own picture of what's going on in your area," said the major. "You don't rely on national agencies." When he first came ashore he walked around with a digital camera, filling a disc with images of the site, which were then taken back to the *Kearsarge* and made into a cyberlandscape to train the troops who would be rotating into the camp.

Force protection—a doctrine that includes morale-boosting quality-of-life comforts such as movies, hot meals, barbells, phone service—had its contemporary roots in Southeast Asia and the bombing deaths of 241 Marines in Lebanon during an ill-fated, ill-conceived, and politically foolish peacekeeping mission in 1983. For the Marines, Vietnam and Beirut were the big lessons, maximum comeuppance. "Now we don't deploy unless we can be self-protected, the rules of engagement have to be decisively clear, and we don't like to stay anyplace too long," said one of the *Kearsarge*'s Cobra pilots, Captain "Bull" Marro. Force protection, however, had been taken to preposterous extremes in Haiti, the 10th Mountain Division apparently believing it had been sent to the island only to guard itself, and although it was miraculously true that no American soldier had been killed by hostile fire since the peacekeeping forces arrived five years ago in Bosnia, it was also true that no French or British soldiers had been killed either, yet the Americans were "turtled up"—required to wear full body armor—and the Europeans weren't. Madeleine Albright's conceit of an "indispensable nation" had trickled down to produce the individually indispensable GI sheltered by a society that expected its military to be not only omnipotent but immortal. Civilians, aid workers, journalists—these are the ones killed in today's war zones, not soldiers.

At the Special Forces conference in April, Brigadier General William Boykin was one of the few top-ranking officers I heard address the issue straightforwardly. "As for force protection," said the general, "we've gone too far with it. It can't be a mission. If you let soldiers believe that their job is to not get hurt and that's how you measure success, then we've made a mistake. . . . We don't want anybody hurt, but we're breeding a generation of young officers that believe that way, and that's a problem."

Many of the commanding officers of infantry units I spoke with in Albania and Macedonia believed that American troops presented a "higher-value target" than troops from other NATO nations, which necessitated not just a more aggressive posture but greater prudence. And as you moved closer to the "front," force protection was a logic few felt the need to question. Task Force Hawk, at the Rinas airfield outside of Tirana, was vulnerable to attack from shoulder-held missiles fired from the surrounding hills, surface-to-surface missiles launched from Yugoslavia, or Serbian MiGs stationed in Montenegro, five minutes' strike time away. Hawk lived on high alert under camouflage netting and walls of stackable bastions; its men turtled up round the clock with armored vests, sweaty helmets, gas masks bouncing on hips as they ran for cover during air raid drills.

"What's interesting to me," said Lieutenant Colonel Paul Brygider, senior commander of the MEU troops, "is the American public's acceptance of civilian casualties [here in the Balkans]. When we start taking military casualties, I wonder if they will accept them any better." "I hate to say it," Lieutenant Colonel Bruce Gandy told me out on the *Kearsarge*, "but there seems to be a parting of the ways between society and the military. We're citizen soldiers, but we're used to getting on ships and sailing away from society, taking care of ourselves. We've asked nothing from our country but to be allowed to go to the forefront and fight, without complaint. The DOD used to be hawkish, State used to be pacifist. Now it's switched. You have to understand the human cost of deploying for fuzzy principles."

Until the day in mid-June when they crossed the border into Kosovo, though, there would be nothing overtly fuzzy about the Marines' immediate mission. When the Kosovars were cruelly herded toward the borders after the bombing commenced on March 24, over twenty nations mobilized assistance to the United Nations High Commission for Refugees, the organization ultimately responsible for managing the welfare of 900,000 displaced people. Israel came as well as Saudi Arabia, the Germans, the Japanese. US Air Force Major Tom Dolney described the scene as kind of like a pickup game on a school lot—"It's not countries getting along, it's a whole bunch of helicopter pilots getting along." Within three months, twenty nations grew to fifty.

In the middle of April, NATO, belatedly, created Operation Allied Harbor, expanding its humanitarian effort, so far limited to hauling cargo and replenishing stocks, to actually building camps and shuttling refugees. Joint Task Force Shining Hawk, commanded by an Air Force three-star general, was conceived by the American military to organize a framework for the United States' humanitarian relief effort but not actually to do the work. The Air Force subcontracted the Bechtel Corporation to build Camp Hope, someone from the Defense Department oversaw quality control, CARE ran the camp, US Army Civil-Military Operations Center (CMOC) orchestrated the contractors and non-governmental organizations such as ADRA (food distribution), Merlin (medical emergency unit), and Save the Children. The French were there, the Turks, dozens of Albanian workers, and about 3,000 refugees.

The foundation for an infantryman, however, would always be the same—combat operations. "But the same principles that made you successful in combat ops," said Major Jurney, raising his voice to be heard over the noise of a nearby well-drilling rig, "will make you successful in humanitarian ops. The key to success is how quickly you can tranistion from humanitarian relief to deadly force."

And therein lies a conundrum. How can we be certain that any humanitarian organization's—especially an army's—self-proclaimed impartiality isn't an illusion, a sinister form of hypocrisy, a tactic, a mask to be whisked away at the appropriate moment, revealing the unforgiving face of an adversary? Certainly the residents of Mogadishu have very little reason to trust the humanitarianism of America or its military. In Haiti the Clinton administration's veneer of altruism became all too transparent when the National Security Council and people in the embassy instructed the Special Forces to treat the blood-drenched FRAPH, a far-right terrorist group, as if they were a legitimate political party, the "loyal opposition" to Haiti's democratic forces. And while Rwanda and Bosnia (to name but two) provided indisputable evidence of our failure to act against massive aggression, why were we so intent on labeling the liberation forces in Kosovo "terrorists"? The blowback of moral equivalency: nobody's right, nobody's wrong, we want to help everybody. Yet the truth is that short of marching on Belgrade and ruling Yugoslavia for the next twenty years, places like Kosovo won't fit nicely into America's multicultural moral template. The Kosovars want what we have—independence and freedom from state-sponsored terrorism. In significant ways it is ours to give, but we hesitate to give it to them. This is not a moral decision. Our moral crusade ends here.

"They [the Clinton administration] are internally inconsistent about moralism," said a senior officer I spoke with in a guarded, no-access command tent at Task Force Hawk who asked to remain unidentified. "When you start drifting into a moral universe, you have to ask, *Whose morals?* It's impossible for those guys to have a consistent, coherent foreign policy, because every time they bump into something, it's a Gordian knot. They're trying to get somewhere, but they bump into inadequate resources and intractable moral dilemmas. They—Sandy Berger, Madeleine Albright—can't help but be inconsistent."

Meanwhile, there was no question among any of the Marines but that they were doing the right thing—helping the suffering

Kosovars—and since no one could yet predict that the war would end so shortly, both the camp and the mission were expanding daily. As far as the eye could scan, green tents were being uncrated and erected to shelter an expected 20,000 refugees within the month, 30,000 if the war continued indefinitely. The Kilo Company had been there long enough to be replaced by Lima Comapny, whose men I watched unstrap their rucksacks and sit down on the ground to be briefed by their company commander, a Captain Dan Sullivan. Each new Marine had brought with him a fresh plastic tub of Huggies disposable wipes, and each man had an extra set of dogtags tucked into the laces of one of his boots, should the set around his neck be somehow blown away.

"The NGOs know we're here to protect them, and they appreciate it," the captain told his assembled company. "This is the first time most of you are doing real-world ops." He didn't want to catch anyone fooling around with his weapon or losing a single round of ammunition.

"The refugees have been through a lot of shit," he said. "There are a lot of kids here that have seen more shit than you've ever seen in a war movie. Treat them with respect. Say hello to them, treat them as you would treat your grandmother if she was a refugee." The captain tried to explain to his troops that they were in one of the poorest countries in the world, a place with strange customs, where it would not be unusual for them to see guys holding hands with each other. "Relax about it," said the captain, and handed over the briefing to First Lieutenant Adam Henrich. "The people here quickly realized we're not the bad guys, we're here to help them," Henrich told the Marines. "The NGOs, in my opinion, are doing the same thing we're doing. In my opinion, we're one big team."

After dinner—trays of huge grilled T-bone steaks delivered from the NGOs kitchen—I walked across the bivouac with Captain Sullivan and Lima Company's gunnery sergeant, Jack Sterling, to the CAAT (Combined Anti-Armor Team) motor pool—Humvees mounted with TOW missiles, Mark 19 automatic grenade launchers, and .50-caliber machine guns—and we took one of the vehicles up to the camp's main gate for a walking tour of the extensive compound. Although the Pentagon had instructed the Marines not to plan for any ground combat operations, few of the soldiers actually believed they weren't headed for a fight. "We thought we'd be in Kosovo right now, kicking ass and taking names," said Sterling, "but here we are with the refugee girls, singing songs."

We strolled down the graveled avenues past row after row of neat tents, families sitting silently in the shadows beyond the thresholds, mothers preparing the evening meal, old men and old women with head scarves nodding at us, teenage girls like any teenage girls anywhere in line at the water fountains, children running toward us to ask our names, take our hands in theirs. Here in Albania the refugees were free to come and go as they pleased, unlike at the dismal, filthy camps I would later see in Macedonia, where the Kosovars were locked in, concentration camp–style, behind fences and barbed wire. Here at Camp Hope, the mood was upbeat, if not uplifting; relieved, if not refreshed. Among the youngest refugees, laughter was not uncommon, nor was the sense of enterprise. People had begun to build primitive kiosks to sell little things, soda and gum and cigarettes; the KLA even had its own clandestine recruiting tent.

For two hours, until well after dark, the gunnery sergeant and I walked the perimeter, visiting the new guards, Lima Company's teenage Marines at their lonely posts for their first night of duty ashore. Despite my hesitation to play along, Sterling made me complicit in a ritual, requiring each young soldier at each scattered checkpoint to articulate his mission. It's good for them, said the gunnery sergeant, to have to explain themselves to somebody who isn't in a uniform, and I was reminded of something Major Jurney had told me, that he himself was a product of lessons learned in engagements past, forced to develop his social skills, to communicate more comfortably, to agree to TV interviews, to be mindful of the diplomacy of community relations.

The nearly full moon had risen by the time I made my way back to the Marines' blacked-out encampment, serene in its constant watchfulness, and crawled into my borrowed sleeping bag, watching the cool mist descend outside the mosquito netting. In the morning the searing heat returned and with it the novelty of Important Visitors. (There was a need for novelty. The days I spent in Albania with Task Force Hawk and its superfluous Apache helicopters were an admirable mix of industry, boredom, and suburban living. "We have some sur-realism around here," I heard an infantry officer say, lounging in front of his tent in a lawn chair. "I feel like I'm in Atlanta, Georgia, sitting on my porch." Soldiers don't go anywhere these days without their TVs, VCRs, PCs and cell phones. The compound bristled with groves of satellite antennae, its boardwalks and grounds coiled with cable hookups. The spring rains had stopped and the mud had dried, and there wasn't much to do but slowly mass forces and matériel, perfect the logistics—communicate, communicate—and be more diligent about physical exercise, given the abundance and quality of chow.)

The brass and the staff from Joint Task Force Shining Hope had planned a major photo op and were being choppered in from their headquarters at Rinas airfield, forty miles away. Before long the crowd of officers had arrived, their every step photographed by a cadre of the military's own spinners. The idea was to do something nice, something fun, for the kids. The refugee children were lined up according to age groups and marched to the far end of the camp, where engineers had scraped a play area and blanketed it with gravel. An Air Force sergeant proudly displayed a blueprint for an extravagant playground he had designed. Lugging sacks of candy, the task force folks divided them-selves up among the groups of children and organized games, assisted by translators and staff from Save the Children.

I lingered behind with one of the civilian watchdogs assigned to the MEU from the Center for Naval Analysis. Although they were civil service, the analysts wore battle-dress uniforms and helmets when they accompanied the Marines ashore from the *Kearsarge*. Even dressed to kill, this man looked like a Beltway technocrat and spoke lovingly, and at great length, about the various types of gravel spread around the camp. As we spoke, I looked over his shoulder at a large African American soldier teaching a circle of refugee children the hokey-pokey, putting his left hand in, his left hand out, twirling all about in his shiny black combat boots. It was a fine sight.

5. The Other Soldiers of Tomorrow

In Kukës, high up in the mountains of the Albainian-Kosovar frontier a week later, it didn't take long to relearn a basic lesson, that no matter how light-footed you walked through a war zone, something's bound to happen. I choppered up from the Rinas airfield with the Italian Coast Guard, seated between an Oxfam engineer and a portly Italian general going up to inspect his troops responsible for guarding the Kukës refugee camp. As we flew in, the reservoir below the city seemed to bob with countless flocks of seagulls, but as we made our descent I saw not birds but a vast spread of rubbish riding the still, blue water.

Barry Davies, the Oxfam engineer responsible for bringing water to the camps, had to tell his younger workers to get a grip when they arrived in town with the first crush of refugees. You're not doctors, he felt obliged to lecture his crew. You're not psychiatrists. The female interpreter would translate the stories of the rapes and executions to the team, and the less experienced workers would come unfocused, frantic with compassion, and Barry would tell them firmly to concentrate on the job, water was what they had come to do, look beyond the suffering and get these people water or things are going to get a lot worse.

Kukës, which had the potential to be a gorgeous alpine town nestled under snow-blotched summits, was a dump of rotting concrete apartment buildings and garbage-laden streets, full of spies and mercenaries, guerrilla fighters and groups of haggard-looking men—the tractor drivers the world had watched on TV. The Oxfam engineer's apartment, which rented for $60 a month back in the spring, now cost $2,000. A toy Uzi lay on the living-room couch, left by the child whose family had moved out instantly, doubling up with relatives, to bank the cash. Everybody's armed, everybody's balanced on the edge, another nation with another festering pathology. There was a battle on the hillside above town last night, two klicks this side of the border, an Italian doctor told me matter-of-factly. NATO bombs, mortar and machine-gun fire, tracers slicing through the air.

Deep inside the Italian camp, filming a queue of women at a water-pipe, I soon find myself in trouble—two AK47s jammed in my face, a cocked fist aimed at my jaw. The KLA were forbidden inside the camp in uniform or armed, but here they were, and furious, mistakenly believing I had captured their presence on my camera. Instead of intervening on my behalf, the local employees of Oxfam who had brought me there averted their eyes and backed away, out of the probable line of fire. Throughout Albania, especially in the north, journalists and aid workers had been robbed and threatened and occasionally roughed up or held hostage by troupes of rogues—the mafia, the police, the KLA—had their cars stolen, their money, their satellite phones, but I didn't know of any Westerner who had been seriously injured, even up here on the border, except by Serb snipers. Nothing much happened now either—the two KLA soldiers demanded my camera, I refused, we yelled at each other in our respective languages, and finally they went away—and the reason I even bring it up is to acknowledge the distance covered by the American military since a sergeant told Philip Caputo in Vietnam, "You're going to learn that one of the most brutal things in the world is your average nineteen-year-old American boy."

I can easily imagine the circumstances that might skyrocket that brutality back to the surface, but as a rule it just isn't there in the ranks. "The truth about the Army," Colonel Volney Warner at Task Force Hawk told me, "is that there's very little difference between me and Private First Class Snuffie. She's bright, intelligent, talented, well-read. If I go to another [country's] army, the private first class is agrarian, uneducated, undisciplined, unprofessional." Because the US Army has had little success recruiting from the middle class, it creates its own middle class, replete with bourgeois values. Because it has mostly eroded racial and gender barriers like no other giant institution in the world, it inculcates open-mindedness and tolerance and good manners. "The Army doesn't look for brutes anymore," said Captain Marty Downie, also at Task Force Hawk. "They want the thinking man, someone who's going to make a smart decision, someone with a conscience." It's a smokeless, lite beer, nice guy/gal culture that prides itself on calculated lethality. I was offended (absurdly) by the very nature of these two KLA fighters who, compared with American GIs, were so quick to stick their guns in my face. It's not a question of who are the more effective, efficient killers—we Americans are. But these guys were more dangerous, period, and the distinction is not a small one, here in the Balkans, or the Middle East, or Africa.

It was the seventy-second day of bombing—six more days to go. I walked up a mountain road toward the border. The war was almost over but no one knew that yet, and the exodus of refugees continued to trickle down the slope toward Kukës, cars with license plates ripped away, tiny tractors pulling wagons stuffed with people and foam mattresses and pots and pans, women in wool coats and head scarves on this hot, bright day, pretty young mothers cradling swaddled infants. It was a lovely day for a ride out of hell. The last tractor I saw before I turned back to the Italian camp was pulling a cart loaded with children, two dozen little ones, presided over by one old man wearing a white skullcap, the de facto patriarch of a wayward future.

Overhead, American jets and their surging, pulsing roar had been continuous since midafternoon. Occasionally I would spot their metallic specks, gleaming in the sun. Back in the refugee camp, I was surrounded by children who didn't want to let go of my hand, who wanted to play with my camera, wanted to introduce me to their sisters, their brothers, their mothers. *Where are your fathers?* They pointed to the mountains. *In Kosovo.*

The oldest, a fifteen-year-old boy, with raven-black hair and a grim smile, slashed his hand from ear to ear, again and again, holding an invisible knife, as he explained what had happened back in his village. There was an immense explosion, like the snap of a woolen blanket amplified a hundred thousand times. *"Aviones, aviones!"* squealed the children. The earth tremored lightly underfoot.

Would you like to know that if the bomb doesn't fall on you, it is a wonderful, terrible thing to behold?

Again, on the other side of the hill above Kukës, the earth exploded with a single, solid, indescribably powerful boom. *"Aviones, aviones!"* cheered the kids. So very high above us were the twin contrails of a B-52 bomber. The children were all over me, jumping up and down, dancing crazily, singing, *singing*. It was power itself, sheer and absolute and disembodied, that enchanted them, they who had known only the fate of the powerless. For a moment, believe me, they were happy amid the horrors of the world. There was one tenacious little boy in a Mickey Mouse T-shirt who positively refused to let go of my hand, and it was this child, I know, who was leading us all into the next century.

The children, I should add, were singing songs of war.

(December, 1999)

Leave

When you teach grad students, as I do every winter, especially those would-be masters, the brainy, dreamy, slack-ass selves who have been squeezed directly through the educational intestine from high school through university and into the relatively expansive bowl of highest, never-ending education, you keep having a recurring thought, each time you enter a seminar room and scan the robust, nascently cynical faces of the whatever generation horseshoed around the table, receptive to the morsels of your wisdom and the tricks of your trade, and the thought is an admonishment, and the admonishment is this: When are you guys ever going to get the fuck out of here?

And I don't mean finish the degree, get a job, a life. I mean turn your life upside down, expose it raw to the muddle. *Go. Put out*, as the New Testament would have it (Luke 5:4), *into deep water*. A headline in the *New York Times* on gardening delivers the same marching orders: "If a Plant's Roots Are Too Tight, Repot." Go among strangers in strange lands. Sniff, lick, and swallow the mysteries, even if you can't digest them. Learn to say clearly in an unpronounceable language, *Please, I very much need a toilet. A doctor. Change for a 500,000 note. I very much need a friend. I very much need an air strike.*

It's not the traditional Grand Tour I'm advocating, though some of the most enduring lessons of traveling are inaccessible until you're out there moving and then they're indelible upon the soul. One thing

377

about crossing borders, going into the world—you quickly learn that despite your marvelous ideals, you can't change it, at least not easily, but the world beyond the horizon can easily change you, and not just a little. Unless perhaps you are cursed, even at a young age, with being unchangeable.

Wandervogel is good for starters, tramping around as the accepted right-of-passage stuff for postadolescents who will wire home for return passage when their boots wear out. Travel per se isn't so bad—sampling, moving on; sampling, moving on—lovers, cities, pilsners; achieving a sort of existential velocity through which everywhere is nowhere (as Seneca warned aimless wanderers millennia ago). Learn a lot, forget a lot—the road as another type of consumerist school.

But let the road end; stop at a crossroads where the light is surreal, nothing is familiar, the air smells like a nameless spice, and the vibes are mesmerizing or just plain alien and stay, long enough to truly be there. At least once in your life, you have to do that, and why you should is finally pretty simple. If you want to know a man, the old proverb goes, travel with him. And if you want to know yourself, travel alone. If you want to know your own home, your own country, and your own place in your own country, go make another home in another country (and I don't mean Canada or England or most of Western Europe). Become an expatriate, a self-inflicted exile for a year or two. Stutter through a second language. Sink into an otherness that reflects a reverse image of yourself, wherein lies your identity, or woeful lack of one. Teach English in Japan, aquaculture in the South Pacific, hygiene in Bangladesh, accounting in Brazil. Join the Peace Corps, volunteer for Save the Children, work in the oil fields of Saudi Arabia, set up a fish camp on the beach in Uruguay, join the diplomatic corps, become a foreign correspondent, study Islamic architecture in Istanbul, sell cigarettes in China.

And here's the point, despite the fun, the challenge, the risk, the discomfort, the seduction and sex in a fog of communication, the tax-free money, the servants and thieves, the disease, the great food, the shitty food, your new friends and your new enemies, the grand dance between romance and disillusionment. You found out a few true things you really needed to know, that you thought you knew but really didn't until you lived it.

You've learned to engage the world, not fear it, or not be paralyzed by your fear of it. You found out, to your everlasting surprise, how American you are—Guess what, it's 100 percent, you can never be anything but—and that is worth knowing. You discovered that going native is self-deluding, a type of perversion. If you're black and you went to Africa, you found out you weren't a black guy in Africa, you were an American in Africa. If you were a white woman in Pakistan, you found that the only thing that provided you with an illusion of security was the troubling fact that you were an American. Whatever gender or race you were, you found out how much you are eternally hated and conditionally loved and thoroughly envied, based on the evidence of your passport. You learned that life is despairingly cheap, justice uncommonly rare, and people more beautiful than you ever imagined.

You found out what you needed to know to be an honest citizen of your own country, patriotic or not, partisan or nonpartisan, active or passive. And you understood in your survivor's heart not to worry too much about making the world better. Worry about making it worse.

For once in your life, you have some hefty context to work with.

And it's true: When you come back home, it's never quite all the way, and only your dog will recognize you.

(2002)

Author's Note for *Kingdoms in the Air*

Thomas Laird is by instinct a preservationist and curator of the old, a documentarian and archiver of the birth of the new and all its complications. He continues to devote his intellect and his energies to the art and religion of Central Asia. There are many like him out in the world, some more practiced and some less deft with gracious manners and diplomatic acumen and the appropriate sensitivities. Handbooks don't help. You are either guided by your heart or you are driven by your heartlessness. Ultimately the Lairds wandering the planet are an antidote against culture-destroying monsters like the Taliban or the imperial lusts of corporations and the corporate state. In a world rapidly spending its inventory of blessings, Laird, and the people like him, are a persistent blessing, and they deserve our everlasting respect and gratitude.

Please read:
Into Tibet: The CIA's First Atomic Spy and His Secret Expedition to Lhasa, by Thomas Laird
East of Lo Monthang, by Peter Matthiessen; photographs by Thomas Laird
The Dalai Lama's Secret Temple, by Ian Baker; photographs by Thomas Laird
The Story of Tibet: Conversations with the Dalai Lama, by Thomas Laird
The Murals of Tibet, photographs and forward by Thomas Laird; text by Robert Thurman
Horses Like Lightning: A Passage Through the Himalayas, by Sienna Craig

Acknowledgments

Ah, editors. What to say about editors?

When I am otherwise occupied in my life, I don't much miss editors, except for the very few great ones who aren't insulated morons or breathtakingly negligent and careless, who aren't shameless lying bastards, who aren't visionless mandarins of the status quo, air-headed cheerleaders for fatuous trends, or tyrants of self-aggrandizing little fiefdoms. The truly good ones, though, are like second, better selves— precious and indispensable, a writer's grace and blessing. To these guardian angels, I offer my endless gratitude.

Mark Bryant, Elizabeth Hightower, Colin Harrison.

Kathy Rich, Dan Coyle, Lisa Chase, Catherine Parnell, Josh McCall, Ryan Krogh, Abe Streep, Jonah Ogles, Will Blythe, Katie Raissian, Gail Hochman, Jeff Hilliard, Lee Jackson, Kevin Fedarko.

And, as always, my first, best reader, Barbara Petersen.